How Free Can the Press Be?

THE HISTORY OF COMMUNICATION

Robert W. McChesney
and John C. Nerone, editors

A list of books in the series appears at the end of this book.

How Free Can the Press Be?

RANDALL P. BEZANSON

University of Illinois Press
URBANA AND CHICAGO

First Illinois paperback, 2008
© 2003 by the Board of Trustees
of the University of Illinois
All rights reserved
Manufactured in the United States of America
1 2 3 4 5 C P 5 4 3 2 1

The Library of Congress cataloged the cloth edition as follows:
Bezanson, Randall P.
How free can the press be? / Randall P. Bezanson.
p.   cm. — (The History of communication)
Includes bibliographical references and index.
ISBN 0-252-02866-x (cloth : acid-free paper)
1. Freedom of speech—United States—Cases. I. Title. II. Series.
KF4770.A7B49   2003
342.73'0853—dc21   2003002148

PAPERBACK ISBN 978-0-252-07520-9

For Elaine, Melissa, and Peter

Contents

Introduction

America enjoys a love-hate relationship with the press. The press often evokes warm feelings of admiration and respect. But it also evokes hard feelings based on distortion, arrogance, and trivialization. Neither feeling is wrong; neither is right. Can we make some sense out of our conflicting emotions?

The First Amendment to the Constitution states that "Congress shall make no law . . . abridging the freedom of . . . the press." It is from this inspiring and definitive, yet terse and ambiguous, sentence that everything we know as the press's freedom springs. What is this thing we call the press? What should its freedom consist of? The Constitution's meaning, its definition of the press, its definition of freedom, even its definition of "abridge," has been placed largely in the hands of the judicial branch of government, and therefore largely in the hands and minds of the Justices of the Supreme Court.

The Supreme Court has polished and embellished the Constitution's language, offering up memorable encomiums to the press, waxing rhapsodic about its importance in a free society. But the Court's stirring rhetoric is surprisingly lacking in specific and operable principles and rules. To find these one must look beneath the veneer of the Court's opinions, examining cases as they actually arise and unfold in federal and state courts throughout the nation.

But in doing so we find another surprise. By most standards, the number of judicial decisions is remarkably small. This is likely because Americans share a common understanding of the press and its need for freedom, or "breathing room," as the Court puts it. Conventions about the way we deal with the press have built up over hundreds of years and have become, in effect, social habits to which Americans naturally conform. The infrequency of press cases may also reflect another fact of life. The press is itself a very powerful social, economic, and political force, a force to be challenged only with trepidation and great, great care.

But the relative paucity of judicial decisions cannot disguise the fact that there are many important and interesting questions about the press and its freedom, some of which have been addressed, though only implicitly, in the Supreme Court's opinions, and others of which have been judiciously—and consciously—avoided. What, exactly, is the press? What function does the Constitution assign to a free press? Does the very idea of the press and its function in our society place the press in a special position under the law? Does the press have a special duty to publish truth and fact? Does the press have a duty to be responsible when carrying out its central function of informing the public, especially when doing so endangers individual interests in privacy and emotional tranquility? Does the First Amendment allow a line to be drawn between fact and fiction, truth and falsity, news and entertainment, history and current affairs, advertising and journalism? Is the press subject to the law, or exempt from it, in the conduct of its business? Are trespass, lies, deceit—even theft—justifiable if done in pursuit of a story?

In the stories that follow, we will explore these questions—the meaning of the press's "freedom," fact and opinion, truth and falsity, publicity and privacy, news and entertainment, newsgathering and lawbreaking—through a series of cases involving press claims for protection under the First Amendment. We will find that the hard questions of press freedom, and the hard answers to those questions, reside not in the general rhetoric the Supreme Court employs but instead in the day-to-day business of journalism and in the way the courts actually treat the press on the rare occasions when its power or authority or freedom has been challenged.

This book is not intended to offer up solutions or even to argue for specific answers to the difficult questions presented by claims of press freedom. It is instead intended to identify interesting and fundamental questions, to give them life in the form of actual cases and people, and then to engage the reader in a form of written Socratic dialogue. My hope is to help the reader understand the competing arguments and principles that might be brought to bear on a question, thus giving *the reader* the means by which to answer the questions.

The cases, or stories, have been organized around five general issues, each reflected in a chapter of the book. The first issue is the nature and purpose of press freedom under the Constitution. This very fundamental question was the subject of perhaps the most famous free press case decided by the United States Supreme Court, *New York Times Co. v. United States*, in which the United States sought a prior restraint against publication of the Pentagon Papers. Why do we have press freedom? Just how free should the press be? How subject must the press be to the choices made by democratically elected government?

The second chapter will probe beneath the idea of press freedom and ask exactly what the press's freedom extends to: freedom to make editorial judgments about the what, whether, when, who, and how of publication decisions. *Miami Herald Publishing Company v. Tornillo*, another famous case, will allow us to explore what editorial judgment means and how far its freedom should extend. *Harte-Hanks Communication, Inc. v. Connaughton*, a libel case, will require us to confront the importance of fact and truth to journalism and, hence, to freedom of the press.

In the third chapter we will test the outer boundaries of press freedom, exploring through *Zacchini v. Scripps-Howard Broadcasting Company*, the Human Cannonball case, the distinction, if any, between news and entertainment. This is a boundary that is often associated with the press's role in a free society, and it is one that the Supreme Court appears to embrace. A second and equally common boundary for press freedom is between news and commerce. The Supreme Court explored this boundary in the *Pittsburgh Press Co. v. Pittsburgh Commission on Human Relations* case, in which a newspaper claimed that freedom of the press gave it the right to employ gender-based column headings in its want-ad section.

After exploring press freedom, editorial judgment, and the meaning of news, the book turns to two quite different, but equally important, questions. The first involves the press's freedom to invade people's privacy in the course of the publication of news. The two stories on privacy are *Bartnicki v. Vopper*, involving publication of illegally intercepted telephone conversations, and *Howard v. Des Moines Register & Tribune Company*, involving publication of the most personal, intimate, and embarrassing information about a named young girl who had been involuntarily, and wrongly it appears, sterilized in a public medical facility. Through these stories we will ask a number of questions about privacy and the press. What does privacy mean? When and why is the press entitled to use private information as news? Should the fact that certain information is forbidden by law to be possessed or disclosed have any effect on the press's right to obtain and publish it?

The last question serves as a transition to the final chapter, which focuses on the press's liability for violating laws that regulate conduct, such as trespass, deceit, misrepresentation, and the like. Does the press's constitutional freedom give it certain privileges, or immunities, from civil and criminal laws to which everyone else is subject? This question is examined through two cases, *Food Lion v. ABC* and *Berger v. Hanlon,* that arose in state and federal courts but did not yield a Supreme Court decision on the claims of press freedom. The cases reveal in striking detail the actual conduct and motives of two major news publishers, ABC and CNN, and thus provide a more concrete and grounded understanding of the dynamics of the newsgathering process and the people caught up in it. They will give us different and useful perspectives on the difficult and largely uncharted legal terrain of the press's freedom to gather information.

This is an illustrative, not an exhaustive, listing of the questions the reader will be invited to consider in the course of reading about the stories told in this book. The point of the stories and the questions is not to provide answers. It is instead to reveal the various ways of thinking about the questions and the competing arguments that can be made. The answers to be found in the cases are always interesting, often confounding, never obvious. And like much in constitutional law, they are always debatable.

1. The Purpose of Press Freedom

Why does the First Amendment guarantee "the freedom of the press"? Is the press's freedom protected as an end in itself, a core principle of liberty? Or is the press's freedom a means to a larger end? Is the press free because its freedom is an essential ingredient of the constitutional order of things, a means by which people can obtain information from sources outside the formal channels of government and its instrumentalities? Does the press's freedom consist, at its core, of independence from government, an independence that, ironically, is necessary to the functioning of government under the Constitution?

The central function of the press is most evident when the press discloses information about government, especially information that the government wishes to keep secret. It is in just such cases, however, that the risks presented by press freedom are the greatest. It is clear that for the press to perform its function of checking government power, it must be free to disclose information about government to the democratic polity. The government's motives for secrecy are not always benign. They are often Machiavellian—politically inspired and self-serving. Yet not all government claims of secrecy are of this type. There are legitimate needs for government secrecy—protection of personal privacy, candid discussion in the making of government decisions, protection of national security. And there are significant harms that can flow from disclosure of such secrets.

Does the First Amendment mean that the press must always be free to publish what it wants, no matter the consequences? Is press freedom like a game in which the government is allowed to do everything it can to protect against the leaking of its secrets, but if government slips up and the press gets the information, there is nothing that can be done, no matter what the consequences? Or is press freedom instead less than absolute? Do the limits of the press's freedom to publish depend on a balance struck between the purposes served by press freedom and the importance of information to the public, on the one hand, and the harms that may follow disclosure of secret information, on the other?

It is the Supreme Court's answers to these questions and the resulting rules of press freedom that give life and shape to the central premises of freedom of the press under the First Amendment. Nowhere are these questions more starkly presented or more thoroughly considered than in the famous case of *New York Times Co. v. United States,* the Pentagon Papers case.

STORY 1

Freedom to Publish
New York Times Co. v. United States
403 U.S. 713 (1971)
(Pentagon Papers Case)

Suppose an enterprising reporter gets hold of a highly sensitive government document alerting the Attorney General and the head of Homeland Security to an imminent terrorist act in a particular city at a known location. The document contains detailed information about the predicted attack, including sources and methods by which the information was obtained. The document specifically recommends that no public announcement of the impending attack be made so that the government can interdict it, thereby apprehending the perpetrators and hopefully obtaining critical information from them about other attacks and the persons, organizations, and governments that are sponsoring the attack.

Assume further that the newspaper for which the reporter works, having decided that the document is genuine and that the reporter's possession of it is legal, decides to publish the document as part of a story on the impending terrorist attack, the probable loss of life, and the huge risk the government is taking in trying to interdict the attack rather than to warn its citizens against it in advance. There is little doubt that the newspaper's decision amounts to constitutionally protected editorial judgment. It is likewise clear that no law of the United States makes the story illegal.

Now assume that the Attorney General and the President of the United States learn of the reporter's possession of the document. They ask the newspaper not to publish it. The paper refuses. So the President decides to seek an immediate injunction against publication on grounds that the document's disclosure will compromise an ongoing law enforcement operation and, in the longer term, will disclose information about methods and sources that will seriously undermine the nation's ability to protect its homeland security.

Does the First Amendment prohibit the government from obtaining such an injunction? Is the newspaper's editorial decision an instance of the press's absolute freedom to publish, irrespective of the consequences?

In the lore of the First Amendment, the controversy over publication of the Pentagon Papers is emblematic of freedom of the press. The case tested the outer limits of the press's freedom to decide what to publish as news, to decide what people should be able to read or hear, and to weigh the harms of publication against the benefits. Does the press's freedom leave no place for a democratically elected government to make and enforce such choices?

If so, what assumptions underlie such a strong preference for the press's power and such a strong distrust of government power? Does press freedom rest on the assumption that private choices, even by private corporations (or perhaps especially by them), are better than public ones made by elected or democratically responsible individuals? Does press freedom rest on an assumption that the press's decisions will be selfless and public-spirited, whereas government choices will be selfish and motivated only by a desire to possess and retain power?

The Pentagon Papers case required two great American newspapers, the *New York Times* and the *Washington Post,* to argue that *they* should be the final judge of the risks and benefits of publishing secret information, weighing the risk of soldiers' deaths and delay of the war's end against the advantages of public knowledge about the conduct of the war. Indeed, the *Times* and the *Post* had to argue that they were *better* able to weigh the risks than the government itself, which was afflicted by the myopia of war and the temptations of political self-protection.

Is this what the First Amendment's freedom of the press means?

* * *

The Pentagon Papers case, as it has come to be called, arose in the early 1970s, during a time when the Vietnam War was raging and distrust of government was rising dangerously.[1] The early stages of peace talks had begun, but soldiers were still dying in the field. Diplomacy was working overtime, struggling to manage a delicate and complex international situation and to find

---

1. Sources for the following account are George C. Herring, *America's Longest War: The United States and Vietnam, 1950–1975,* 2d ed. (Philadelphia: Temple University Press, 1986); Stanley Karnow, *Vietnam: A History* (New York: Viking Press, 1983); Robert S. McNamara, *In Retrospect: The Tragedy and Lessons of Vietnam* (New York: Times Books, 1995); David Rudenstine, *The Day the Presses Stopped* (Berkeley: University of California Press, 1996); Kenneth W. Salter, *The Pentagon Papers Trial* (Berkeley, Calif.: Editorial Justa Publications, 1975); Peter Schrag, *Test of Loyalty: Daniel Ellsberg and the Rituals of Secret Government* (New York: Simon and Schuster, 1974); Sanford J. Ungar, *The Papers and the Papers,* 2d ed. (New York: Columbia University Press, 1989); Tom Wells, *Wild Man: The Life and Times of Daniel Ellsberg* (New York: Palgrave, 2001).

and build on openings for peace or a diplomatic resolution—or, at least, a resolution that might be *called* a "just peace," even if it was not. The diplomacy depended very much on secrecy, on intelligence, and on subtlety in foreign relations. Diplomacy's success would decide the fate of soldiers and citizens in Vietnam, for each day saved in the quest for peace could be counted in lives not sacrificed.

During the ceremonies proclaiming Vietnam's independence on September 2, 1945, U.S. Army officers stood on the dais with Ho Chi Minh and other dignitaries, marking the beginnings of what would be a long and complicated relationship with the Asian country. Americans would first oppose France's attempts to regain control of Vietnam, but then, as the United States became increasingly concerned about the spread of communism in China, American opposition turned to support. The United States would eventually spend 2.6 billion dollars helping France's futile attempts to retain control of Vietnam. Talks between France and Vietnam began in Geneva on May 8, 1954. The resulting agreement to partition Vietnam was supposed to lead to nationwide elections. Instead, it led to war.

By early 1956, the United States had taken over the training of the South Vietnamese army from the French. American advisers were unaware of how deeply the South Vietnamese leader, Ngo Dihn Diem, was resented by the Vietnamese people until civil war broke out in the early 1960s. After President John F. Kennedy's election, American commitments in Vietnam increased to one hundred advisers and four hundred special forces troops to train Vietnamese soldiers. By the end of 1962, the number of men had increased to more than nine thousand.

President Lyndon B. Johnson inherited a morass of misinformation and misunderstanding. He would later say, "I knew from the start that I was bound to be crucified either way I moved. If I left the woman I really loved— the Great Society—in order to get involved with that bitch of a war on the other side of the world, then I would lose everything at home. But if I left that war and let the Communists take over South Vietnam, I would be seen as a coward, and [it would be] impossible to accomplish anything for anybody anywhere on the entire globe."[2]

Johnson ordered top-secret raids against bridges, railroads, and other installations in North Vietnam. The North Vietnamese responded with increased military action, including, on August 2, 1964, firing on the USS *Maddox* in the Gulf of Tonkin. In response, Congress passed the Gulf of Tonkin Resolution, authorizing President Johnson to take "all necessary measures

---

2. Karnow, *Vietnam*, 320.

to repel any armed attacks against the forces of the United States." As the war escalated, Johnson's Secretary of Defense, Robert McNamara, became worried that the war was "acquiring a momentum of its own that must be stopped."[3] He urged Johnson to limit troop increases, to work toward a negotiated settlement, and to impose stringent reforms on the government of Saigon.

While McNamara did not advocate a complete cessation of hostilities, his strategy of restraint was completely at odds with the advice of Johnson's other military advisers. The bitter split in policy would ultimately lead to McNamara's departure. But it also led him while still in office to wonder exactly how and why America was involved in Indochina and what lessons could be learned from it. He wrote:

> By now it was clear to me that our policies and programs in Indochina had evolved in ways we had neither anticipated nor intended, and that the costs—human, political, social and economic—had grown far greater than anyone had imagined. We had failed. Why this failure? Could it have been prevented? What lessons could be drawn from our experiences that would enable others to avoid similar failures? The thought that scholars would surely wish to explore these questions once the war had ended was increasingly on my mind.[4]

With those questions, the Pentagon Papers project was begun. Called the "Vietnam-History Task Force," the study was commissioned on McNamara's orders on June 17, 1967. There appears to have been no awareness of the project in the upper reaches of the Johnson administration. But McNamara denied trying to keep it a secret, claiming that doing so would have been impossible, since thirty-six researchers and analysts were involved. One of the researchers was Daniel Ellsberg.

There are differing views about what led to McNamara's departure as Secretary of Defense. McNamara himself said that he "[did] not know . . . whether I quit or was fired."[5] McNamara left the administration in early 1968. President Johnson announced his decision not to seek reelection only a few weeks later. When Johnson left office, Morton Halperin, Deputy Assistant Secretary of Defense for Internal Security, left also, taking his copy of the secret study of the war in Indochina with him and depositing it in the safe of the RAND Corporation, a Washington think tank. Halperin had only thirty-eight of

---

3. McNamara, *In Retrospect*, 270–71.

4. Ibid., 280.

5. Ibid., 311.

what would later be forty-seven volumes of the study, but those thirty-eight volumes would eventually end up in the hands of Ellsberg.

When President Richard Nixon took office, approximately thirty thousand Americans had been killed in Vietnam, a third of that number dying during his first year as President. Although Nixon began pulling troops out of Vietnam, he did not end the war. Instead, he began an air campaign to bomb Cambodia. Antiwar sentiment erupted around the country, and the protests increased after four young people were killed on the campus of Kent State University on May 4, 1970. The antiwar sentiment would lead Ellsberg, who had worked on the Pentagon Papers project at RAND, to decide that the documents needed to be disseminated to the public.

Daniel Ellsberg was born in Chicago in 1931. Much of his childhood was spent practicing the piano, attempting to fulfill his mother's desire that he become a concert pianist. When Ellsberg was twelve, his parents sent him to Cranbrook, an elite prep school, where he was acknowledged as the school genius. On July 4, 1946, while his family was on a road trip to Denver, his father fell asleep at the wheel. The car crashed into a concrete barricade, killing Ellsberg's mother and younger sister and seriously injuring Ellsberg, who spent three months in a hospital. He returned to Cranbrook for his junior and senior years; went to Harvard, graduating third in his class; and then studied in Cambridge, England. Upon returning from England, he enlisted in the Marine Corps. Ellsberg served in the Mediterranean, and after his discharge he returned to pursue graduate studies at Harvard.

Following his graduate work, Ellsberg joined the RAND Corporation in California. One of his responsibilities was to draft a memo about Vietnam policy during the early days of the Kennedy administration. The memo would become part of the Pentagon Papers. Ellsberg left RAND in 1964 and joined the Defense Department, becoming an aide to John McNaughton, McNamara's Assistant Secretary of Defense. A year later Ellsberg was sent to Vietnam as a civilian consultant. During his time there, he became disillusioned about U.S. policy in Southeast Asia. When he returned to the United States, he rejoined RAND, where he enjoyed access to the entire Pentagon Papers study.

Ellsberg became convinced that the information contained in the Pentagon Papers would be explosive if released. He began removing volumes of the study from his office and making photocopies, often enlisting the aid of his thirteen-year-old son Robert and, on one occasion, his even younger daughter Mary, who was ten. Ellsberg's co-conspirator in this mission was

Anthony Russo, a former colleague at RAND. The two men used the copy machine at Russo's girlfriend's advertising agency.[6]

Ellsberg delivered one set of copies to William Fulbright, Chair of the Senate Foreign Relations Committee, in the hopes that public hearings would be held. When Fulbright did not schedule hearings on the matter, Ellsberg contacted Neil Sheehan, a former UPI correspondent Ellsberg had met in Vietnam, who was by that time reporting for the *New York Times*. In March 1971 Sheehan traveled to Cambridge, Massachusetts, and returned to Washington with photocopies of most of the Pentagon Papers. Ellsberg never turned over the volumes that contained the diplomatic history of the peace talks and the release of prisoners of war. He considered those too sensitive.

Initially, the *Times* was concerned about the reliability of Sheehan's source. Normally, an investigative journalist is not handed thousands of pages of classified material without any effort on his part. Sheehan shared his information and several of the documents with his bureau chief, Max Frankel, who then informed managing editor A. M. Rosenthal about the papers and the magnitude of the information.

By late April, Sheehan and others had gone through the documents and realized their significance. *Times* publisher Arthur Ochs Sulzberger was informed of the study and the plans for publication. Sulzberger told the news department to prepare their stories, but that he and he alone would make the final determination about publication. He then began contacting the legal staff of the *Times* to determine the consequences of publication.

Sulzberger's chief adviser was a former military man with no journalistic experience, Harding Bancroft. Bancroft opposed publication of the Papers. *Times* columnist James Reston and *Times* legal department head James Goodale were both in favor of publication. Goodale was certain an injunction would never be sustained by a higher court, and Reston threatened that if the *Times* did not publish the Papers, he would publish them in his own newspaper, the *Vineyard Gazette*. Sulzberger finally agreed to a ten-part series of stories supported by the documents, and he allotted six pages a day, half the number of pages requested by the news staff. The first part of the series appeared on Sunday, June 13, 1971.

Public controversy immediately erupted over the *Times*'s publication of the first installment of the Pentagon Papers. The controversy was encouraged, if not facilitated, by denunciations of the *Times* coming from the State, De-

---

6. Ultimately, and only following the government's efforts to block publication of the papers in the Pentagon Papers case, Ellsberg and Russo were indicted by a federal grand jury of espionage and theft. The charges, however, were ultimately dismissed on May 11, 1973.

fense, and Justice Departments in the Nixon administration. Despite assertions that national security was being jeopardized and that sensitive foreign policy and intelligence information was being disclosed, the *Times* continued publishing further installments.

On Monday, June 14, the Justice Department sent the *Times* a telegram asking that the paper desist from further publication or face legal action. After the *Times* published another installment of the Papers on Tuesday morning, the government went to federal district court in Manhattan, requesting that the *Times* be enjoined from further publication because grave national security interests of the United States were at stake. Following a brief hearing on Tuesday afternoon, June 15, Judge Murray I. Gurfein granted a temporary injunction pending a full hearing, which was scheduled for Friday, June 18. At that hearing, Judge Gurfein ruled for the *Times* but extended his injunction to allow the government time to appeal. The government appealed to the Second Circuit Court of Appeals, which reversed Judge Gurfein's decision, ordered that further hearings be held to evaluate the government's claims of serious national security risks, and continued the injunction pending the further proceedings.

Immediately following the *New York Times*'s first publication on June 13, the *Washington Post* began seeking a way to cover the Pentagon Papers story other than by merely reprinting the story from its competitor. The *Post*'s assistant managing editor for national affairs, Ben Bagdikian, had met Ellsberg at the RAND Corporation while working on a book about the media. When the Papers were first published by the *Times,* he immediately suspected Ellsberg had been the source. Bagdikian attempted to contact Ellsberg several times on Wednesday, June 16, and finally reached him on Wednesday night. He was told he could obtain a copy of the Papers if he flew to Boston that night. Bagdikian consulted with the managing editor of the *Post,* Eugene C. Patterson, who gave him permission to get the Papers. He was told to call the paper from the airport and confirm the decision with Benjamin Bradlee, the *Post*'s executive editor.

Bagdikian traveled to Boston and returned with the Papers in a flimsy cardboard box. The suitcase he had brought with him was too small. He brought the box to Bradlee's home and was met by a horde of *Post* staff and lawyers. The lawyers were against publication. Katharine Graham, publisher of the *Post,* was called. After listening to the legal and journalistic arguments on both sides, Graham decided in favor of publication. The *Washington Post,* under the byline of columnist Chalmers Roberts, began publication of a series of stories based on the Pentagon Papers in the late edition of Friday, June 18.

Following the *Post*'s publication, Assistant Attorney General William Rehnquist telephoned the newspaper and requested that publication be stopped. The paper refused, and the government then sought an injunction against the *Post* in federal district court in Washington, D.C. At 5:00 P.M. on June 18, a hearing was held before Judge Gerhard Gesell. Judge Gesell refused to issue an injunction, ruling in favor of the *Post*. The government immediately appealed, and a hearing was held at 9:45 P.M. that evening before the Court of Appeals for the D.C. Circuit. The appellate court issued a temporary injunction halting further publication until the full court could hear the appeal and thereafter issued an opinion denying the injunction and ruling in favor of the *Post*.

Both the New York and Washington, D.C., cases were appealed to the United States Supreme Court. The Supreme Court granted certiorari on Friday, June 25, and scheduled oral argument for the next day, Saturday, June 26, an extraordinary step that had never before been taken in the history of the Supreme Court.

The Supreme Court that gathered for oral argument at 11:00 A.M. on Saturday, June 26, 1971, was a remarkable, perhaps a great, one. The Chief Justice was Warren Burger, who had been appointed in 1969 by President Nixon to replace Earl Warren. Chief Justice Burger was relatively new to the job, but by 1971 it was clear to knowledgeable observers that he was not there to lead a revolution. The earlier, and controversial, Warren Court precedents were quite secure and indeed were often extended by the Burger Court in the 1970s.

Accompanying the Chief Justice were the other eight Justices. They were seated on the raised bench on either side of the Chief, with the most senior next to the Chief and the most junior at the ends. Seven of the Justices had served on the Warren Court, and among them were some of the truly great Justices in the Court's history. The most senior was Justice Hugo Black, an Alabaman appointed to the Court from the United States Senate by President Roosevelt in 1937. The year 1971 would be his final one on the Court. Justice Black and the next most senior Justice, William O. Douglas, appointed by President Roosevelt in 1939, were by 1971 well known for their absolutist interpretation of the First Amendment. For them, "no law" meant *No Law!* The freedoms of speech and press could not be traded off against interests in public order or morality.

Next in order of seniority was Justice John Marshall Harlan, appointed by President Eisenhower in 1955. Harlan had been a New York lawyer of great distinction and then a judge on the United States Court of Appeals. His was perhaps the most analytically powerful and exacting intellect on the Court. Also appointed by President Eisenhower was Justice Harlan's colleague William Brennan, appointed in 1956 and, like Harlan, possessed of a great analytical mind—one that tended, on the liberal side of the scales, to offset Harlan's more conservative inclinations.

The terms *liberal* and *conservative* are widely used in common parlance, but they can be misleading when applied to the Supreme Court. They are best understood as representing a frame of mind employed by Justices when interpreting the Constitution. The Justices' job is to interpret the meaning of the Constitution's provisions, such as the guarantees of free speech and press. It is not to enact their own political preferences, as legislators do. Yet the Constitution's language is spare and often ambiguous, requiring the Justices to give the language meaning in the context of history and the circumstances of cases. A Justice who is "conservative" will, as a general matter, be less willing to interpret words broadly but will instead feel more bound to the text and specific history of the Constitution. A Justice who is "liberal," on the other hand, will look to the purposes and values reflected in a constitutional term when confronted with uncertain meaning, extrapolating from those purposes and values and thus freeing himself or herself of the restraints of the Founders' exact language and specific intentions two hundred years ago.

Liberal and conservative interpretations, so understood, do not necessarily yield politically liberal or conservative results. The absolute protection of speech and press voiced by Justices Black and Douglas, which some might deem to be politically liberal, was a product of a very literal and thus conservative interpretation of the First Amendment, which provides that "Congress shall make no law . . . abridging the freedom of speech, or of the press." Justices Harlan and Brennan, in contrast, did not interpret "no law" in the First Amendment to mean literally *no* law. They both looked beyond the text—or to other terms in the text, such as "abridge"—to give the amendment meaning. Justice Harlan, the more judicially conservative justice, placed great weight on the meaning intended by the Founders, believing that limiting his interpretation to original intention served as a necessary restraint on his own power. Justice Brennan, the more judicially liberal, looked also at historical meaning, but if that meaning was insufficient to answer a question, he was willing to look also for the general purposes of a constitutional provision and translate the text's meaning in a way that would serve those original purposes in different and unanticipated circumstances.

Justices Harlan and Brennan did not bind themselves to the text. They both went beyond the words themselves in order to give the words "new" meaning. Justices Black and Douglas, in contrast, stuck to the text of the Constitution alone. Yet the Black-Douglas approach, which was the most "judicially" conservative, yielded the most expansive meaning of press freedom. The Harlan-Brennan approaches, each less judicially conservative, led to a less expansive interpretation of press freedom, one that made the press's freedom dependent on the risks of harm to other social values that the press's publication might create. The liberalism or conservatism of a Justice or a Court thus has more to do with the methods of constitutional interpretation than with the specific results reached in cases.

The final three members of the Warren Court who would decide the Pentagon Papers case were, in order of seniority, Justice Potter Stewart, appointed by President Eisenhower in 1958; Justice Byron White, appointed by President Kennedy in 1962; and Justice Thurgood Marshall, appointed by President Johnson in 1967. Justices Stewart and White were ideologically unattached, so to speak, and thus occupied the middle of the Court and cast deciding votes in many close cases. Justice Marshall was avowedly liberal, a lawyer who had cut his teeth on the civil rights struggle and, among many accomplishments, had argued the case of *Brown v. Board of Education* before the Supreme Court.

The final Justice was Harry Blackmun, appointed to the Court in 1970. Justice Blackmun was still feeling his way along, as most Justices do for the first few years. He would often remark, in his style of self-deprecating humor, that he was nominated as Nixon's third, and least worst, choice; that he was confirmed easily as a lawyer and judge from the Midwest because he had kept his nose to the grindstone and no one knew anything about him; and that he was then unceremoniously plopped into the center of the Court and handed a bunch of cases on which oral argument had already been held and on which the Court had divided 4-4, therefore requiring his deciding vote. Having survived a first year like that, the Pentagon Papers case still wasn't a breeze for him.

This was the Court that the lawyers in the Pentagon Papers case would confront at oral argument. Three lawyers argued the case, one for the United States and one each for the two newspapers. The United States was represented by the Solicitor General of the United States, an officer of the Justice Department who is responsible for representing the United States before the Supreme Court. The Solicitor General was Erwin Griswold, a person of near mythic proportions, who was unanimously revered and respected as an advocate by the members of the Supreme Court. Before becoming Solicitor General, Griswold had served for many years as the dean of the Harvard Law School.

The newspapers were represented by two distinguished lawyers. The *Washington Post*'s counsel was a highly respected private lawyer, William Glendon, of Washington, D.C. Perhaps the most interesting lawyer was Alexander Bickel, who represented the *New York Times*. Bickel was a professor at the Yale Law School, a law school that ranked with Harvard as the best or second best in the world. Bickel was one of the most distinguished constitutional law scholars in the country. His writings were known, and read, by all of the Justices on the Court.

Oral argument in the Pentagon Papers case would match two public and intellectual giants in the legal profession, and two of the greatest advocates ever to appear before the Court.

Chief Justice Burger: We will hear arguments in Nos. 1873 and 1885, The *New York Times* against the United States, and United States against *Washington Post Company.*

  Mr. Solicitor General, you may proceed.

Solicitor General Griswold: Mr. Chief Justice, it is important, I think, to get this case in perspective. The case of course raises important and difficult problems about the Constitutional right of free speech and of the free press. But it also raises important questions of the equally fundamental and important right of the Government to function, a fundamental question of separation of powers [involving] the power and authority which the Constitution allocates to the President as Chief Executive and as Commander-In-Chief of the Army and Navy.

  The problem lies on a wide spectrum, and like all questions of Constitutional law involves the resolution of competing principles. [Of course,] if we were to start out with the assumption that never under any circumstances can the press be subjected to prior restraint [that is, legally prohibited from publishing in advance of publication by an injunction against a newspaper], then of course we come out with the conclusion that there can be no injunction here. But I suggest that there is no such Constitutional rule, and never has been such a Constitutional rule.

  We have, for example, the copyright laws. My son was in Toronto earlier this week, and he sent me copies of the *Globe and Mail* of Toronto, [containing the] series the Pentagon is trying to kill, each one headed "Copyright New York Times Service." I have no objection to that, but these stories which have been published have been copyrighted by the *New York Times* and I believe by the *Washington Post,* and I have no doubt that the *New York Times* and the *Washington Post* would seek to enforce their copyright [by enjoining other papers from publishing in violation of their copyright].

I suppose it is very likely that in one form or another they have obtained royalties because of their copyright on this matter.

But let us also consider other fields of the law. There is a well known branch of the law that goes under the heading of literary property. In the Court of Appeals I gave the example of a manuscript written by Ernest Hemingway, let us assume, while he was still living, [but] unpublished, perhaps incomplete, subject to revision. In some way the press gets hold of it. Perhaps it is stolen. Perhaps it is bought from a secretary through breach of fiduciary responsibility, or perhaps it is found on the sidewalk. If the *New York Times* sought to print that, I have no doubt that Mr. Hemingway or now his heirs could obtain from the courts an injunction against the press printing it.

Next, we have a whole area of law, a traditional branch of equity, involving participation in a breach of trust. There cannot be the slightest doubt, it seems to me, no matter what the motive, no matter what the justification, that both the *New York Times* and the *Washington Post* are here consciously and intentionally participating in a breach of trust. They know that this material is not theirs. They do not own it. I am not talking about the pieces of paper which they may have acquired. I am talking about the literary property, the concatenation of words, which is protected by the law of literary property.

The point of the Solicitor General's references to copyrights and intellectual property is to illustrate that these property interests are often protected by injunctions like the one the United States was seeking, and therefore, that injunctions against newspaper publication are not flatly prohibited by the First Amendment. Fair enough, but the Solicitor General also knows that the Pentagon Papers case was much different, and the property rights, or copyright, cases were of limited relevance, if any at all. The government was not seeking an injunction to protect its copyright or its ownership interests in the Pentagon Papers. It was instead seeking to prevent publication because of the harm that the publication might cause to other interests, such as national security, the safety of soldiers in Vietnam, and the like. Prohibiting publication of a specific story because the government dislikes the story or believes it to be dangerous is different from Hemingway protecting his right to control when his writings will be released. When government seeks the injunction, when the material to be barred from publication is an account of the government's own conduct, and when the government's motive is not to protect its ownership or copyright but its ability to conduct foreign affairs in secret, the Supreme Court must scrutinize the government's actions very carefully, for the actions look a lot like censorship.

But the Solicitor General's point is crucial, for he is trying to negate from the outset any idea that the First Amendment flatly and absolutely prohibits injunctions against publication and gives the press complete power over publication decisions, permitting legal sanctions to be brought to bear *only after* publication in the form of punishment or damages. For Griswold—and, as it turns out, for both the *Times* and the *Post*—the only question in the case was whether the government could prove that the harm occasioned by publication of the Pentagon Papers was great enough to justify enjoining publication from the outset.

Solicitor General Griswold: Again I say I don't regard this as controlling or conclusive in this case. I am simply trying to advance the proposition that there are many factors and many facets here, and that there is no Constitutional rule that there can *never* be prior restraint on the press or on free speech.

Question: Mr. Solicitor General, I did not understand your brother counsel on the other side [representing the *New York Times* and the *Washington Post*] to really question any of this. I thought at least for purposes of this case they conceded that despite the First Amendment an injunction would be permissible in this case if the disclosure of this material would in fact pose a grave and immediate danger to the security of the United States.

The Solicitor General: Mr. Justice, if they have conceded it, I am glad to proceed on that basis.

Question: I am not conceding it for them, but that had been my understanding of what the issue is.

The Solicitor General: I may say that their briefs were served on me within the last hour, which was entirely in accordance with this Court's order, but I have not seen their briefs. I do not know what is in their briefs.

Question: In other words, I had thought—and I have not had the benefit of much more time than you have had—that this basically comes down to a fact case, that the issues here are factual issues.

The Solicitor General: And that, Mr. Justice, is extremely difficult to—

Question: To argue here in this Court, I understand.

The Solicitor General: In open court.

This exchange focuses on defining the question the Court must address. The Solicitor General's definition of the question facing the Court was clarified and, effectively, accepted. The question was not whether an injunction could *ever* be obtained by government to prevent a newspaper from publishing a story, but instead what the government must show to get such an injunction in this case, and whether the facts of the Pentagon Papers case satisfied the standard.

On the first issue, the standard to be met, the Solicitor General's position is that a grave but general harm—such as interference with the conduct of ongoing negotiations—that would almost certainly, though not immediately, result from publication, should suffice to satisfy the First Amendment. The *Times* and *Post,* in contrast, argue that the harm from publication must be very concrete and specifically identified, that it must be very serious and irreversible, and that it must follow directly and immediately from publication.

The second question is whether a grave harm existed in the case and whether it was sufficiently likely to be caused by publication of the Pentagon Papers. This is the fact question to which the Justice's question refers.

The Solicitor General: Now, with respect to the actual factual situations, the only thing I can do is point to the closed brief, which I have filed, in which there are ten specific items referred to.

I have brought here the 47 volumes [of the Pentagon Papers] that are supposed to be the background of this case. [To narrow the issues upon which the government relies,] I delegated to able and conscientious associates the preparation of a "supplemental statement," which [consists of] the materials specified in the special appendix before the [Court of Appeals in New York], and such additional items added in a supplemental statement filed at five P.M. yesterday.

I had nothing to do with preparing the supplemental statement. However, when I had a chance to see it last evening, after the State Department called me at eight or nine-o'clock at night and [asked to add] four additional items, I examined it. Here is a copy of it. I find it much too broad. In particular it has at the end a statement in view of the uncertainties as to the precise documents in the newspapers' custody—we do not know now, and never have known, what the papers in the possession of the *Times* and the *Post* are.

Question: I thought the *New York Times* was required to and did give you a list of what they had.

The Solicitor General: They prepared an inventory, but it is not possible to tell from it whether they are the same papers that we have. . . . Therefore, I am saying with respect to the factual question [presented in this case—

i.e., the harm that may result from disclosure—] that we rely *only* on items specified in the supplemental appendix filed in the Second Circuit and on such additional items as are covered in my closed brief in this case, which total 10 items. I spent all of yesterday afternoon in constant successive conversations with the individuals from the State Department, the Defense Department, the National Security Agency, and I said, "Look, tell me what are the worst, tell me what are the things that really make trouble." They told me and I made longhand notes of what they told me. From that I prepared the closed brief.

Question: Well, Mr. Solicitor General, if we disagreed with you on those [ten items] that you have covered, [would that end the case, because we would not need to look at] the remainder of the items?

The Solicitor General: Mr. Justice, I think that the odds are strong that that is an accurate statement. I must say that I have not examined every one of the remainder of the items.

The Solicitor General is at a considerable disadvantage here. He does not know exactly what the *Times* and *Post* have in their possession. He has not been able to read all of the forty-seven volumes of the papers in the very short time available to him. He therefore can't be very specific about the risks presented by publication of the Pentagon Papers, and of course, he can't speak to those risks and the documents posing them in the open oral argument before the Court. He has had no choice but to accept, after discussion and (one suspects) some debate within his office, the government officers' claims of harm, which he has reduced to ten items specified in the closed brief.

Question: Are you making an argument that even if those ten items that you have covered do not move us very far that nevertheless the cumulative impact of all of the others might tip the scale?

The Solicitor General: Yes, and that there ought to be an opportunity for a full and free judicial consideration of each of the items covered in the supplemental appendix. It is perfectly true that there was a trial before Judge Gesell in the District Court in Washington, D.C. I referred to it in my closed brief as "hastily conducted." Judge Gesell started the trial at eight o'clock last Monday morning, and was under orders from the Court of Appeals to have his decision made by five P.M. There are 47 volumes of material, and millions of words. There are people in various agencies of the government who have to be consulted, and Mr. Glendon [the *Washington Post*'s lawyer] quite appropriately conducted cross examination, which took time. Much of the material had to be presented by affidavits, and there simply has not been a full careful consideration of it. To the best of my knowledge, based on what was told me yesterday afternoon by the concerned persons, the ten items in my closed brief are the ones on which we most rely, but I have not seen a great many of the other items in the special appendix simply for sheer lack of time.

Question: What was the length of the trial before Judge Gurfein in the New York case?

Mr. Seymour [an Associate Solicitor General]: The *in camera* proceedings [i.e., those conducted in private before the judge alone and not open to the public or the press], your Honor, were approximately four hours, including cross examination and argument.

Question: What was the length of the hearing in the Court of Appeals for the Second Circuit?

Mr. Seymour: The total argument there, public and *in camera,* was just over three hours. The *in camera* portion was about an hour, I would guess.

Question: Decisions were rendered in the New York case by the District Court within two days afterwards?

Mr. Seymour: Within less than 24 hours, your Honor. The hearing finally finished at 10:45 P.M., on Friday night. Decision was rendered at 2:25 P.M., Saturday afternoon.

Question: What was the time interval in the decision by the Court of Appeals?

Mr. Seymour: I believe it went one full day, that is, the decision was rendered late on the day of the 23rd. The argument was finished shortly after five on the 22nd.

Question: And in the proceedings in the District of Columbia?

The Solicitor General: The trial in the District of Columbia occurred between eight A.M. and five P.M., including the decision last Monday. I participated in the oral argument in the Court of Appeals, and it occupied two hours and forty-five minutes. It started at about 2:15 and was over I think just before five. That is the entire amount of judicial time which has been devoted to millions of words.

Question: Mr. Solicitor General, do you also say that the ten items you have talked about fully justify the classification that has been given them and which still remains on them?

The Solicitor General: Mr. Justice, I am not sure whether this case turns on classification.

Question: I agree it probably does not.

The Solicitor General: My position would be that as to those ten items—it is more than ten documents, but ten items—they are properly classified "Top Secret". One of the items, I should make plain, is *four volumes* of the 47 volumes, four related volumes all dealing with one specific subject, the broaching of which to the entire world at this time would be of extraordinary seriousness to the security of the United States. As I say, that is covered in my closed brief, and I am not free to say more about it.

Question: As I understand it, Mr. Solicitor General, your case does not really depend upon the classification of this material. In other words, if the *New York Times* and the *Washington Post* had this material as a result of the indiscretion or irresponsibility of an Under Secretary of Defense who took it upon himself to declassify all of this material and give it to the papers, you would still be here.

The Solicitor General: I would still be here.

Question: Your case depends upon the claim, as I understand it, that the disclosure of this information would result in an immediate grave threat to the security of the United States of America.

The Solicitor General: Yes, Mr. Justice.

Question: However it was acquired, and however it was classified.

The Solicitor General: Yes, Mr. Justice. But I think the fact that it was obviously acquired improperly is not irrelevant in the consideration of that question. I repeat, it was obviously acquired improperly.

The legality of the Pentagon Papers's acquisition by the newspapers was a tricky matter in the case. The United States was not claiming that the *Times* or the *Post* had acted illegally in receiving the records and documents from the Pentagon Papers, nor that the papers' mere possession of the material or even its publication as news violated any criminal law. Were it otherwise, the government would not have had to seek an injunction and face the very difficult proof requirements about serious harm immediately caused by publication.

On the other hand, the government took the position that the person or persons (Daniel Ellsberg, as it turns out) who had removed the information from the government's control and disclosed it to the newspapers did, in fact, violate one or more criminal laws of the United States. Those persons could be charged with a crime and prosecuted.

But why, if the material was stolen by Ellsberg and if the *Times* knew it, shouldn't the *Times* be guilty of violating the law? Part of the answer is that there was at the time no law making the *Times*'s knowing receipt of the Pentagon Papers a crime. And if there had been such a law? This part of the answer is more complicated and won't arise for many years until the *Bartnicki* case in 2001, when the Court will have to answer the question. The *Bartnicki* case will be discussed in a later chapter of this book, in story 6.

But for the time being, and in the absence of a criminal statute making the newspapers' receipt of the Pentagon Papers a crime, the Solicitor General is forced to admit that the "theft" from the government and the breach of security involved in that theft are *legally* irrelevant to the government's case for an injunction against the *Times* and the *Post*.

Question: May I ask, Mr. Solicitor General, am I correct that the injunctions so far granted against the *Times* and the *Post* have not stopped other newspapers from publishing materials based on this study or kindred papers?

The Solicitor General: It is my understanding, Mr. Justice, that except with respect to the items in the *New York Times,* the *Washington Post* and the *Boston Globe,* there has not been anything else published which was not already published either in this series, or elsewhere.

Question: Mr. Solicitor General, to the extent anything has been published and has already been revealed, the United States is not seeking an injunction against further publication of that particular item?

The Solicitor General: No, Mr. Justice. I think at that point we would agree that it becomes futile. It is useless.

Question: Mr. Solicitor General, this brings me back to my original question of a few moments ago as to what the real basic issue in this case is. As I understand it, you are not claiming that you are entitled to an injunction simply or solely because this is classified material.

The Solicitor General: No.

Question: Nor do I understand you to be claiming that you are entitled to an injunction because the material was stolen from you, that it is the government's property. You are claiming rather that whether or not it is classified, and however it is classified, and however it was acquired by these newspapers, the public disclosure of this material would pose a grave and immediate danger to the security of the United States of America, period.

The Solicitor General: In large part, yes, Mr. Justice, but I am still trying to get some help from the background and the setting, which, I repeat, is not irrelevant: the fact that the concatenation of words here is the property of the United States, that this has been classified under Executive Orders approved by Congress, and that it obviously has been improperly acquired.

Question: That may have a great deal to do with whether or not somebody is guilty of a criminal offense, but I submit it has very little to do with [the newspaper's freedom to publish, which is] the basic First Amendment issue before this Court in this case.

The Solicitor General: All right, Mr. Justice—we must also show that publication of this material will [result in] "grave and irreparable harm to the security of the United States."

The oral argument is now turning to the heart of the case: the standard the government must satisfy to justify an injunction. The Solicitor General argues that an injunction is constitutional if the government proves that publication will result in "grave and irreparable, but not immediate and specific," harm. The background facts that the Pentagon Papers were classified or stolen are not strictly relevant to this standard, but those facts make it easier to claim that *immediacy and specificity* of the future harm are less critical because the material was classified, its classification was known, the material was purloined, and the *Times* and *Post* both knew it.

Question: I would think with all due respect to my colleague that the question of classification would have an important bearing on the question of the scope of judicial review of an Executive classification.

The Solicitor General: I think, Mr. Justice, that is true, but I also think the heart of our case is that the publication of the materials specified in my closed brief will, as I have tried to argue there, materially affect the security of the United States. It will affect lives. It will affect the process of the termination of the war. It will affect the process of recovering prisoners of war. I cannot say that the termination of the war or recovering prisoners of war is something which has an *immediate* effect on the security of the United States. I say that it has such an effect on the security of the United States that it ought to be the basis of an injunction in this case.

I would refer to the standard which was used by the District Court in this case. Judge Gesell found, after a hearing, that publication of the documents in the large may interfere with the ability of the Department of State in the conduct of delicate negotiations now in process—not in the past—now in process, or contemplated for the future, whether these negotiations involve Southeast Asia or other areas of the world. This is not so much because of anything in the documents themselves, but rather results from the fact that it will appear to foreign governments that this government is unable to prevent publication of actual government communications when a leak such as the present one occurs.

[Judge Gesell denied the injunction notwithstanding this finding, however, because he rejected] as a standard the whole question of damage to the ability of the Department of State, and that means the President, to whom the foreign relations are conferred by the Constitution, to conduct delicate negotiations now in process or contemplated for the future. I suggest to the Court that it is perfectly obvious that the conduct of delicate negotiations now in process or contemplated for the future has an impact on the security of the United States.

Judge Gesell required the government to prove that there will be a definite break in diplomatic relations, that there will be an armed attack on the United States, that there will be an armed attack on an ally, that there will be a war, that there will be a compromise of military or defense plans or intelligence operations, or a compromise of scientific and technological materials.

If the [Constitution requires proof of such specific things before they happen, the government could never] prevent the publication of improperly acquired material. The standard Judge Gesell used is far too narrow. My own view would be that in the present parlous state of the world—considering negotiations in the Middle East, considering the SALT Talks now going on—it is perhaps not inappropriate to remember that SALT is Strategic Arms Limitation Talks, the consequences of which will not be the prevention of a nuclear attack tomorrow, or next week. But only by success in this kind of negotiation can we have any hope that our children and our children's children will have a world to live in.

I suggest that when publication of documents may interfere with the ability of the Department of State in the conduct of delicate negotiations now in process or *contemplated for the future,* that should be enough by itself to warrant restraint on publication, [and such a standard would support enjoining publication in this case of the] quite narrowly selected group of 10 items covered in the special appendix and dealt with in some detail in my closed brief.

It is [the government's] view that in rational terms in the modern world, the proper standard should be great and irreparable harm to the security of the United States, [not proof of imminent danger of war or death of troops]. In the whole diplomatic area, things don't happen at 8:15 tomorrow morning. It may be weeks or months. People tell me that already channels of communication on which great hope had been placed have dried up. I haven't the slightest doubt myself that the material which had already been published and the publication of the other materials affects American lives and is a thoroughly serious matter. To say that it can only be enjoined if there will be a war tomorrow morning, when there is a war now going on, is much too narrow.

The Chief Justice: Thank you, Mr. Solicitor General.

The Solicitor General has made a quite good and earnest, if factually vague and highly theoretical, argument. His argument rests implicitly on the assertion that in a democracy no compelling reason exists to reject the sober judgment of elected officeholders in favor of the private, and perhaps selfish, profit-seeking judgment of a news corporation. He did not make this argument explicitly, a fact that he may later come to regret. But he thought it safest, it appears, to concede that the government must make a strong showing of harmful consequences arising from publication, amounting to a fair certainty of serious consequences at some time in the future and manifested in a presently unknown way.

The Solicitor General really couldn't do much better or much else than this, for he had no specific knowledge of the facts revealed in the forty-seven volumes of the Pentagon Papers, much less knowledge of exactly what the newspapers had in their possession. So he was left to argue that general diplomatic consequences, for example, were sure to follow, even though there was no way to know specifically what they would be, when they would happen, or the magnitude of their felt impacts. This simply had to be enough to satisfy the Constitution, for it was all that a court could reasonably be expected to determine. It would be a sufficiently specific and demanding standard to enable a court reviewing an injunction request to protect against the inherent self-interest, convenience, and penchant for secrecy that could color the executive branch's sober judgment.

The difficulty, of course, was threefold: (1) the government's standard was very open ended and general; (2) it required no real factual proof of specific consequences of publication; and (3) in deferring heavily to the Executive's (President's) judgment about serious harm to ongoing international and diplomatic activities or plans, it assumed the good faith and sober, nonpolitical judgment of the President. The President's good faith cannot, of course, be adjudicated in a court of law. As a consequence, a reviewing court would almost always have to take the President's word on the likelihood of future harm. This would effectively eviscerate judicial review and make injunctions against newspapers freely available in matters involving foreign affairs or national security, a dangerous invitation to politically motivated actions by the political branches against the press.

Fortunately for the Solicitor General, the oral argument and the Justices' questions never got to this level. He would have been in serious trouble had it done so. Instead, Griswold was able to focus his argument on the meaning of his proposed standard: on the gravity of the predicted harm rather than on exactly how or when it would occur, and on the discretion accorded the

President in the conduct of the nation's foreign affairs and thus the deference that should rightly and necessarily be paid to the President's expressions
of concern. The President's good faith and seriousness, in other words, should
be presumed.

Griswold, of course, had no way of knowing the President's personal views,
the strength of his concerns, the grounds on which they rested, or the types
of harms feared. Nor did he have any basis on which to question the good
faith and soberness of the President's judgment. But today we know much
more about these matters, thanks to the Oval Office tapes President Nixon
himself made. We now know President Nixon's actual reactions to the Pentagon Papers' publication and the reasons that led him to seek an injunction
against the newspapers. These things are starkly revealed in the tape record-
ings of phone conversations between President Nixon and H. R. Haldeman,
Alexander Haig, Secretary of State William Rogers, and Henry Kissinger.

The subject of the *Times*'s publication of the Papers appears to have first
come to President Nixon's attention during the course of a telephone conversation between Nixon and Haig, shortly after noon on Sunday, June 13,
1971. The conversation began with a discussion about the Vietnam War casualty figures for the prior week. The President then asked if there was anything else interesting going on in the world.

Haig: Yes sir—very significant—this, uh goddamn *New York Times* exposé
of the most highly classified documents of the war [...] Sir, the whole study
that was done for McNamara, and then carried on after McNamara left
by Clifford and the peacenicks over there. This is a devastating—uh, security breach, of—of the greatest magnitude of anything I've ever seen.
Nixon: Well, what about the, ... what about Laird, what's he going to do
about it. [...] I'd just start right at the top and fire some people.
Haig: Yes sir. Well, I'm sure it came from defense, and I'm sure it was stolen
at ... at the time of the turnover of the administration.
Nixon: Oh, it's two years old then?
Haig: I'm sure it is, and they've been holding it for a juicy time, and I think
they've thrown it out to affect Hatfield-McGovern. [...] But it's, it's something that [is] a mixed bag ... it's a tough attack on Kennedy ... it shows
that the genesis of the war, uh, really occurred during sixty-one [...]
Nixon: Yeah, Yeah. That's Clifford (perhaps laughter).
Haig: And ... it's brutal on President Johnson; they're gonna end up in a
massive gut-fight in the Democratic Party on this thing.[7]

----

7. All transcripts by Eddie Meadows, National Security Archives, George Washington University, from the Nixon Tapes, Nixon Presidential Materials Project, WHT-5-70.

The second phone call to the White House that day was from Secretary of State William Rogers. The two men began the conversation by discussing the wedding of the President's daughter in the White House the previous weekend. The conversation moved on to a discussion of the casualty figures. Then the conversation continued:

President Nixon: I don't know whether you—I didn't read the piece, but Haig was—is, uh—was telling me about it that—uh he's—uh, that—that piece in the *Times* is of course a-a massive security leak from the Pentagon you know. [. . .] It—it all is—it all relates to—it all relates, of course, to everything up until we came in.

Rogers: Yeah.

Nixon: And its—uh—it's ver—it's hard on Johnson; it's hard on Kennedy; it's hard on Lodge. Of course the . . . the difficulty from our standpoint, and I suppose the *Times* is running it now because of McGovern-Hatfield—it's also hard on the Vietnamese. [. . .]

Rogers: Isn't it awful?

Nixon: Goddamn.

Rogers: Of course McNamara looks lousy too.

Nixon: Yeah. I didn't read the piece, but he looks—apparently [. . .] McNamara started [the project] then Clifford got in—he makes McNamara look bad.

The two men then make some uncomplimentary remarks about Robert McNamara and Clark Clifford and move on to a discussion of political strategy on another matter.

It was not until the third phone call of the day, from Henry Kissinger, that the tenor of the conversation regarding the Pentagon Papers turns serious.

President Nixon: Of course it's [. . .] unconscionable on the part of the people that leaked it. Uh, fortunately it didn't come out in our administration . . . uh . . . according to Haig, it all relates to the two previous administrations. [. . .] But I hope . . . But my point is if there are any of the people there who participated in the thing—who, in leading it, that's my point. Do we know?

Kissinger: In public opinion, it actually, if anything, will help us a little bit, because this is a gold mine of showing how the previous administration got us in there. [. . .] It just shows massive mismanagement of how we got there, and it [. . .] pins it all on Kennedy and Johnson.

Nixon: Yeah? (Apparently laughing)

Kissinger: From the point of view of the relations with Hanoi it hurts a little because it just shows a further weakening of resolve.

[Later the subject of harm caused by the papers comes up again.]

Kissinger: Basically, it doesn't hurt us domestically, I think [. . .] It hurts us with Hanoi, because it just shows how far our demoralization has gone.

Nixon: Good God.

Kissinger: But basically [. . .] the decision they [Hanoi] have to make is do they want to settle with you [. . .] they know damn well that you are the one who held firm, and [. . .] no matter how much [. . .] anyone else is demoralized doesn't make any difference.

Nixon: Yeah, right, right.

On Monday afternoon President Nixon spoke with H. R. Haldeman, Chief of Staff.

President Nixon: I think the thing to do is to [. . .] find out what the statute of limitations is. [. . .] I don't think we can do much now, but if the statute of limitations is a year, and we've got a year [. . .] I know that we can charge them [. . .] and . . . uh, subpoena all these bastards and bring the case. [. . .]

Haldeman: Well this thing too is clear, it seems to me it . . . it hurts us in that it puts the war back up into a high . . . tension level, but the facts in it . . .

Nixon: Hurt the other side.

Haldeman: Don't hurt us politically so much [. . .] they hurt the others, but what they really hurt—and this is what the intellectuals [. . .] and the *Times* [. . .] is that it hurts the government. What it says is [. . .] to the ordinary guy, "all of this [Vietnam War] is a bunch of gobbledygook." But out of the gobbledygook comes a very clear thing: you can't trust the government, you can't believe what they say; and you can't rely on their judgment; and the . . . the implicit infallibility of Presidents, which has been an accepted thing in America, is badly hurt by this, because it shows that people do things the president wants to do even though its wrong, and the president can be wrong.

Nixon: Well, so much for that; the story is out. [. . .]

Haldeman: My feeling is that we shouldn't [. . .] at least Haig's urging was that, that we shouldn't do anything about it . . . until we know what—see what we've got—and that by doing anything we would only escalate it.

Nixon: I think he's right.

The reactions to the *Times* stories were a mixture of anger at the person who leaked the Pentagon Papers, political calculation, generalized concern about the ongoing Vietnam negotiations, glee at the damage done to the Democrats and specifically to Kennedy and Johnson, and an emerging appreciation of the opportunity presented to get even. In a later conversation with John Erlichman, President Nixon would say, "Hell, I wouldn't prosecute the *Times*. My view is to prosecute the goddamn . . . that gave it to 'em." The tapes speak loudly for themselves on the mix of motives and the primary ingredients leading to later legal action.

There is no reason to believe that Solicitor General Griswold had any knowledge of the tapes or the President's motives as he presented the government's argument to the Court. His job was to defend the injunction in terms of the harm it might do to the national interests.

The Court suffered under the same disability, as we will see in the exchanges with the attorneys arguing for the *Times* and the *Post*. Chief Justice Burger next called Alexander Bickel, representing the *New York Times,* to the podium.

Mr. Bickel [representing the *New York Times*]: Mr. Chief Justice, may it please the Court, we began publishing on June 13. We published on the 14th and 15th, with no move from the Government until the evening of the 14th, despite what is now said to be the gravest kind of danger, which one would have supposed would have been more obvious than it turned out to be.

Question: Mr. Bickel, aren't you going to allow some time for somebody to really see what this means before they act and some pleadings get drawn, and lawyers come into the courts?

Mr. Bickel: I plan to return briefly to that point. I point out now only what was evident to us at the hearings when we cross examined some of the Government witnesses, high ranking people in the Government, who quite evidently read these things on Sunday morning, and on the following day, and no great alarm sounded.

We were then enjoined, under prior restraint, on the 15th, and we have been under injunction ever since. The hearing [in the District Court in New York] was before Judge Gurfein. It took place on Friday last, I believe. It started first thing in the morning with open hearings. We went *in camera,* for something upward of four hours. The record will clearly show that the Judge's sole purpose, *in camera,* and his continuously expressed intent, was to provoke from the Government witnesses something specific—to obtain from them a degree of guidance that he felt he needed in order to penetrate this enormous record. It is our judgment, and it was his, that he got very little, perhaps almost nothing.

The point, however, that I want to leave with you is that at no time in the course of these hearings did the Government object to the speed or rapidity of them; at no point was more time asked for. Of course, we all labored, as I think is only proper under the knowledge that a great newspaper was being restrained from publishing, and that expedition was desirable. But there is no evidence, that I know of, that Judge Gurfein rushed the proceedings, or would have rushed them, if the Government had asked for more time. I think the Government gave Judge Gurfein all it had.

Bickel's argument is that an injunction prohibiting publication can be justified only upon proof by the government of facts establishing that a clearly identified and serious harm will be directly and imminently caused by the publication. The standard is exacting, but its key feature is the requirement of factual proof, not projection, surmise, or speculation. There is really little doubt that the government failed to produce facts proving that serious injury would be caused by publication of the Pentagon Papers. Indeed, this is the weakness in the government's case, and the reason the Solicitor General's standard is considerably looser than Bickel's standard—and a good bit less demanding of facts and of specificity in injury and causation.

Bickel starts out his argument by striking at the soft factual underbelly of the government's proof. The government, he says, gave "all it had," and that amounted to nothing concrete or specific or real. He will continue pressing this line of argument, now broadening his focus to the legal standard within which the argument gains its legal and persuasive force.

Mr. Bickel, continuing: If I may, at this point, take up Mr. Justice Stewart's question to the Solicitor General, referring to our position. We concede, and we have all along in this case conceded for purposes of the argument, that the prohibition against prior restraint, like so much else in the Constitution, is not an absolute. But beyond that, Mr. Justice, our position is a little more complicated.

   Our ultimate First Amendment point rests, of course, on the narrow exception [to the strong rule disfavoring] prior restraints on speech. Prior restraints fall on speech with a special brutality and finality and procedural ease all their own, which distinguishes them from other regulations of speech. If the criminal statute "chills" speech, prior restraint "freezes" it.

What are "prior restraints," and why are they especially disfavored under the Constitution? On a technical level, a prior restraint is nothing more than an enforceable order in advance of publication that prohibits a publisher from publishing or speaking a specific message. If the publisher violates the order by publishing the banned material, the publisher can be fined or held in contempt or punished in other ways without being able to defend his or her action by reference to the First Amendment. The wrong the publisher committed is, simply, violating the order restraining publication.

Prior restraints are, for obvious reasons, very handy ways of preventing harm from speech before it occurs—whether the harm is an invasion of a person's privacy; the piracy of copyrighted material; or the disclosure of information that would produce great harm, such as the formula for making fine anthrax. The First Amendment has never been interpreted absolutely to bar prior restraints, for obvious reasons that these examples reveal. On the other hand, the efficiency of prior restraints in keeping a lid on information or knowledge can also lead to mischief, for the prospect of keeping embarrassing or bothersome information secret is mightily tempting, especially in a democratic society in which information is power. This is the reason that prior restraints, while permitted in limited situations, are viewed with great legal suspicion when it comes to speech and press publications, and this is why Bickel argues that the claimed risk of great harm must be more than surmise and speculation about an indefinite future.

Yet in another sense the special significance of prior restraints is a bit harder to understand or defend. The only legal distinction between a law enjoining publication of a secret in advance and one that imposes criminal punishment on a person after he or she published the same secret is timing. The second kind of law, which throws the discloser into jail, is really no different or less constitutionally troublesome than the prior restraint. The purpose of the threat of criminal punishment is to deter the publisher from publishing— or else he or she will go to jail. The criminal law's purpose, in other words, is to exact a prior restraint by the *in terrorem* consequences of publishing. And if the law is clear and effective and exacts substantial punishment, this is precisely what it will accomplish.

So, we might ask, why is a law that imposes criminal punishment on a publisher deemed preferable under the First Amendment to an injunction imposed in advance of publication, at least if the injunction is imposed by a judge who can consider the First Amendment issues before deciding whether or not to issue the injunction? In both cases there is nothing that absolutely prevents a newspaper from publishing, as long as the newspaper decides to accept the consequences. And in both cases the consequences are that the publisher will go to jail.

We will return to this question later. It is a very important question, and one that may not, in the end, have any very good answer. For now, it is enough that we understand the question as we read the give and take of the oral arguments presented by the lawyers for the *Times* and the *Post*.

Mr. Bickel, continuing: A prior restraint might be possible to prevent "actual obstruction of the recruiting service," or the publication of sailing dates of transports, or the number and location of troops. I suppose that under the present law, the "recruiting service" part of that exception is problematic, but on the sailing dates of ships and the location of troops, there is a very specific statute authorizing speech restraints, but that law has not been cited against us because that is not what the newspapers have reported. That is not in our paper. That being the case, there is no applicable statute under which we are covered.

The question then necessarily arises, as a matter of *inherent Presidential authority,* what kind of feared event would give rise to an independent power on the part of the President? My suggestion would be that whatever that case—that extremity [in which presidential lawmaking power unchecked by the legislative branch exists,] when the President has independent, inherent authority to act domestically against citizens, including newspapers, and to impose a prior restraint—whatever that case may be, it cannot be this case.

Whatever that case may be, it surely is of a magnitude and of an obviousness that would leap to the eye. I submit that that cannot be this case. It cannot be that it has to take the Government, which has been reviewing these documents for many months, not just in connection with this case, but in reply to an inquiry made by Senator Fulbright, it cannot be that a Government consisting, after all, of more than just the five witnesses we heard in New York, or the ones that were heard here, over this length of time, has an unfamiliarity with these documents, substantial as they might be, which is so great that, when news of their publication comes up, nobody in the Government knows that somewhere in those documents is one which presents a mortal danger to the security of the United States.

Question: Professor Bickel, reading from Judge Wilke's dissent [in the *Post* case, he defines] "'harm' to mean the death of soldiers, the destruction of alliances, the greatly increased difficulty of negotiation with our enemies, the inability of our diplomats to negotiate, as honest brokers, between would-be belligerents."

I take it that you disagree fundamentally with that statement?

Mr. Bickel: Not entirely, Mr. Justice Blackmun. For example, [I would argue that] the death of soldiers, as in the troop ship, [could justify an injunction]. I would disagree that impairment of diplomatic relations can be a case for prior restraint, even under a statute.

Nothing that any of these judges, including Judge Wilke, have seen [in the government's proof in this case] is related by a direct, causal chain to the death of soldiers or anything grave of that sort. I have heard it all, and everything that I have read—what characterizes every instance in which the Government tries to make its case factually—is a chain of causation whose links are surmise and speculation, all going toward some distant event, itself not of the gravity that I would suggest—

Question: You know these records better than I do, but Judge Wilke says, "But on careful, detailed study of the affidavits and evidence, I find the number of examples of documents which, if in possession of the *Post*," and I repeat, this is the *Post* case, "would clearly result in great harm to the nation."

Now I repeat my question. You, therefore, disagree fundamentally with what he seems to say?

Mr. Bickel: I beg your pardon, Mr. Justice. I had thought that Judge Wilke dissented on the ground that he would like more evidence to come in. If this is a statement about the evidence, then, depending on what the standard is that he has in mind, I would think that that language does not quite communicate to me what the standard is, and I doubt that it is the narrow standard that I would contend for.

Depending on the standard that he has in mind, he is either wrong about his standard, or seven judges disagreed with him. I am sorry. I am not sufficiently familiar with the *Washington Post* case.

Question: Professor, the standard that you are contending for is "grave and immediate," is it not? Is that too general for you?

Mr. Bickel: Let me say that the difficulties of words are simply enormous—one has to bring into one's mind an image of some event and try to describe it. Let me first say that I would differentiate between a standard applicable to the President, acting on his own, and a prior restraint being imposed pursuant to a well-drawn statute, which defines the standard and the case. I would demand less of the statute than I would demand of the President.

But the standard, in general, that I would have in mind would, at one end, have a grave event—a grave danger to the nation. At the other end would be the fact of publication, and I would demand that the link between the fact of publication and the feared danger, the feared event, be *direct* and *immediate* and *visible*.

Question: I take it then that you could easily concede that there may be documents in these 47 volumes which would [properly] satisfy the definition
of "top secret,"and nevertheless would not satisfy your standard?

Mr. Bickel: That is correct, Mr. Justice. I would say that—

Question: I have not read anything in any of your documents that suggests
that no document in these 47 volumes satisfies properly the definition of
top secret.

Mr. Bickel: I don't know about that.

Question: You do not deny that, do you?

Mr. Bickel: I have no knowledge. I have never been near the documents, Mr.
Justice.

Question: But your position must be then that even if there is a document
or so, none of them satisfies your standard.

Mr. Bickel: If [I were] asked that question on the day I appeared before Judge
Gurfein, on a temporary restraining order, my answer would have been,
"I expect not, I trust the people at the *Times.*" I am fairly certain by now,
Mr. Justice, after all of this time, having read the submissions of the Government—although I was hit with another one this morning—that there
is nothing in there that would meet my standards, because if there were,
it surely should have turned up by now.

I gather the Solicitor General had the same experience yesterday afternoon that I saw Judge Gurfein having: "Please show me. Now, which are
the three, which are the five, which are the ten? Which is the most important of these?" All that I have ever heard, have been statements of the feared
event in terms of effect on diplomatic relations. If it is a military matter,
then it was in terms of the addition of a possible cause to a train of causal
factors, to a train of events that is well on the rails as is, and propelled by
sufficient other facts.

That sort of statement is the only thing we have heard, and I would submit that that does not meet any possible First Amendment standard. It does
not meet it either in the statement of the seriousness of the event that is
feared, or what is more important and more obvious in this case, in the
drawing of the link between the act of publication as the cause of that event
and the event that is feared. In the government's case here, that link is always, I suggest, speculative, full of surmises, and a chain of causation that
after its first one or two links gets involved with other causes operating in
the same area, so that what finally causes the ultimate [predicted] event
becomes impossible, [because one simply can never] say which the effective cause was.

The standard I would propose under the First Amendment would not be satisfied by such things.

Question: Your standard is that it has to be an extremely grave event [or harm] to the nation and it has to be directly and proximately caused by the publication.

Mr. Bickel: That is exactly correct.

Bickel has conceded in his argument that the government may, in the proper case, enjoin a newspaper. This is a quite remarkable—and disarming—concession, and it has the effect, among other things, of making his proposed test appear so reasonable that it need not be subjected to much challenge.

But before we accede to Bickel's brilliant legal strategy, it is useful to consider the hypothetical terrorism case at the very beginning of this story. It is very easy to view the alleged dangers only in retrospect and thus to fail to appreciate the grave concerns that were being sincerely presented to the Supreme Court. We now know that the probable dire consequences of publication of the Pentagon Papers were greatly inflated. We know of the terrible mistakes that were made in Vietnam and the imperative, clear to us now but not then, that America get out as soon as possible. And we now know about the cynicism, manipulation, and purely political motivations behind the Nixon administration's efforts to stop the Papers' publication.

But can we extrapolate from the single example of the Pentagon Papers to reach the conclusion that the press should *never* be stopped from publishing allegedly dangerous material? Can we assume that all dangers are exaggerated, if not imagined? Can we discount all politicians' motives, assuming hypocrisy and political machinations only?

And can we conclusively presume the good and tempered motives of publishers? In 1971 the world of newspaper publishing consisted mostly of a small, tight club of professionally dedicated journalists working for a relatively small number of elite newspapers. Today's newspaper world is very different. More to the point, today's national *news* world is different, consisting of large and small organizations and individual publishers whose abilities range from professional to incompetent to consciously prevaricating, and who practice in all media and in real time. The news industry today shares fewer common values and is less able to exercise self-regulation at an industry or professional level.

If a planned terrorism strike were known by the government, if the knowledge were kept secret in order to interdict the strike, and if a newspaper or a cable news organization or a Web site or an interest group or a talk show came into possession of the information and threatened to publish it, would we be highly skeptical of the risks? Would we demand proof of very specific, yet future, deaths to soldiers or agents or particular civilians, at a time certain? Would we demand that the specific and exclusive causal connection between publication of the information and the deaths be proved to a virtual certainty? Would we require the government to prove that the predicted consequences would not have happened anyway—say, by some inadvertence or incompetence?

As it turns out, one of the Justices was not prepared to let Bickel off quite as easily as his recitation of the exacting clear and present danger test implies.

Question: Mr. Bickel, it is understandably and inevitably true that in a case like this, particularly when so many of the facts are under seal, it is necessary to speak in abstract terms, but let me give you a hypothetical case. Let us assume that when the members of the Court go back and open up this sealed record, we find something there that absolutely convinces us that its disclosure would result in the sentencing to death of a hundred young men whose only offense had been that they were nineteen years old and had low draft numbers. What should we do?

Mr. Bickel: I am addressing a case of which I am as confident as I can be of anything that your Honor will not find such a document when you get back to your chambers. It is a hard case. But it is almost impossible to resist the inclination not to let the information be published, of course.

Question: I suppose in a great big global picture this is not a national threat. There are at least 25 Americans killed in Vietnam every week these days.

Mr. Bickel: No, sir, but it is a case in which the chain of causation between the act of publication and the feared event, the death of these 100 young men, is obvious, direct, immediate?

Question: That is what I am assuming in my hypothetical case. You would say the Constitution requires that it be published, and that these men die, is that it?

Mr. Bickel: No, I am afraid that my inclinations to humanity overcome the somewhat more abstract devotion to the First Amendment in a case of that sort. . . . But I do honestly think that that hard case would make very bad separation of powers law [if the President could make it without the support of a statute enacted by Congress].

Bickel proves himself once again the master of the legal sleight of hand. *Assuming,* he asks, *that the causation is proven to be direct, clear, and immediate,* would he prohibit publication to save one hundred men from death? "Of course," he says. In saying so, he concedes nothing, really, for the difficult problem is not in the number of people who would die—one or ten or one hundred or more—but rather proving that which Bickel is *allowed to assume, but which can never really be proved:* direct, clear, and immediate causation of an event that is yet to occur.

Question: Let me alter the illustration a little bit. Suppose the information was sufficient that Judges could be satisfied that the disclosure of delicate negotiations having to do with the possible release of prisoners of war would delay the release of those prisoners for a substantial period of time. I am posing that so that it is not immediate. Is that or is that not in your view a matter that should stop the publication and therefore avoid the delay in the release of the prisoners?

Mr. Bickel: On that question, which is of course a good deal nearer to what is bruited about in the record of this case, I can only say "no" unless—which I cannot imagine can be possible—the link of causation is made direct and immediate, even though the event might be somewhat distant. But unless it can be demonstrated that it is really true if you publish this, that will happen, or there is a high probability—rather than as is typical of those events, where there are seventeen causes feeding into them, any one of those entirely capable of being the single effective cause, and the real argument is, well, you add publication to that, and it makes it a little more difficult—I think, Mr. Justice, that is a risk that the First Amendment signifies that this society is willing to take. That is part of the risk of freedom that I would certainly take.

Question: I get a feeling from what you have said, that you do not think that the courts should weigh heavily the impairment of sources of information, either diplomatic or military intelligence sources. I get the impression that you would not consider that enough to warrant an injunction.

Mr. Bickel: In the circumstances of this case, Mr. Justice, I am perfectly clear in my mind that if the President, without statutory authority, goes into court, and asks for an injunction on that basis, he should not get it.

The Chief Justice: Thank you. Mr. Glendon?

Mr. Glendon [representing the *Washington Post*]: Mr. Chief Justice, your Honors, General Griswold, Mr. Bickel. We have heard here a familiar plea, familiar to us who have been involved in this case over this last intense week, that some more time is needed while the First Amendment is suspended.

Question: Can anyone know in any certain sense the consequences of disclosure of sources of information—for example, of upsetting the negotiations, if that were hypothetically true, in Paris, or possible negotiations that we don't know anything about—on the release of war prisoners, and that sort of thing? How does a government meet your burden of proof? Such a publication does not bring any battleships to the outer limits of New York Harbor, or set off any missiles, but would you say that it is not a very grave matter?

Mr. Glendon: Your Honor, I think if we are to place possibilities or conjecture against suspension or abridgement of the First Amendment, the answer is obvious. The fact, the possibility, the conjecture or the hypothesis that diplomatic negotiations would be made more difficult or embarrassed does not justify suspending the First Amendment—this is what we have in this case. Conjecture can be piled upon surmise. Judge Gurfein used the words up in New York . . . he said when there is a security breach, people get the jitters. I think maybe the Government has a case of the jitters here. But that, I submit, does not warrant stopping the press from publishing news on this matter, in the absence of a much stronger showing.

To say now that we need more time does not measure up. You are being asked to consider restraining two newspapers, while others are publishing, from giving their readers the news. It is, of course, their readers whose rights are involved, too, their right to know.

The country is now engaged in an intense national debate. Things are happening this week on that score. These lawsuits undoubtedly precipitated the Executive to turn over these documents to the Congress. Senator Fulbright, as I am sure you are all aware, has been trying for some two years to get these documents. These documents were classified Top Secret. They were classified Top Secret because some unknown individual who was never presented to the Court decided that they were Top Secret. They were all Top Secret because one was Top Secret. There has been no review of these documents except for one individual who said that he had been reviewing them for some two years for sensitivity, and the sensitivity arose from Senator Fulbright's frequent request to get these documents so that Congress could exercise its responsibility and the public could be informed.

This has been a case of broad claims and narrow proof. Substantial claims have been made. If you accept them, anyone would be worried, but we are talking here about proof. I was starting earlier to refer to a district judge telling the Government to show the top secret documents. They were in the courtroom, and the Government was invited to show them—let us look at what we are talking about—instead of dealing just with abstractions and conjectures. This was on the so-called "secret" transcript, and I

am not going to advert to it, other than to say that the one document that
the Government produced in response to this invitation set forth certain
options with reference to the war which I think any high school boy would
have no difficulty in either putting together, himself, or readily understanding. All of them are in the public press.

Now this is the sort of proof that we have been faced with, and this is
the will of the wisp that we have been chasing. Your honor, the Government came into court, they suspended the First Amendment, they stopped
us from printing, and they said they were going to prove their case. Now
it may be that the Government would feel that the courts should become
the Defense Department's security officer, and that the courts should delve
into this pile of paper, 47 volumes, on its own, from time to time, whenever the Government is so moved—that the courts should work for them.
I say, your Honor, that under our system, as I understand it, when you bring
a case, you are supposed to prove it, and when you come in claiming irreparable injury, particularly in this area of the First Amendment, you have
a very, very heavy burden.

The Chief Justice: Thank you, Mr. Glendon. Mr. Solicitor General, you have
about 12 minutes or thereabouts left.

The Solicitor General: Mr. Chief Justice, and may it please the Court, I should
like to make it plain that we are not at all concerned with past events in
this case. We are not interested in protecting anybody. That should be
obvious enough simply from the date of the materials which are involved.
We are concerned with the present and future impact of the publication
of some of this material. When I say "future," I do not mean in the 21st
Century, but I also do not mean to limit it to tomorrow, because in this
area, events of great consequence to the United States happen over peri-
ods of six months, a year, perhaps two or three years.

Reference has been made to the fact that, oh, there are leaks all the time.
There are a great many leaks, but I would point out that there is also a very
wide respect for the security classification system and its potential impact
on the security of the United States. Senator Fulbright did not publish this
material. He requested of the Secretary of Defense what use he could make
of it, and I have seen on the television other members of Congress who
said that they had some of the material but felt it not appropriate to use
it, because it was classified Top Secret.

Question [from Justice Hugo Black]: Mr. Solicitor General, what particularly worries me at this point is that I assume that if there are studies now
being made, in the future there will be studies made about Cambodia, Laos,
you name it. If you prevail in this case, then in any instance in which any-

body comes by any of those studies, a temporary restraining order will automatically be issued. Am I correct?

The Solicitor General: It is hard for me to answer the question in such broad terms. I think that if properly classified materials are improperly acquired, and that it can be shown that they do have an immediate or current impact on the security of the United States, that there ought to be an injunction.

Question: Wouldn't we then—the Federal courts—become a censorship board—

The Solicitor General: That is a pejorative way to put it, Mr. Justice. I do not know what the alternative is.

Question: The First Amendment might be.

The Solicitor General: Yes, Mr. Justice, and we are, of course, fully supporting the First Amendment. We do not claim or suggest any exception to the First Amendment. We do not agree with Mr. Glendon when he says that we have set aside the First Amendment, or that Judge Gesell or the two courts of appeal in this case have set aside the First Amendment by issuing the injunction. The problem in this case is the meaning and interpretation of the First Amendment.

Now Mr. Justice [Black] your construction of the First Amendment is well-known, and I certainly respect it. [The First Amendment reads: "Congress shall make no law abridging the freedom . . . of the Press. . . ."] You say that "no law" means no law, and that should be obvious. I can only say, Mr. Justice, that to me it is equally obvious that "no law" does not mean "no law," and I would seek to persuade the Court that that is true.

As Chief Justice Marshall said, so long ago, it is a *Constitution* we are interpreting, and all we ask for here is the construction of the Constitution in light of the fact that the First Amendment is a part of the Constitution, and there are other parts of the Constitution that grant powers and responsibilities to the Executive, and that the First Amendment was not intended to make it impossible for the Executive to function or to protect the security of the United States.

It has been suggested that the Government moved very slowly in this matter. The *Times* started publishing on Sunday. On Monday, the Attorney General sent a telegram to the *New York Times,* asking them to stop and to return the documents. That is pretty fast as the Government operates, in terms of the consultations that have to be made, the policy decisions that have to be made. The *New York Times* refused the government's request. On Tuesday, the United States started this suit.

It is suggested that there have been full hearings, that everything has been carefully and thoroughly considered. But there is clear evidence of haste in both records. The only hearings that have been held in any courts are as to whether a preliminary injunction should be granted. They were not intended to be full, plenary trials, but merely sufficient to show the probability of possible success. There simply was not time to prepare a comprehensive listing or a comprehensive array of expert witnesses. The Government relied on the fact that the District judge would examine the study, and on the record, he concededly refused to do so. This was at the heart of the decision of the Court of Appeals for the Second Circuit, in its decision to remand for a full week of hearings on the merits.

Question: Which case are we talking about now?

The Solicitor General: I am talking about the *New York Times* case in the Second Circuit. The Second Circuit sent it back to the judge for a hearing—

Question: As I understood it, there was no claim that Judge Gurfein did not consider everything that was then before him, but that new matter was brought to the attention of the Court of Appeals for the Second Circuit?

The Solicitor General: On the contrary, Mr. Justice, the full 47 volumes were offered to Judge Gurfein, and he refused to examine them.

Question: He did not. He did not refuse to, he failed to.

The Solicitor General: No, Mr. Justice, he said that he would not examine them.

Question: He said that he did not have time to, but he did ask the Government to please bring forward the worst.

The Solicitor General: No, I think that really came at a later stage.

Question: Then a new matter was brought to the attention of the Second Circuit—

The Solicitor General: Brought to the attention of the Second Circuit Court of Appeals, and they sent it back for a hearing. Everything about this case has been frantic. That seems to me to be most unfortunate.

Question: No. The reason is, of course, as you know, Mr. Solicitor General, that unless the constitutional law, as it now exists, is changed, a prior restraint of publication by a newspaper is presumptively unconstitutional.

This means that the government bears the burden of proof, indeed a heavy burden of proof, to demonstrate that an injunction is warranted. To meet that burden, the Justice is saying, *at least some evidence* must be offered by the government. Having failed to offer any concrete claim of harm flowing from publication, much less any evidence supporting the claim, the government's complaint that it had insufficient time to prove its case amounts to little more than a plea that the government deserves more time to root around in the Papers at its leisure, which would mean until the *Times* no longer really cares about publishing the Papers any more.

The Solicitor General: It is a very serious matter. There is no doubt about it. And so is the security of the United States a very serious matter. We have two important constitutional objectives here which have to be weighed and balanced, and made as harmonious as they can be. But it is well known that the *Times* had this material for three months. It is only after the *Times* has had an opportunity to digest it, and it took them three months to digest it, that it suddenly becomes necessary to be frantic about it. It was not so terribly important to get it out and get it to the public while the *Times* was working over it, but after that, now the *Times* finds it extremely difficult to accept an opportunity for the courts to have an adequate chance, first, to resolve the extremely difficult question of the proper construction of the First Amendment in this situation, and I concede that it is an extremely difficult question. If the proper construction is the one which Mr. Justice Black has taken for a long time and is well known, of course, there is nothing more to be said. But our contention is that that is not the proper construction.

Question: And the counsel on the other side do not disagree with you, Mr. Solicitor General. They do not take Mr. Justice Black's position, at least for purposes of argument in this case.

The Solicitor General: Frankly, I do not think it is much of a limitation [i.e., concession by the newspapers] to say that it can be enjoined if it will result in a break of diplomatic relations or a war tomorrow. As I have already said, we think the standard used by Judge Gesell is wrong. The standard which Judge Gesell used is to say that unless publication presents a direct and immediate, grave harm, and satisfies the definition of top secret, that it does not meet the First Amendment requirement. I contend that that is wrong.

I have sought to show in the closed brief, which is filed here, that there are items in this material which will affect the termination of the war in Vietnam, which will affect negotiations such as the SALT Talks, which will affect the security of the United States vitally over a long period, and which will affect the problem of the return of prisoners of war. I suggest that however it is formulated, the standard ought to be one which will make it possible to prevent the publication of materials that will have those consequences.

The Chief Justice: Thank you, Mr. Solicitor General.

The case is submitted.

(Whereupon, at 1:13 o'clock P.M. the argument was concluded.)

The oral argument in *New York Times v. United States* was about as good as oral argument gets in the Supreme Court. The differences between the two sides were clearly marked; the reasons for the positions taken, as well as their practical consequences, were clearly set out. The lawyers responded to the Justices' questions forthrightly and specifically, with no hemming and hawing. They were obviously well prepared.

But the lawyers, and the Court, too, labored under a substantial disability: there was really no concrete evidence of well-defined and factually specific harms that would result from the publication of the Pentagon Papers; thus it was hard to argue exactly how and why the balance should be struck between freedom of the press and national security. This problem was particularly difficult for Solicitor General Griswold. He had the forty-seven volumes of the Pentagon Papers before him, but it was impossible for him to review such a mountain of material in the time available to him. Even if he had been able to read all of the materials, he would have been hard pressed to identify or evaluate the national security risks they presented. He was thus forced to rely on the ten or so specific documents or sets of documents that people in various parts of the government had supplied to him and to accept with little questioning the asserted risks that publication of the documents posed.

The legal strategy available to Griswold was thus forced upon him by circumstance. He would, first, candidly acknowledge the fact that he had had no opportunity to examine, much less carefully consider, all the documents. Moreover, he would express considerable doubt even about many of the materials to which he was directed by the relevant agencies of the government, stating openly that he could give credence only to ten items, and qualified credence even as to them. The Solicitor General's responsibility as an officer of the Court required that he make such admissions. In any event, were he not to make them, the Court would surely press him to be more specific, and he would have to demur.

And another hard fact also presented itself: if the Solicitor General hadn't the time or experience to read and interpret all of the documents, the Supreme Court Justices would certainly find themselves in the same position once they began to look at any portions of the mountain of material. This fact might actually help his argument. If the Justices found themselves in the same fix that the Solicitor General was in, they might be more sympathetic to the difficulties presented by cases like this one and thus better appreciate the nature and force of his arguments on the merits.

The circumstances then drove the Solicitor General to a second, and inevitable, tactic. He would have to argue that the First Amendment requires a showing of grave and probable harm in order to stop a newspaper from publishing publicly significant material in its possession. But he could argue that the grave harm need not be specifically identified and need not be imminent. Under such a standard the Solicitor General could make an argument for the government without blushing: forty-seven volumes of classified material were, by virtue of bulk alone, likely to present serious national security risks; in any event, the relevant agencies of government—the CIA, State Department, Defense Department—had all expressed great concern, as had the President of the United States.

The Supreme Court, the Solicitor General would argue, is the head of an unelected branch of government unfamiliar with the conduct of war and removed from ongoing foreign relations. It therefore *must* defer to the Chief Executive's judgment of the facts, the risks to ongoing peace negotiations, confidential intelligence activity, and the likelihood of lives lost. Such judgments communicated to the Supreme Court by the President simply must be accepted without the Court requiring the President to reduce them to a specific number of lives that would be lost at a particular place at a particular time. It matters not in the larger global scheme of things whether lives would be lost in a specific battle or by virtue of a prolongation of a war; or whether the harm would be damage to the country's ability to successfully engage in negotiations with another country (Russia, for example) on another front (an Anti-Ballistic Missile Treaty, for example); or, indeed, whether lives would be lost as a result of future terrorist acts unless adequate intelligence information is obtained now. The fact of probable adverse consequences from publication of secret documents, attested to by the executive branch, should be enough. As to timing, a harm's inevitability, not its imminence, should matter. Are one hundred deaths next week more serious than the heightened risk of nuclear conflagration if the ABM Treaty is not successfully negotiated? Can a court possibly make such a judgment?

This was the argument the Solicitor General made, and made well. He began it with allusions to the many settings in which publication of material is now stopped in advance, such as copyright violations, invasion of privacy, and disclosure of trade secrets in commercial settings. But these examples were, as he said, just background observations—facts that put the government's claim in a more sympathetic perspective. He then argued that the First Amendment was not an absolute bar to prior restraints, even as to publication of information about government. In this he was helped by the agreement of the opposing lawyers. The question in the case, therefore, was simply how grave the harm, how specific its definition, and how imminent its occurrence must be to satisfy the First Amendment. Viewed against this background, the government's argument is far from unreasonable; indeed, when combined with the inability of the Supreme Court to determine the significance of particular documents and assess their risk, the argument for deference to the President's judgment of risk is very strong.

Bickel's argument, by contrast, was both easier and harder. It was easier because both sides agreed that the government bore the burden of justifying an injunction. Bickel, therefore, did not have to address the specifics of the Pentagon Papers or the particular risks they might present. He could just sit back and say to the government, "Show me," and then "Prove it," without more. The *New York Times,* in other words, didn't need to explain or defend its decision to publish. Its reasons for publication were constitutionally irrelevant.

Bickel could therefore say, as he did, that he had never even looked at the Pentagon Papers and didn't consider it his place or duty to do so. He was both wise and right in this statement. And the government assisted him in this line of argument by failing to bring forward any specific evidence about any concrete, imminent harm. If, then, concrete evidence of imminent and specific harm is the standard the government must meet, Bickel will win the case.

But in another sense Bickel's strategy was more difficult. By resting his argument on the proposition that the First Amendment imposes a burden on the government that can rarely if ever be met, Bickel *should* have to explain why the First Amendment should be so read—why it so strongly prefers private rather than public action in the first place. As it turned out, Bickel effectively was able to duck this question—indeed to prevent its coming up at all in oral argument—by conceding that the First Amendment did not prevent the government from enjoining a newspaper. The government may, he said, enjoin newspapers; the only question is whether it has the facts to justify it. The Supreme Court, apparently comfortable with this nonabsolutist, balancing legal position, found no need to argue or inquire about constitutional basics, focusing in its questions instead on the narrower and essentially technical question of *how* specific and *how* soon and *how* directly caused the harm must be.

Having successfully avoided the fundamental—and harder—constitutional questions, having defined the issue in the case to be whether the government had offered enough factual proof of its predictions of doom, and hav-

ing made sure that the judicial proceedings moved too fast for the government to have done anything else but present a muddled factual record, Bickel
assured his client's ultimate victory. It was a brilliant strategy—of which the
Solicitor General was aware, and in the face of which the Solicitor General
was helpless. The government not only failed to provide any evidence about
a specific harm directly caused by and imminently to follow from publication, but it also *failed to present any concrete factual evidence of harm whatsoever.* The government's case was all surmise and intuition. No one, not even
the Solicitor General, would argue the government needn't provide any evidence at all. No one would seriously argue that a court should just take the
President's word for it.

But that, in the end, was the case the government handed to the Solicitor
General. He did the best he could with it. But he lost. The Supreme Court
decided the case for the *Times* and the *Post,* issuing a very brief and unsigned
opinion just four days after oral argument. The opinion was short and sweet.
"The Government," the Court said, "'carries a heavy burden of showing
justification for the imposition of [a prior] restraint.' . . . The Government
ha[s] not met that burden."

Yet the Court, like Bickel, avoided the more fundamental constitutional
question: why is it that the First Amendment should be understood to place
such a near-absolute restraint on the government's ability to control the
publication of potentially harmful information? To some this will seem like
a silly question. They will say that the proposition is obvious. The First
Amendment can mean nothing without a rule keeping the government completely out of the editorial rooms of newspapers.

But others can respond that nothing in the text of the First Amendment—
"Congress shall make no law abridging . . . the freedom of the press"—gives
us much guidance about its meaning in a case like the Pentagon Papers case.
And in any event, "abridging" is an ambiguous—and certainly far from absolutist—word, as is "freedom," not to mention the possible range of meanings that might be given to "press." The government's authority to enjoin
the press is, by the admission of all the lawyers in the case and the Supreme
Court itself, a matter of *balancing* the press's interest in its own freedom
against the government's interest in self-preservation, the protection of lives,
and the accomplishment of important governmental purposes. And the reason the question is one of balancing government interests against the private interests of the *New York Times* is because the United States is a democracy in which all citizens participate and, by their participation, make laws
that subordinate private property and profits and interests to the public good.
To put the point somewhat differently: Why in a democracy should private

power be supreme over public will? Why should an editor—even one for a great newspaper such as the *Times*—have more power than a legislature, or a President in the midst of war? Who elects the editor?

This serious and important question requires us to think about democracy and its relation to individual freedom of belief; about the connection between freedom of belief and access to knowledge and information; and about the relationship between the availability of information and knowledge, and freedom of the press. How much press freedom is needed in order to assure that citizens can arrive at their own views and preferences as they vote for legislators or Presidents? Is the disclosure of secret information about war, or terrorism, that is likely to cause a serious harm at some time in the future, essential to our ability to vote, to be free individuals, or to engage in government oversight?

It is hard to argue that having access to *any and all* secret information is essential to freedom and democracy. After all, the Pentagon Papers would never have been disclosed if the government had only done its job and kept Daniel Ellsberg from getting hold of it. Nothing in the Constitution prohibits the government from protecting against disclosure of secret information. And just how much secret information does the government now possess and protect? A great deal, and some of it relates to important foreign policy subjects but is likely to present no specific, immediate threat of deaths of soldiers. Indeed, in the contemporary age of global terrorism, government is criticized for not having enough secret information and is often excoriated for releasing what little it has to the press and the public. Yet freedom and democracy persist. Legally, at least, the First Amendment has absolutely nothing to do with the government's ability to obtain information and to keep the information secret, thus preventing us from knowing it.

The argument, then, must not be about the importance of the information itself to our freedom or self-government but instead about the importance of giving *someone other than the government* the final say about what to publish about the government. Here the newspapers' First Amendment argument is a bit more cogent: an independent, outside check on the government's policies and actions may be important to keeping the government in line and to making people aware of possible problems on the horizon—self-dealing, fraud, corruption, and so on. But having that independent private party—the press—untethered to government, as important as that is, does not mean that the press needs to have absolute freedom to publish whatever it wants no matter the consequences. At some point the clash between the press and the government must be understood as a competition between an unelected, private, and profit-motivated party responsible to the morally and politically agnostic capitalistic marketplace, on the one hand, and, on the other hand, a government consisting of legislative, executive, and judicial branches, its members largely elected by the public at large under a system that does not privilege money or power in the weight given each vote cast.

Solicitor General Griswold argued, in effect, that neither of these competing interests ought to control the other. That's why the First Amendment question is one of balance between the government's claimed interest, on the one hand, and the importance of the editor's role in advancing freedom and democratic self-government, on the other. If the government can identify no harm likely to result from a publication, the editor should win. But if a substantial government and public harm is likely to result, Griswold argued that the government should win because the democratic process (even if just the democratically elected Chief Executive) is the better place for judging whether avoidance of the harm is more important than the editor's freedom from restraint. Indeed, the force of this logic is the precise reason that Bickel saw the equation the same way, as a balance. Bickel simply argued that the scales should be set strongly in favor of the private editor, given the government's natural and inevitable desire to aggrandize its own power, especially through secrecy, and given that too much secrecy would undermine basic assumptions of democracy. The harm should be specific and direct and imminent. But when it is—and only when it is—the job of weighing the harm against the editor's freedom (and through it, our own freedom) is best left to the government.

Yet, as Bickel himself admitted, if the government could prove that only one or two people would be killed as a direct and immediate result of publication, that would be enough to justify an injunction, for the editor's job is not to make judgments about the value of life. Indeed, the editor's publication decisions rarely even allow such factors to be considered, thus the oft-voiced press view that "we, the press, are not responsible for the consequences that may flow from our publication of news; we only decide whether the news we publish is useful to the public."

So the question in the Pentagon Papers case, and in the terrorism case, too, is one of balance, not of absolutes. Here both lawyers had a field of fair disagreement and space to make interesting and important arguments to explore the meaning and value of freedom and the press. But without a factual setting more certain than the shifting sands in the Pentagon Papers record, such an argument was hard, perhaps impossible, to have. Only broad theory could be offered. And in the end, broad theory, alone, is unsatisfying—

for all sides. It is unsatisfying for those inclined to agree with the government because the actual contents of the Papers and an understanding of the risks would surely be persuasive and would give muscle and skin to the skeleton of First Amendment theory. It is also unsatisfying to those more skeptical of the government and more trusting of the editor, for understanding the editors' choices and how they are actually made would be useful information for all persons who are asked to place great faith in them. More fundamentally, knowing enough to see President Nixon's apparent indifference to the publication of the Pentagon Papers for any reasons other than political expediency—knowing, in short, of the seeming hypocrisy and political shallowness of the government's motives and the utter lack of any perceived harm (except a political harm to Democrats)—would have concretely reinforced the importance of being skeptical of government and its motives. It would have shown the importance of a private press to maintaining needed skepticism.

Nixon Tapes, Monday, 14 June 1971
Telephone Conversation with John Mitchell, 7:19 P.M.
Source: Nixon Presidential Materials Project, WHT-5-70
Transcribed by Eddie Meadows, National Security Archive, The George Washington University

Nixon: Hello

Mitchell: Mr. President

Nixon: What is your advice on that—uh, *Times* thing John? Uh—you—you would like to do it?

Mitchell: Uh—I would believe so Mr. President, otherwise we will look a little foolish in not following through on our—uh, legal obligations, and—uh

* * *

Nixon: How—how do you go about it—you do it sort of low key?

Mitchell: Low key—you call them, and then—uh, send a telegram to confirm it.

Nixon: Uh-huh, uh-huh—say that we're just—uh, we're examining the situation, and we just simply are putting you on notice

Mitchell: (Unclear) we're putting them on notice that they're violating a statute, because we have a communication from Mel Laird as to the nature of the documents, and they fall within a statute. Now, I don't know whether you've—you've been—noticed it, but this thing was—uh, Mel is working

Nixon: Henry—Henry's on the other—I just—he just walked in—I'll put him on the other line—go ahead.

Mitchell: Uh, Mel—uh, had a pretty good go up there before the committee today on it, and it's all over town, and all over everything, and I think we'd all look a little silly if we just didn't take this low-key action of advising them about the publication

Nixon: Did Mel—did Mel take a fairly—uh, hard line on it?

Mitchell: Uh, yes, he—hahaha—gave a legal opinion, and it was a violation of the law, which—uh, of course puts us at where we have to get to

Nixon: Well look—look—as far as the *Times* is concerned, hell, they're our enemies—I think we just oughta do it—and anyway, Henry tell him what you just heard from Rostow

Kissinger: Well, Rostow called on behalf of Johnson, and he said that it is Johnson's strong view that this is an attack on the whole Integrity of government—that if you—that if whole ca—if whole file cabinets can be stolen and then made available to the press—uh, you can't have orderly government anymore. And he said if the president defends the integrity, any action we take he will back publicly.

Mitchell: Well—uh, I—I think that we should take this (unclear), do some—uh, undercover investigation, and then open it up.

Nixon: Yeah

Mitchell: Uh, we've got some information we've developed as to where these copies are, and who they're likely to—uh, have leaked them, and the prime suspect, according to your friend Rostow, you're quoting, is a gentleman by the name of Ellsberg, who is a left-winger that's now with the RAND Corporation, who also have a set of these documents

Nixon: Subpoena them—Christ, get them

Mitchell: Uh, so I would—I would think that we should advise the *Times* we will start our covert check [later] . . . just open it up

Nixon: Right, go ahead

Nixon Tapes, Tuesday, 15 June 1971
Telephone Conversation with Charles Colson, 6:21 P.M.
Source: Nixon Presidential Materials Project, WHT-5-81
Transcribed by Eddie Meadows, National Security Archive, The George Washington University

Operator: Mr. President, I have Mr. Colson for you

Colson: Yes—yes sir, Mr. President

Nixon: I was thinking on our—uh, this—uh—uh, *New York Times* thing Uh (stammering) maybe you could generate some support from some of our—our constituent groups on this—you know—uh, like for example— uh, I think veterans and—uh—uh

Colson: Yes sir

Nixon: And—uh fellow like Meany ought to pop-up on this one, you know

Colson: Uh-huh

Nixon: I mean this—and also I think that on the congressional side that what is really needed—here's a great opportunity for a—a young congressman, or—uh, a vigorous congressman and or senator or so, to really—uh, go— go—go all out on a thing like this. . . . You know now they're—they have the privilege of the—you know—they—they're—what they have is—uh, of course—uh, they can say anything they please—uh, on the floor—uh, and even though the case is gonna be in the courts

Colson: Right

Nixon: We're gonna be stuck with it; but on the other hand—uh—uh, we can't say much; but—uh, but I—I think that it's very important to—to— to build a backfire on these people. Understand, I—I personally think that if we cast this in the right direction, Chuck, this could backfire on the *Times*—I (unclear)

Colson: Oh I think absolutely (unclear)

Nixon: They're playing by their own constituency. Now, we've got to get across several points; one, it's the Kennedy-Johnson papers

Colson: Uh-huh

Nixon: (Unclear, stammering) basically—that's what we're talking about— the Kennedy-Johnson papers, and that gets it out of our way. Second, It's a family quarrel; we're not gonna comment on (unclear)

Colson: Yes sir

Nixon: But what we have is the larger responsibility, to maintain the Integrity of government—

Colson: Wholly unrelated to these papers

Nixon: and—as Rogers said in his press conferences, he had inquiries from foreign governments today, as to whether their papers were s—uh, classified—er, you know

Colson: Right

Nixon: And that—I mean it really involves the ability to conduct government—how the hell can a president, or a secretary of defense, or anybody do anything

Colson: That's right

Nixon: And—uh, how can anyone make a contingency plan if it's gonna be taken out in a trunk and given to a goddamn newspaper

Colson: Well, I don't think there's any question Mr. President that it'll ba—my own feeling is that it will backfire against the *New York Times,* and we can help generate this . . . We can certainly get the veterans groups—uh, (unclear)

Nixon: Yeah—uh—you know, I think some of them should—they ought to put—cast this—(stammering) listen—uh, the main thing is to cast it in terms of doing something disloyal to the country

Colson: That's right

Nixon: This risks our men you know—just—uh, all that sort of thing—secret—uh, things that—uh, aid and comfort to the enemy—I mean, after all—(unclear) Jesus, its—uh,

Colson: I think the *Times* position is indefensible; I think that—uh, it's—it's distinguishable from any other case, in that here we went to them and said you can't publish that; it's a violation of security, and they said to hell with you we're going ahead and publish anyway. So we—we—we would have been very, very remiss in our duties had we not taken whatever legal means were available to prevent it—and—uh, I think we (unclear)—I think you'll find a great deal of popular support for—uh,

Nixon: If we can generate

Now, they're—they're running the line, Chuck, a right to know—b—raise that with Price; ask him how do you answer "right to know"?

That's of course a Goddamn code-word: right to know—the public has no right to know secret documents

Colson: And (unclear, stammering) you can make the point that—that "right to know" does not include things which will compromise the—either the security (unclear, both talking)

Nixon: (Unclear) which will injure the country, and—and right—and—and freedom of the press does not—is not the freedom to—uh, destroy the integrity of the government—to print—uh, well

Colson: And if you—if it were the battle plan for the withdrawal of troops next week, that could subject boys to attack, why there'd be no argument about it. Now the integrity of the system as a whole is at stake

Nixon: That's right

Colson: You simply cannot allow a newspaper to publish classified documents

Nixon: If they justify this, then in any future ca—case. then the publisher of a paper will put himself—that was really what Alger Hiss did you see. . . . Well, pour it on them.

Colson: We'll—we'll pour it on—we're coming up with

Nixon: Get some congressmen stirred up

Colson: We'll get the congress, and some editorials, and (unclear) our groups
Nixon: Good

Nixon Tapes, Tuesday, 15 June 1971
Telephone Conversation with John Mitchell, 6:35 P.M.
Source: Nixon Presidential Materials Project, WHT-5-86
Transcribed by Eddie Meadows, National Security Archive, The George Washington University

Mitchell: Yes Mr. President
Nixon: I wondered—uh, (unclear) if you had any—uh—uh, success with Rogers
Mitchell: Yes, he's agreeable to do it.
Nixon: And he'll get out a sort of a general statement of some sort (unclear)
Mitchell: Yes sir, it will not—uh, be limited solely to the foreign affairs (unclear)
Nixon: I think what is very important in this is to find a way to get some strong language—like a massive breach of security—things of that sort, so that we can get something in the public mind—we're not just interested in making the technical case for the lawyers.
Mitchell: Exactly

Nixon Tapes, Tuesday, 15 June 1971
Telephone Conversation with William Rogers, 6:44 p.m.
Source: Nixon Presidential Materials Project, WHT-5-89
Transcribed by Eddie Meadows, National Security Archive, The George Washington University

Rogers: Hello Mr. President
Nixon: You had a long day
Rogers: Yeah, sort of (laughing)
Nixon: (Unclear) I started at eight o'clock with a congressman and I've been going like a chicken with my head cut off—but I—uh, wanted to tell you I just—uh, got a chance to go over the—uh, press thing—I just think you couldn't have done it better. And I think par—(unclear, stammering)—particularly effective is what you said about the fact that—uh, some foreign—uh, governments have raised questions about the security of their own cables, and that sort of thing
Rogers: Right
Nixon: Because Goddamit it's true

Rogers: Right

Nixon: How can we—uh, how can they—uh, they wonder if—uh—if we just allow wholesale—uh, publication—declassification I should say—did you know that the documents—uh, with regard to Pearl Harbor have not been de—declassified yet?

Rogers: Isn't that something!

Nixon: This thing is—uh—uh, we can talk about somebody placing themselves above the law and all that, but on this—uh, statement thing, they—my feeling is that first I cannot say anything, I feel because it's in the courts. I think you can, solely from a—

Rogers: Sure

Nixon: A foreign—can you—don't you think so?

Rogers: Sure. I'll be glad to say anything that'd be helpful. . . .

Rogers: But—uh, the—uh—dammit they never carry the good things—I said that when they talked about this thing—I—(unclear) McNamara papers, I said that I was not gonna get involved in—in passing judgment on it. I said we've got other things to do; we're trying to get this nation out of war

Nixon: Yeah

Rogers: I said we—what—w—I would hope that when President Nixon leaves office we can have a study made of how we got the United States out of Vietnam—uh (laughter)—and uh

Nixon: Also as I say, basically this is a family quarrel—we've—I—I think the papers could well be called the Kennedy-Johnson papers is what they are you know—

Nixon: And—uh, I've told the boys here just call them Kennedy-Johnson—you know (both laughing)

Rogers: That's good

It's—uh, really a shameful, shameful (unclear)

Nixon: I just—I just—I just can't really how—see how the *Times* could do it

The private press is powerful—perhaps too powerful. The press is often unfair, protective of its own interests, corrupted by the conflict between its public and its profits. Yet while private companies, including newspaper companies, may be captives of the capitalist market and the profit motive, in the end they do not possess the attributes of government: a monopoly on the use of violence, on the enforcement of law, or on the conduct of elections. Those powers, very dangerous if abused, all belong to government.

Perhaps the burden of proof in prior restraint cases has little to do with the risk of harm. Perhaps the high, indeed nearly impossible, burden placed on government is instead a function of the risks of corruption. If a newspaper becomes corrupted—indifferent to truth or public need, for example—readers can just stop buying it. But if the government becomes corrupted, the entire constitutional scheme—individual freedom of action and belief, democratic self-government, due process, separated government powers—is in jeopardy.

Perhaps this is what the First Amendment's freedom of the press is about: the choice at its extreme between a rotten editor or an ethically corrupt President.

But why should we be put to such a stark and dark choice? We can do many things to prevent the corrupted President: pass restrictive laws, require disclosure of information, oblige the other branches to engage in oversight through committees or lawsuits. Can't we also do things to prevent the rotten editor? Does the First Amendment prevent government from passing restrictive laws, from requiring disclosure of information, and from subjecting the press to the oversight of the legislative and judicial branches?

This is the subject of the stories that follow. As it turns out, there is much that government can do, and does, to regulate the press. The First Amendment is not an absolute. As Solicitor General Griswold said, "no law" does not really mean No Law!

Additional Reading

Anderson, David. "The Origins of the Press Clause." *U.C.L.A. Law Review* 30 (1983): 455ff.

Bollinger, Lee. *Images of a Free Press.* Chicago: University of Chicago Press, 1991.

Fiss, Owen. "Why the State?" *Harvard Law Review* 100 (1987): 781ff.

Jeffries, John C., Jr. "Rethinking Prior Restraint." *Yale Law Journal* 92 (1983): 409ff.

Levy, L. *Emergence of a Free Press.* New York: Oxford University Press, 1985.

Lewis, Anthony. *Make No Law: The Sullivan Case and the First Amendment.* New York: Random House, 1991.

Meiklejohn, Alexander. "The First Amendment Is an Absolute." *Supreme Court Review* 1961 (1961): 245ff.

2. Editorial Judgment

The First Amendment provides that "Congress shall make no law abridging the freedom of speech or of the press." What distinguishes press expression from free speech, which is separately mentioned? Some scholars have argued that there is no difference. The press's freedom was mentioned simply to make certain that newspapers, pamphlets, and other publications were not left out. This is a possible explanation. Yet redundancy is not a common feature of the Constitution. And considering the notes and writings surrounding the drafting and ratification of the Bill of Rights, there seems little doubt that the drafters of the First Amendment had something different and special in mind when they used the words "freedom of the press."

The press's freedom was often described as a means of enabling publishers of news and opinion to serve a function that secures and perpetuates individual liberty of belief and a social order in which government is controlled by the governed. To achieve such ends the people would need access to useful and objective information about political, economic, and social matters, emanating from sources other than government or its agencies or instruments. This, in turn, requires that publishers and editors and writers be free to make their own, fiercely independent choices about what to publish. Free editorial judgment, in other words, is a central feature of the press's freedom under the First Amendment.

Just what does editorial judgment mean? To whom must an independent editor or publisher be responsible when making publication judgments? What assumptions about private ownership, competition, and selflessness underlie an editor's freedom? What part does truth play in the editor's choices? The two stories in this chapter force us to confront these and other questions that go to the heart of the press's editorial freedom.

STORY 2

Freedom to Decide What to Publish
Miami Herald Publishing Company v. Tornillo
418 U.S. 241 (1971)

Miami is a big, hungry, boisterous, ethnically diverse city. Politics are often divisive, contentious, and played for keeps, hardball style. Miami's newspaper, the *Miami Herald,* is also big, dominant, and aggressive. If the desirable condition of a free press in America is "uninhibited, robust and wide-open," as the Supreme Court has said, the *Herald* fits the bill. Our story involves a candidate for the Florida legislature from Miami, Pat Tornillo, whose campaign for office in the fall of 1972 collided head-on with the editorial preferences of the *Miami Herald.* The *Herald* did not like Tornillo one bit, and it didn't mince words in saying so. Pat Tornillo responded in kind by challenging the *Herald*'s facts and its motives.

But the *Herald* had the edge. It owned its pages. And Pat Tornillo's responses were not going to be seen there.

There's the rub.

* * *

THE MIAMI HERALD
September 20, 1972
The State's Laws and Pat Tornillo

> LOOK who's upholding the law!
>
> Pat Tornillo, boss of the Classroom Teachers Association and candidate for the State Legislature in the Oct. 3 runoff election, has denounced his opponent as lacking "the knowledge to be a legislator, as evidenced by his failure to file a list of contributions to and expenditures of his campaign as required by law."
>
> Czar Tornillo calls "violation" of this law inexcusable.
>
> This is the same Pat Tornillo who led the CTA strike from February 19 to March 11, 1968, against the school children and taxpayers of Dade County. Call it whatever you will, it was an illegal act against the public interest and clearly prohibited by the statutes.
>
> We cannot say it would be illegal but certainly it would be inexcusable of the voters if they sent Pat Tornillo to Tallahassee to occupy the seat for District 103 in the House of Representatives.

* * *

September 27, 1972

FROM: PAT L. TORNILLO, JR.
 CTA Executive Director
 1809 Brickell Avenue
 Miami, Florida 33129
 Legislative Candidate, District 103

TO: *MIAMI HERALD*
 One Herald Plaza
 Miami, Florida

Pat Tornillo and the CTA Record
 Five years ago, the teachers participated in a state-wide walkout to protest deteriorating educational conditions.
 Financing was inadequate then and we now face a financial crisis.
 The *Herald* told us that what we did was illegal and that we should use legal processes instead. We are doing just that through legal and political action.
 My candidacy is an integral part of this process. During the past four years:

—CTA brought suit to give Dade County its share of state money to relieve local taxpayers.
—CTA won a suit which gave public employees the right to collectively bargain.
—CTA won a suit which allowed the School Board to raise $7.8 million to air-
 condition schools and is helping to keep this money.

Unfortunately, the *Herald* dwells on past history and ignores CTA's totally legal efforts of the past four years.
 We are proud of our record.

* * *

THE MIAMI HERALD
September 29, 1972

 FROM the people who brought you this—the teacher strike of '68—come now instructions on how to vote for responsible government, i.e., against Crutcher Harrison and Ethel Beckham, for Pat Tornillo. The tracts and blurbs and bumper stickers pile up daily in teachers' school mailboxes amidst continuing pouts that the School Board should be delivering all this at your expense. The screeds say the strike is not an issue. We say maybe it wouldn't be were it not a part of a continuation of disregard of any and all laws the CTA might find aggravating. Whether in defiance of zoning laws at CTA Towers, contracts and laws during the strike, or more recently state prohibitions against soliciting campaign funds amongst teachers, CTA says fie and try and sue us—what's good for CTA is good for CTA and that is natural law. Tornillo's law, maybe. For years now he has been kicking the public shin to call attention to his shakedown statesmanship. He and whichever acerbic prexy is in alleged office have always felt their private ventures so chock-full of public weal that we should leap at the chance to nab the tab, be it half the Glorious Leader's salary or the dues checkoff or anything else except perhaps mileage on the staff hydrofoil. Give him public office, says Pat, and he will no doubt live by the Golden Rule. Our translation reads that as more gold and more rule.

* * *

FROM: Pat L. Tornillo, Jr.
   CTA Executive Director,
     and Candidate (Dem.) for
     State Rep., Dist. 103
   1809 Brickell Avenue
   Miami, Florida 33129
   Phone: 854–0220
September 30, 1972

EDITORIAL REPLY

Since the *Herald* has chosen to publicly attack my record, accomplishments, and positions on various issues, and those of the CTA, I again request that under Florida Statute 104.38, the *Herald* print the following record of affirmative and legal action.

In 1968, CTA signed a no-strike affidavit.

In 1969, CTA filed and won a suit in the Supreme Court of Florida, which gives all public employees the right to bargain collectively without the right to strike.

In 1971, CTA filed the Tornillo suit, which enabled the School Board to receive $7.6 million and are presently cooperating with the Board in their effort to retain this money and avoid further financial chaos.

Since 1968, CTA has reimbursed the taxpayers of Dade County for the full salary and all fringe benefits of its president.

Since 1970, CTA has not used the school mail service to communicate with its members.

Since 1970, CTA has paid all costs of payroll deduction of dues for its members.

We have attempted to obey all the laws of the state, not intentionally violating any, while continuing our efforts to alert the public to the impending financial crisis facing the schools.

We have, however, also retained our belief in the right of public employees to engage in political activity and to support the candidates of our choice, as is the right of any citizen in this great country of ours.

Aye, there's the rub.

* * *

While the *Herald* was having its say against Tornillo on its editorial pages, Tornillo couldn't even get in the door, much less on the *Herald*'s pages. Tornillo was out in the cold, with few choices. There wasn't another paper as large or as powerful as the *Herald* for Tornillo to turn to. The *Herald* dominated the Miami market, and it worked hard to keep it that way. So Tornillo took the only alternative open to him: he sued the *Miami Herald,* demanding that he be given space to respond to the *Herald*'s attacks on him. And Tornillo had some ammunition of his own, because Florida law required that candidates for office be given free space for reply in the pages of newspapers that launch personal attacks on them.

The problem, Tornillo claimed, was not that the *Miami Herald* was too uninhibited, wide-open, and robust, but that it was too big, too strong, too dominant. It monopolized speech and thus could act like a bully by choking off debate and ideas. This is not what freedom of the press is supposed to be all about. Freedom of the press, Tornillo claimed, assumes a competitive press, not a monopolistic one, for the press's freedom is an essential means by which wide public debate and the airing of diverse views and opinions can be assured. A press that prevents debate and squelches diversity of views and opinions doesn't deserve the Constitution's full protection. The government should be able to take steps (as Florida had) to assure that differing views are heard even if the press refuses to do so voluntarily. The *Herald* must be forced to open *its* pages to Tornillo.

It was a battle between ownership, on the one hand, and fairness, on the other. Ownership, the *Herald* said, wins that battle.

There's the rub.

* * *

Pat Tornillo's lawsuit was quickly and unceremoniously thrown out by the Florida district court on the ground that Florida's requirement that the *Herald* publish a column it did not agree with or did not want to publish was classic censorship. Whether, how, and what to publish are matters left exclusively to editors of newspapers, not arms of government. The decision was unsurprising.

What was surprising, however, was what happened next. Tornillo appealed to the Florida Supreme Court. And he won.

On July 10, 1973, the Florida Supreme Court issued its opinion agreeing with Tornillo and upholding the constitutionality of the Florida law that required the *Miami Herald*—on threat of damages and possibly criminal punishment—to make room in its pages for candidates such as Tornillo to reply to newspaper articles and editorials criticizing their personal characters or official records. According to the Florida Supreme Court:

> The right of the public to know all sides of a controversy and from such information to be able to make an enlightened choice is being jeopardized by the growing concentration of the ownership of the mass media into fewer and fewer hands, resulting ultimately in a form of private censorship. . . . Freedom of expression was retained by the people through the First Amendment for all the people and not merely for a select few. The First Amendment did not create a privileged class which through a monopoly of instruments of the newspaper industry would be able to deny to the people the freedom of expression which the First Amendment guarantees.

The Florida court's decision shocked the legal world—or at least the newspaper and media segments of the legal world. The idea of government-imposed obligations of balance and fairness was anathema to the press, especially to the large private newspapers that owned their pages and their markets, too. A rule of balance and fairness was not, however, without precedent. In the broadcasting industry the government had for many years attempted to impose certain public obligations on the highly regulated and concentrated radio and television media. But government-imposed obligations of balance and fairness had never before been visited on the print medium, especially on newspapers.

The *Miami Herald* promptly appealed the Florida Supreme Court's decision to the United States Supreme Court. The Supreme Court agreed to hear the case and scheduled the oral argument at the end of the 1973 Term.

* * *

At 2:14 P.M. on Wednesday, April 17, 1974, the case came for argument before the United States Supreme Court. The Justices hearing the case were Warren E. Burger, Chief Justice of the United States, and Associate Justices William O. Douglas, William J. Brennan, Potter Stewart, Byron R. White, Thurgood Marshall, Harry Blackmun, Lewis F. Powell Jr., and William H. Rehnquist. The Court was well into a transition from the Warren Court of the 1960s to a more moderate—and later increasingly conservative—Court in the 1970s. Four of the Justices had been appointed in the previous five years by President Nixon. But a more moderate, or even more conservative, Justice would not necessarily be inclined to interpret the press's First Amendment freedoms narrowly. Indeed, more conservative Justices would be likely to sympathize with the *Herald*'s claim of complete control over its paper. The First Amendment, after all, does say that "no law . . . [shall] abridge . . .

freedom of the press." Indeed, the Florida Supreme Court's decision upholding Tornillo's right to force the *Herald* to print his reply in the interests of
fairness and balance reflected the more liberal position in the case.

The lawyers presenting the oral arguments were Daniel P. S. Paul, of Miami, Florida, for the *Miami Herald;* and Jerome A. Barron, of Washington,
D.C., for Pat Tornillo.

Mr. Chief Justice Burger: We will hear argument next in No. 73-797, Miami
Herald against Tornillo.

You may proceed whenever you are ready, Mr. Paul.

Mr. Paul: Mr. Chief Justice, and may it please the Court.

Compelling a newspaper to print is the same as telling it what not to
print. It is censorship forbidden by the First Amendment. There is a national policy that has been expressed in the First Amendment that newspapers should not be deterred in printing what they choose, particularly
about political candidates.

The First Amendment protects newspapers from the intrusive editorial thumb of Government. If there is any area where the role of the press
under the First Amendment must remain unfettered, it is criticism of
political candidates of the very kind expressed in this case. One of the chief
roles of the press is vigorous criticism of candidates and of public officials.
Newspapers historically have been in the business of grinding axes, particularly political ones. Editorial discretion and judgment must mean freedom to choose what to print and what not to print. As this Court has said
in an earlier case, "Editing is what editors are for, and editing is the selection and choice of material."

The only restraints on the autonomy of the press in its nonbusiness
aspects are the restraints imposed by its readers and by its journalistic
integrity. The attempt at regulation of fairness or balance of newspapers
strikes at the very core of the First Amendment and would lead to the press
being treated as a public utility.

Freedom of the press, not fairness, is what the First Amendment is concerned with. Fairness has been left to the editors.

This is tough, muscular talk. Paul's argument simply slams the door on
Tornillo's claim. The *Herald* is a publisher. The *Herald* owns its newspaper.
The *Herald*'s freedom is the complete freedom to exercise dominion over its
pages, its property—period. The decision about what to put in the pages is
an editorial decision for the owner, for the *Herald,* and for no one else, in-

cluding the Florida legislature that enacted the right-to-reply law or the courts that enforce it.

The argument, if its premises are accepted, leaves no room for questions. But that does not mean there aren't plenty of questions that might be asked. How, for example, can the *Herald*'s absolute dominion over its pages be squared with the more qualified right to publish agreed by all parties and the Court in the Pentagon Papers case? How can complete control by the *Herald* be squared with libel laws or rights to privacy, to which we shall later turn?

Is the press's freedom "just there" in the Constitution, without any qualification or explanatory purpose, beyond question or debate? Isn't the press's freedom intended to provide a forum for exchange of information and opinion in a democracy—and in this case in a contested election? Can it be that the *Herald*'s freedom is the freedom to voice its view on the election and then to squelch all others? Is the *Herald*'s freedom, in other words, something like an argument that newspapers have been constitutionally anointed to tell the voters how to vote, an unelected elite in whose hands democracy's well-being rests?

What does Paul's remarkable freedom consist of? It consists of the choice of material to publish, a choice that he calls editorial judgment. Just what is editorial judgment? Is it the absolute right to decide? Or is it the right to decide *provided that* the decision is of a character and serves the purposes that make it worth making free? If a newspaper decided on what it would publish simply by flipping coins or by running competing stories through a random number generator, would that be editorial judgment that should be made free—absolutely free—under the First Amendment? Isn't someone's choice, based at least on some criteria or reasoning process, necessarily assumed in the phrase "freedom of the press"? What about a decision not to publish either a story or a response from a candidate, simply and only because the newspaper's editors personally hate the candidate and wish to wreck his or her prospects, even though the positions taken by the candidate are within the realm of reason? Would a decision governed by personal animus of an editor be one that should qualify for the Constitution's freedom of the press?

These are real and serious and hard questions. They have answers, or at least they can be supported by well-reasoned arguments on both sides that reveal important insight into the issue of press freedom presented in the *Tornillo* case. Paul had no interest in addressing those issues. He wanted, instead, to build a wall of unchallengable assumptions or premises that would close off any more searching discussion. This he was entitled to do. But ordinarily the Supreme Court puts a pretty quick halt to such a strategy, honing in with questions, probing beneath the surface. But the Court instead just listened and then let Paul turn to the second part of his argument, which was that the Florida statute was vague and overly broad and thus would foster a parade of horribles, some of which Paul would describe. The fact that it had not done so over the course of its more than sixty-year history wasn't mentioned.

Mr. Paul: The Florida statute is broad in scope. It may be invoked by any candidate who has filed for local, State, or Federal office. In fact, it may be invoked by an incumbent public official as soon as he qualifies for reelection and becomes a candidate. It applies to any criticism of a candidate published in the newspaper. It's not limited to editorial criticism. It applies, at the very least, to news articles, to syndicated columns, to cartoons. In fact, the statute could be triggered by a news article in which one candidate assails another, a reply is demanded, the other candidate demands a counter-reply, and an entire round-robin *ad infinitum* could be set up in the newspaper. One article which criticized several candidates would trigger as many replies as there were candidates criticized; each candidate would be entitled to his separate reply. It would apply to newspapers whether or not they were published in Florida.

Question: What would happen if a newspaper published an editorial against all of the candidates of one political party? Would each one of them have an answer?

Mr. Paul: Under the Florida statute, each of the candidates would have a right to demand publication of their answer. A *New York Times* story, for example, on Florida politics would trigger the statute and the *New York Times* under penalty of criminal sanctions would be required to accept replies of Florida candidates.

And I emphasize, this statute applies without regard to the truth or the falsity or the fairness of the original article, regardless of whether there was any malice involved. In fact, this statute produces a peculiar result: newspapers which publish something that is true may be required to publish a totally false reply.

As I said, the statute carries criminal penalties. The editor could be put in jail for up to a year and fined a thousand dollars in addition to the civil remedies which have been implied by the Florida Supreme Court.

Now, Mr. Tornillo seeks to justify this sweeping incursion on the First Amendment on the ground that the State has an interest in fair elections and that this justifies this abridgement. Moreover, we are told by Florida that its right of reply statute is justified because of economic concentration of the media. However, there is nothing in the record to justify appellee's argument that the media is now one vast monolith. The facts are that there is much more diversity in the media and in the number of media than at the time the First Amendment was adopted.

Of course the press has power. It's obvious that the press has to have power to assure its editorial independence and to assure that it can fulfill its role under the First Amendment.

Interestingly enough, the statute would have exactly the opposite effect the State of Florida claims. Newspapers, particularly small ones with space limitations, would be deterred in publishing political criticism for fear of triggering the statute. Publications, for example, with a distinct editorial viewpoint would have the greatest dilemma of all. Will the twelve black newspapers serving the black community in Florida have to give equal time to George Wallace to reply as a candidate despite the views of the particular editor of that newspaper and the community which it serves?

There are many other examples, but we submit that an examination of this statute on its face dictates that the opinion of the Florida Supreme Court must be reversed.

I would like to save the rest of my time for rebuttal.
Mr. Chief Justice Burger: Very well.

Paul's argument is remarkable because, with but one small and unsubstantive question by a Justice, it was uninterrupted. This rarely happens. Oral argument is an opportunity for the Justices to probe the reasoning of both sides of an issue presented in a case (why should the press have absolute power over what it publishes, no matter what the cost?); to test out different ways of looking at the facts (what exactly is editorial judgment?) or the terms of a challenged law (doesn't the law's requirement that a candidate merely be able to respond to what the press has already said serve to increase speech and promote debate, not to limit or censor it?); and to explore the implications of a line of argument for other cases (does the *Herald's* argument mean that a court could not order an opportunity to reply as a remedy in a libel case or order a newspaper to correct a false advertisement?). Nothing of this sort happened with Paul. Was this because the Justices had already made up their minds before the oral argument and were simply sitting through the ritual? Was it because the Justices, despite their life tenure, were reluctant to publicly challenge the press's legal arguments, especially because the *Miami Herald* is a very big and influential newspaper, joined in its argument by virtually the entire news industry?

The reason was clearly not because the *Herald*'s argument was so good that it could not be questioned or probed or challenged in any way. No argument is that good. One could not have come much closer than Paul did to a bold declaration that the press is above the law. And Paul got away with it, met only with silence.

Was the silence a sign of agreement, or of indifference? One wonders whether this very question was going through Paul's mind as he sat down— before his time was up and simply because he ran out of things to say.

It was now time for the other side, Pat Tornillo and the state of Florida, represented by Jerome Barron, a well-recognized law professor who had written an influential article in the *Harvard Law Review* in which he claimed that the concentration of power in the media required government to take remedial steps in order to protect the First Amendment rights of the public.

Mr. Barron: Mr. Chief Justice, and may it please the Court. Pat Tornillo is the executive director of the Classroom Teachers Association of Dade County, Florida, and he is a very controversial fellow, and he intends to remain being a very controversial fellow. Mr. Tornillo led the school teachers of Florida in a strike which angered the Governor of Florida, and it also angered the *Miami Herald,* as we are reminded in the *Herald*'s editorials.

It is everybody's right to be angered and to say what they please under our Constitution. What Mr. Tornillo wanted, however, when he read the editorials, was the right to fulfill *his* role, as a citizen critic of Government.

Mr. Tornillo had an advantage over other people who had had media problems: he lived in a State which has had a right of reply statute since 1913. To me the paradox of this case is that everyone in the media is claiming censorship, and the only person who has been censored in this proceeding is Pat Tornillo.

The question before the Court is this: if a candidate during the course of an election is editorially attacked by a daily newspaper in his community, may a state statute afford him a similar amount of space to reply? That is the question before the Court.

Question: Or to put it another way, for instance, an ordinary person cannot reply to an editorial, but by merely becoming a candidate that person automatically gets that right.

Mr. Barron: That's right, Mr. Justice Marshall. In other words, the position, of course, is that generally there are no access rights to the media. That is the law. That point is that if one becomes a candidate and one is attacked, then—

Question: If the editorial is written against Joe Doakes calling him anything and really condemning him to high heaven and Joe Doakes says, "I know how to fix him. I'll become a candidate." But under this statute, even if a man does that deliberately, this statute covers it.

Mr. Barron: Not quite, Mr. Justice Marshall, because the media would still have the upper hand because if they have attacked him prior to the time he became a candidate and then he becomes a candidate, they still would be able to refuse to print his reply, as long as they don't editorially attack him.

Question: Well, let me put it another way. If he is an ordinary citizen and he is attacked, he can get no redress unless he becomes a candidate.

Mr. Barron: As I read the statute, the attack would have to come after he has become a candidate.

Question: That's what I'm saying.

Mr. Barron: If that's what you are saying, I agree with you.

Question: Then he's insulated from then on.

Mr. Barron: He is insulated from not being able to respond.

Question: That's right?

Mr. Barron: Correct. Yes, sir.

At this point, the Justices' questioning of Barron is not much better than the questioning of Paul. The exchange between Justice Marshall and Barron is a pretty silly one. The point Justice Marshall is trying to raise is that the Florida law is peculiar because it only applies to political candidates. If forcing newspapers to give space for responses by candidates is all to the good, then shouldn't the law apply to all speech and speakers, too (bond-issue elections, public-office holders, corporate executives)? There is a good response—the law is part of the election laws, and debate on questions related to contested elections is particularly important under the First Amendment—but Barron gets stuck in making a highly technical distinction that, while important in a sense, is pretty well beside the general point of the question. So the Justice and Barron get all tied up in a side question, and the main point becomes lost. When Barron resumes his argument, he slides right over Justice Marshall's issue about the law's limited application.

Mr. Barron (continuing): This statute can be justified on two very familiar propositions of constitutional law. The first is that some regulation of the press is permissible so long as it serves a valid overriding government purpose. This statute does not detract from expression one iota. It *adds* to the realm of discussion. This statute has the unique feature of both better assuring free and fair and honest elections, *and* implementing the Constitution's profound commitment to debate, which is vigorous, free and wide open.

Question: Nothing in this Court's First Amendment decisions has suggested that one person would have a right to commandeer somebody else's printing press and make his expression that way, [has] it?

Mr. Barron: No, Mr. Justice Rehnquist. But let me answer your question this way.

Florida has precisely the statute geared to fulfill the constitutional objective of wide-open debate: to let harm from falsehood and strident criticism of government officials be cured, but yet to have more debate.

Question: What if Mr. Tornillo, in the course of his campaign, had announced after this editorial attack that on next Friday night he was going to take care of the *Miami Herald* and had announcements throughout the week in advertising to build up an audience on that conflict and that on Wednesday the *Miami Herald* said they wanted equal time and would like to have one of their editors or someone present to answer him. Do you think Mr. Tornillo would have to yield half of the time on the platform in the hall he had rented for that occasion?

Mr. Barron: He would not, Mr. Chief Justice, because Florida—

Question: The statute doesn't apply to him.

Mr. Barron: The statute does not apply to him. May I just speak a little further to your point, because it's a fundamental point in this case? This case has occasioned a good deal of interest. This case has nothing to do with the establishment as a matter of constitutional law of a right of reply, with all the problems of establishing parameters that that would involve. This case raises a much narrower and more conventional constitutional question, and that question is: if a State, by statute that goes directly to implementing its Election Laws, passes a statute which also happens to respond to the interests of public debate, is such a statute constitutional? And it seems to me, Mr. Chief Justice, that this is a much more limited and a much more familiar task for constitutional adjudication.

Question: Now, suppose Florida had a statute which required a candidate for office who attacks a newspaper to give equal time in the place and setting in which he made the attack on the newspaper, would you then have an approximate parallel to this statute?

Mr. Barron: No, Mr. Chief Justice, I do not believe you would. I am not frankly worried about the access problems of the *Miami Herald,* with its circulation of 350,000, the dominant paper in the State of Florida with 82 percent of the circulation in Dade County. The other newspaper, the *Miami News,* has only about 80,000 in circulation. So that under this Court's own principle regarding alternative means of obtaining access for reply it seems to me that the constitutional case for a statute protecting Mr. Tornillo, an individual, is much greater than a statute protecting a newspaper's right to reply, when the newspaper has a circulation of 350,000.

We do not want the newspapers of this country to say anything in their editorials that they do not wish to say. Let them say what they please. But what we have is a situation in the 20th century where economics and technology have given us a world we did not want—one of concentrated media power and monopoly control over the channels of public communication. And our task is to try to make an adjustment so that freedom of speech and press as we understand it and as we believe in it can endure. That's our problem. It seems to me that we can get guidance from what the First Amendment is all about. I do not believe it is completely beyond the power of the State to say that if someone is attacked to the point of destruction, he can reply. I do not believe the First Amendment prohibits such a law.

Question: But you can attack to destruction anybody in Florida except a candidate.

Mr. Barron: That is true, your Honor, and it is a situation I regret, but it is a fact. But we make progress in life incrementally, and I believe that sustaining of this statute would be progress in terms of the First Amendment.

Many years ago Mr. Justice Brandeis said that we have First Amendment protection because public discussion is a political duty. Then he said something else. He said that the opportunity to air supposed grievances is the path of safety. What did he mean by that? Obviously, he meant that if we are going to have things like freedom of speech and press, if we are going to have a free society, then people have to have a sense of justice about existing institutions. He believed that if people could reach an audience, that if we could have real debate, then our institutions, our free institutions, would be secure.

It seems to me that the Florida right of reply statute accomplishes these objectives.

Question: Professor Barron—

Mr. Barron: Yes, Justice Blackmun.

Question: Your eloquence prompts me just to ask one question. Perhaps you can help me over the hurdle. For better or for worse, we have opted for a free press, not for free debate.

While almost casually put, this question is a very important and, for Barron, difficult one. It asks whether a tension exists between a First Amendment based on the press's freedom and one based on the need for more speech and debate for the public to receive and act upon. Or can these two ideals be reconciled? Paul's argument rested on the press's freedom being just like the individual's liberty to speak. The First Amendment protects the individual's expressive free will and keeps the government out of the business of regulating the beliefs people hold and express. The greatest diversity of opinions will be produced by competition in ideas among free individuals in the open market of speech, not by government taking over the market and imposing government's view of the competing opinions on it. Forcing the *Herald* to carry Tornillo's response to its editorial would be like forcing any person making an argument to refrain from making it unless, once finished, he or she also makes the counterargument.

But why should a newspaper be treated just like a living, breathing, free-willed individual under the First Amendment? Barron must argue that newspapers should not be so treated. Newspapers are profit-making enterprises, not human beings. Their "freedom" should not and need not be the same as the individual citizen's. Indeed, if the Framers had intended that conclusion, they would not have provided separately in the First Amendment for freedom of the press. The press's role, Barron must argue, is to facilitate and foster the dissemination of useful information and to encourage debate, especially on matters left for decision to the democratic process. The press, in other words, is an instrument of the individual's political and expressive freedom. *Its* freedom does not extend to monopolizing and controlling information and debate.

Mr. Barron: Well, Mr. Justice Blackmun, I hope that is not so. I hope that we can work out an accommodation between the two. It seems to me it is not necessary to change any of our ideas about what should be in the content of editorials. On the other hand, in terms of the realities that I adverted to before, I think it is possible, if we go with a statute that is careful enough and a situation that cries out for some redress of injustice as this one does to have both.

The cry we have heard from the press in this case is that if newspapers must give their opponents a forum, they would rather say nothing. To call that a chilling effect, I think we have to ask a question: Who, then, is putting the chilling effect on the expression of constitutional rights?

Question: Of course, the only entity that the First Amendment is directed against is the Government. I take it the *Miami Herald* can chill anybody's rights to their heart's content and they are not violating the Constitution.

What you are saying is in effect that the real chilling here comes from the *Miami Herald.*

Mr. Barron: That is correct.

Question: Well, there is nothing in the Constitution that prevents a private person from chilling anybody's First Amendment right.

Mr. Barron: But I would suggest, Mr. Justice Rehnquist, that since this Court has held that the First Amendment is not an absolute, a State statute that imposes some duties on the *Miami Herald* changes that situation.

Question: Then you come down to the question whether a State statute can impose duties. You are back to your—

Mr. Barron: Exactly, Mr. Chief Justice, that is the question. The question is whether this statute is consistent with the First Amendment. And our position is that since the law *adds to* expression rather than detracts from expression it does not offend the First Amendment; instead it *implements* it.

Question: What's the difference between the State saying you shall publish A and the State saying you shall not publish A under the First Amendment?

Mr. Barron: Mr. Justice Marshall, I believe there is a great difference. To respond directly to your question, if the State says, "You shall not publish," then I think we are by anyone's reckoning in the area of censorship. Whereas if a State says you shall publish a reply, then you are not telling the newspaper it may not print something or even that it must take a position that it dislikes.

Question: You said it would not make them take a position they dislike?

Mr. Barron: That's right.

Question: The *Miami Herald* didn't want to publish it.

Mr. Barron: What I mean, Mr. Justice Marshall, is that institutionally the *Herald* is still free, every paper in Florida will still be free, editorially to attack anyone they wish.

Question: And then publish what they don't want to publish.

Mr. Barron: That is correct.

Question: And that is not governmental control.

Mr. Barron: I would suggest that it is not *unconstitutional* government control.

Question: Suppose the State says that every newspaper must publish any material that can be classified as debate by any politician who offers it? Would that be constitutional?

Mr. Barron: I would have great doubt about the constitutionality.

Question: That sure would build up the debate you have been talking about.

Mr. Barron: No, Mr. Justice Marshall, I don't believe it would because—

Question: You don't believe it would? If you gave a politician a right to print something in the newspaper?

Mr. Barron: [It would not assure] responsiveness, [which is necessary to debate]. The whole idea of the right of reply is responsiveness. If we have attack and reply, then it seems to me we are in a debate.

Question: I see.

Mr. Barron: It is a danger, really, to free expression if we subordinate the free expression right of the American people to the property rights of those who own communication facilities. This is not to say that those who own and work in such facilities do not have First Amendment rights; of course they do. The question is: can we afford some slight, legislative aid, to make the debate we have all been talking about a reality. And it is my position that this statute leads precisely to that result.

Mr. Chief Justice Burger: Thank you.

The questioning is more frequent in Barron's argument than in Paul's, and it focuses often on important points of substance and theory, as well as on the practical application of the Florida law. Yet there is still a sense that the Justices are somewhat disconnected from the case before them. Barron is not pressed on the evidence, if any, of newspaper monopoly and control over information and opinion, and whether such control is serious enough to warrant a law forcing newspapers to publish responses to their own articles and editorials. The evidence on the point is far from clear: in 1974 many towns still had competing newspapers; competing media also existed for news and opinion, including radio, television, magazines, and the like. And while no one at the time could foresee the information explosion produced by the computer and the Internet and telecommunications, many could have predicted that technology would almost certainly make any market definition of monopoly power obsolete within a matter of years.

Nor, of course, had there been any pressing of Paul on the same questions. The *Herald* did, in fact, have very considerable power and influence; it had little competition in Miami and Dade County; and it did, in fact, have very considerable power to define the issues for the public. Given this, why should the *Herald* be able to complain (via the First Amendment) about giving over a few inches of column space to a candidate who simply wants to respond to what the *Herald* already had decided to print? If the editorial was important enough to print, surely it was important enough to set aside a small amount of space for a competing view.

All in all, the argument was disappointing, and the fault lay with the Justices, not with the lawyers.

Chief Justice Burger: Do you have anything further, Mr. Paul?

Mr. Paul (Rebuttal Argument): Mr. Chief Justice, and may it please the Court.

Mr. Barron keeps talking about Mr. Tornillo being censored. There is absolutely nothing in this record to support any such assertion that Mr. Tornillo didn't get his message across. Mr. Barron describes Mr. Tornillo as a public figure and as a controversial man. We would have to be very naive to think that Mr. Tornillo was relying entirely on a paragraph statement in the *Miami Herald* in order to get his message across in his campaign. There is nothing that shows that he was muzzled.

But I think the nub of it comes down to the remarks that Professor Barron made when he says that this case poses First Amendment interests in conflict. There are no competing First Amendment interests in conflict here. There is no First Amendment right to use the press. There is no right of a citizen to be interviewed by the press. There is no right to have a letter that a citizen may write to the press printed. A judicial inquiry into editorial discretion and the editorial function is not permissible under the First Amendment. Compulsion is the same as censorship and there is no difference between saying that you shall publish and you shall not publish under the First Amendment.

Paul's statement of the press's freedom is striking, for it reflects the absolute freedom that the *Herald* is arguing for in the case, and it states the elements of that freedom in no uncertain terms. This is a bold statement for Paul to make, especially in the immediate post-Watergate period when the President's claim of absolute power (executive privilege) had been denied by the Court with the statement that no one, not even the President, is above the law under the Constitution. Of course, the press was still seen as the hero in the Watergate matter, so perhaps the bitter pill of a press that is above the law was easier to swallow.

But surely the press's power is not absolute; the press is not above the law. Isn't the press responsible if it knowingly libels someone? Is the press free to steal the words of other newspapers or writers and print them as its own without any regard for the copyright laws? Can't the press be held responsible for false advertising carried in its pages or for advertising itself falsely? Can't the press be stopped from advertising jobs that are available only to men or white persons? What if a newspaper buys up all the competition, shuts it down, and then jacks up prices and keeps any future competition out of the market? May the press do what the antitrust laws would prohibit any other company from doing?

Mr. Paul, continuing: As Mr. Justice Blackmun pointed out, our founding fathers in writing the First Amendment opted for a free press, not a fair press. They decided fairness was too fragile an issue for them to deal with. It's the only First Amendment we have, and it is not the function of the Court to rewrite it. The issue is really who decides what gets into the newspaper, the Government, the Florida legislature, or the editor of a free newspaper?

I understand that Professor Barron says this statute reflects a noble concept of fairness, but motherhood, as one editor pointed out, is also a noble condition, although motherhood under compulsion is rape and it begets illegitimacy. And to force an editor to print what he does not desire and his conscience does not wish to print, is a clear violation of the First Amendment.

Mr. Chief Justice Burger: Thank you, gentlemen. The case is submitted.

As it turns out, it did not take the Court long to decide the *Tornillo* case. On June 25, 1974, the Court announced its unanimous decision in favor of the *Miami Herald* and against Pat Tornillo. Every Justice joined the opinion written by Chief Justice Burger. Two Justices wrote separate concurring opinions, which did not disagree with the Chief Justice but simply added a thought or two.

Reaching a decision in the case seems to have been easy for the Court. The Justices' seeming disconnection with the case at oral argument may, indeed, reflect the fact that even at that early stage the Justices were pretty well of one mind, going through the process of argument but without their hearts in it, because they already had decided to support the press's claim of complete freedom to decide what to publish in its pages and to reject Jerome Barron's monopoly argument.

The decision was also quick and easy because, as it turns out, the Court appears not to have thought it necessary to explain its decision in detail. Although the opinion ranged widely, its central holding and the reasons for it were stated concisely:

> A newspaper is more than a passive receptacle or conduit for news, comment, and advertising. The choice of material to go into a newspaper, and the decisions made as to limitation on the size and content of the paper, and the treat-

ment of public issues and public officials—whether fair or unfair—constitute the exercise of editorial control and judgment. It has yet to be demonstrated how governmental regulation of this crucial process can be exercised consistent with the First Amendment guarantees of a free press as they have evolved to this time.

Any . . . compulsion [that newspapers] publish that which "'reason' tells them should not be published" is unconstitutional. A responsible press is an undoubtedly desirable goal, but press responsibility is not mandated by the Constitution and like many other virtues it cannot be legislated.

But can a decision in the *Tornillo* case be explained so easily? Is the conclusory incantation of a rule of absolute press freedom enough to satisfy those who would seek to *understand* the Court's action and those who would seek also to know its limits? Should the Court be able to get away with little more than banal and overbroad statements?

Is every decision about publication that someone bearing the title editor makes absolutely protected by the First Amendment, no matter the harm it causes, or whether it relates to the placement of ads for used Chevies or full information about candidates for office? Is government always and absolutely forbidden from requiring a newspaper to publish something? Is the press's freedom the freedom from the antitrust laws? Must a person have the title editor to possess this substantial constitutional power? Or may someone writing a letter or a magazine or an e-mail claim to be an editor, too?

Many of the stories we will turn to in the succeeding chapters will explore these questions directly. We will thus defer until later stories the questions of copyright and ownership of news; the line between news and entertainment; the status of advertising and commercial activity, libel, and invasion of privacy, to name a few. For now we will address briefly two questions at the center of the *Tornillo* case: First, why should the press have absolute power over publishing decisions, since who controls the press is a matter over which no one but the owners of the press have any control? Second, does the First Amendment necessarily assume that competition exists among distributors of news and opinion? If it does not exist, why shouldn't government correctives, such as a right of reply, be permitted in the interest of the public and the functioning of a free and democratic system of government?

The contest for power between government and the press has already been discussed in story 1, the Pentagon Papers case. There the question was the magnitude and certainty of predicted harm resulting from publication. A near-certain harm might justify government "abridgement" of press freedom through a prior restraint. Anything less, however, would leave the publication decision firmly and finally in the hands of the press. In Pat Tornillo's case, his harm, and perhaps the public's, too, was specific, imminent, and directly caused by the *Herald*'s editorial and its refusal to allow Tornillo to respond. Should this be enough to fit within the exception to press freedom crafted in the Pentagon Papers case?

In the Pentagon Papers case, the anticipated harm was lives lost, war prolonged, military plans scuttled. In Pat Tornillo's case, however, the harm, if it is that, was very different. Tornillo's harm was the criticism leveled against him by the *Miami Herald* and the potential of losing an election because of it. The offending editorial was not claimed to be false. Instead, it was embarrassing and, well, unfair. May criticism and embarrassment and unfairness be counted as harm under the First Amendment? Does that go too far, at least as a justification for government regulation of the *Miami Herald*?

At first blush, most people would say yes. Criticism is part of everyday life, as is embarrassment and unfairness. We may not like it, but we ordinarily cannot demand that the law do anything about it. But on reflection the answer may not be quite so easy. What about some similar kinds of harm that the law does protect against, even from the press? How about damage to one's reputation, for example? If a newspaper knowingly libels me by a false statement, the law weighs in with great force, allowing me to sue the newspaper and, if successful, recover lots of money—much more money, in fact, than the *Herald* would have spent giving reply space to a year's worth of Tornillos. Is a false statement about me a more serious harm than an unfair criticism?

How about embarrassment? The law allows me to sue a newspaper for damages if it invades my privacy, even if the private facts disclosed are true, as long as the facts are embarrassing. Is this kind of embarrassment—an unfair disclosure of my private life for no good reason—different than the embarrassment Pat Tornillo felt? The point of the libel and privacy examples, of course, is not that they are the same as Tornillo's case, but rather that they rest on forms of personal harm or hurt that may ultimately be hard to distinguish from the kind of hurt felt by Tornillo.

Tornillo clearly suffered some harm because of the *Herald*'s editorial. So let's ask the harm question from a different angle. Whatever we think of his harm, are we comfortable leaving decisions about publishing such harmful material to the final editorial judgment of a private newspaper rather than (in some part) to the government? Why? Is it because the *Herald* is better equipped to judge the facts than a court? Is it because the *Herald* is in the best position to make a disinterested and fair judgment about whether to allow Tornillo space for a reply? Are newspapers inherently fairer than government? These questions—how serious the harm, who can best judge it—

are difficult ones. Frankly, the Supreme Court's opinion in Tornillo's case did not treat them seriously. It didn't even address them.

There are further difficulties with the Court's answer to Tornillo's claim. The Florida statute whose constitutionality was questioned did not in any way censor the *Herald*. Unlike the Pentagon Papers case, it did not prevent the *Herald* from publishing its editorial. It did not impose a penalty of any sort on what the *Herald* published. The government made no attempt to correct any falsity, award any damages, or force any apology by the *Herald*. Instead, the statute sought only to require that the *Herald* allow Pat Tornillo to reply in its pages to the article the *Herald* had written about him. This is neither government censorship nor government control over what positions or views the *Herald* may choose to express.

The *Tornillo* case is also different from the Pentagon Papers case, or a libel or privacy case, in terms of the Florida law's impact on editorial freedom. The *Herald* freely and fully exercised its editorial freedom when it decided to publish its editorial. No one denied its freedom to do so. No one required that the *Herald* amend or alter its stated position. Tornillo only wanted to add to the discussion of a topic—his candidacy—that the *Herald* had freely decided was important enough to editorialize about. In other words, the *Herald* denied Tornillo the chance to *increase,* not correct or diminish, speech on the *Herald*'s own chosen topic. The *Herald*'s claim of freedom, therefore, looks like a freedom to have the first, last, and *only* word on a subject.

The *Miami Herald* effectively claimed freedom in its own pages to express its view and to prevent others from saying anything inconsistent with it. This right is much more than the familiar claim that the press is free to decide what it deems important and to provide information for the public on that subject. How, we might ask, is the *Herald*'s broader claim consistent with the press's role as a provider of information and opinion for democratic self-government? Democracy rests on the assumption that the people decide contested questions, not the press. How is the *Herald*'s claim to speak and also to prevent others from speaking consistent with the press's function of checking government and private power in society? If the checking function implies, as it surely does, the right of the press to criticize government, allowing the subject of criticism the chance to reply does not compromise that function at all; it serves it—unless, of course, the press is free not only to criticize but also to be free from criticism of itself.

The *Herald* also makes two additional arguments: (1) requiring a newspaper to give space for reply will inhibit the newspaper from publishing about important and controversial matters in the first place; and (2) the space that would be given over to reply will necessarily prevent the paper from publishing another, perhaps important, story (or cost it money by increasing the number of pages printed). Therefore, the argument goes, the First Amendment must give the press complete control over its pages.

The inhibition argument is, frankly, beneath the dignity of the press to make and surely beneath the dignity of the *Miami Herald*. Is the *Herald* seriously saying that the prospect of disagreement with its editorial view will keep it from taking positions in the future? Isn't the press claiming freedom in the name of providing information and opinion about controversial matters for the public? Doesn't the checking function assume a press dedicated to taking on those in power and challenging accepted beliefs? The argument made by the *Herald* implies a very different kind of press, one that is timid, uncertain, dependent, and weak-willed.

The argument about giving up needed space is similarly unavailing, at least as a general matter. In Tornillo's case it cannot be said that much space was involved at all; the statute was narrow in its application and limited in its requirements. And one might conclude that what space is given over to response is well worth it, for the readers and for the newspaper, too. Tornillo's reply would give the public full information about the controversy concerning his ethics and qualifications. It would allow the readers to weigh both sides of the question and make their own decisions. Does the press really claim a freedom to protect the readers, and the public in general, from weighing all facts and arguments because individuals are not deemed capable of making their own decisions? Is the press's freedom based on an assumption that the press is always right, and therefore the press must be free to assure its correctness by preventing publication of any competing views?

Finally, the *Herald* argues that committing space to Tornillo would either prevent it from publishing other important stories or cost it money. Is this always the case, or might it depend on the circumstances? Exactly what other stories would be preempted by Tornillo's replies? How important are they? Are they really more important than more facts about a story so significant that the *Herald* decided formally to editorialize on it? Indeed, might the space preempted be something other than a story? Perhaps an advertisement? Or a recipe published in the style section in order to fill out the page?

In fairness, the *Herald*'s argument is a serious one, for can we really have a free, independent press if the paper doesn't control its pages? The press can rightly claim that its role is not to be converted into a community bulletin board obliged to print everyone's contrary view on any topic the *Herald* has written about. If the newspaper could be domesticated in this way, much of its energy would be sapped from its central mission of informing people and serving as an independent source of information, obliged to no one but the public's interest as the paper sees it.

This is the classic formulation of the press's function and freedom. But this conception of the press's freedom rests on the assumption that any given newspaper is operating in a larger market in which there is competition by other newspapers for the minds of the same readers. No single speaker, no single newspaper, controls public dialogue. In such a competitive environment, there would be no need to respond to Pat Tornillo's demand for space to reply in the interest of fairness or public enlightenment. There would be other newspapers able, willing, and anxious to call the *Herald* to account, to editorialize with the opposite view. Tornillo's demand for fairness would dwindle, for the market would function naturally in a way that guards against unfairness.

In Miami at the time of Tornillo's case, there was little, if any, competition for the *Herald*. No other newspaper in the *Herald*'s market reached a similarly wide audience. And the situation has gotten worse, not better. Today there are virtually no cities with newspaper competition; most of the rare exceptions involve two newspapers operated together by the same company, giving only the impression of competition. More than 50 percent of the daily newspaper circulation in the United States is owned and controlled by about fifteen large firms. For most of these firms, the driving force in the newspaper business is not the press's contribution to information and opinion or its service as an independent check on public and private power. These firms are themselves aggregations of great private power and public influence. For these large firms the driving forces are revenue yields and the market price of their stock. Reporters, editors, and publishers more often than not enjoy stock options in the companies—enjoy them, that is, as long as the stock price rises. News personnel have a direct, personal, and often significant stake in the financial performance of the company and its stock price. In the case of Pat Tornillo, that means the newspaper's employees might have a stake in the advertising revenues that could be earned if they could sell the space that Tornillo's reply would otherwise occupy.

What are the necessary conditions for a free press? If a free press means a private press, not a government-owned one, as it surely does, must the private press function in a competitive world that prevents it from monopolizing information and opinion, thus effectively exercising governmentlike power? Is the market in which we should judge the presence of competition the market of daily newspapers, or should the competitive market include also the larger markets for television journalism, radio news, magazines, and

Internet sites? Do newspapers, at least today, still serve as a uniquely respected and influential source of information to the broadest of audiences in communities, regions, states, and the nation? Do we think of the newspaper's straight news and opinion as different from, and indeed better than, most news provided in other media of communication? Can the *Herald,* in the end, successfully argue that although it monopolizes (or at least dominates) Miami's newspaper market, its real market includes also radio, television, and millions of Internet sites? Can the *Herald* argue that the First Amendment thus frees it of any duty to make space for replies to those it attacks because the competitive market assures that its refusal will produce no serious harm to Tornillo or to the function of a free press?

"Editing is what editors are for" is the only explanation the Supreme Court gave in awarding victory to the *Miami Herald.* Frankly, Pat Tornillo deserved more than the hollow rhetoric the Supreme Court gave him. So did the press, whose function in a free society goes much deeper than that. If this is all that needs to be said in Tornillo's case, then perhaps we need to think further about the definition of *editors* and *editing.* Somewhere a more compelling understanding of the press's freedom must be found.

Additional Reading

Anderson, David. "Freedom of the Press." *Texas Law Review* 80 (2002): 429ff.

Bezanson, Randall. "The Developing Law of Editorial Judgment." *Nebraska Law Review* 78 (1999): 754ff.

Blasi, Vincent. "The Checking Value in First Amendment Theory." *American Bar Foundation Research Journal* 1977 (1977): 521ff.

Commission on Freedom of Expression (The Hutchins Commission). *A Free and Responsible Press.* Chicago: University of Chicago Press, 1947.

Nerone, John, ed. *Last Rights: Revisiting "Four Theories of the Press."* Urbana: University of Illinois Press, 1995.

Story 3

Truth and Uncertainty
Harte-Hanks Communications, Inc. v. Connaughton
491 U.S. 657 (1989)

Libel law is not really about truth. At least this is so when the press publishes a libelous statement about public officials, prominent public figures, or even ordinary persons who have injected themselves into a public controversy. In such cases libel law is about "actual malice"—whether the publisher knew the statement was false but published it anyway or had serious doubts about a statement's truth and recklessly published it notwithstanding those doubts, indeed with indifference to them. To be sure, if a statement can be proved true, the publisher will be free of liability. But even if it can't be proved true, and indeed even if the statement is proved false, the publisher is still off the hook as long as he or she didn't know or seriously suspect its falsity at the time of publication.

Libel law, in other words, is about what was *believed* about truth at the time of publication, about a publisher's motive, about the journalistic process of gathering and checking information. None of these questions go to truth per se. A story believed true when published, but which turns out to be false, is not libelous, no matter how much harm comes to its victim. Likewise, a story that may actually be true, but whose truth the publisher doubted at the time of publication, may be subjected to liability to a person whose reputation was harmed, even though (as it turns out) deservedly. This is especially likely if the publisher failed to take steps to check the facts or corroborate the story and thus, perhaps purposely, avoided finding out more in order to avoid knowing the truth. For these reasons and others, many observers of the law have criticized libel law as irrational, bizarre, even perverse, and as highly intrusive into the journalistic and editorial process.

What should libel law be about? Should it be about truth? Fairness? Responsibility? Maintaining professional standards? What does truth have to do with journalism and, therefore, press freedom? If libel isn't about truth, should the law at least require that the journalistic enterprise be a truth-seeking one? These are surprisingly complex and difficult questions, as we will see in our story. It is a story about the different forms of truth that often exist in a story or event, about a newspaper's motive in publishing a story and how motive is related to journalism and news, and about sloppiness and indifference in finding and checking facts. It illustrates why and how libel law is not about truth. It also makes us ask, if it is not about truth, then is libel law worth all the trouble?

* * *

Daniel Connaughton was a lawyer in Hamilton, Ohio, a city of about sixty-five thousand people located twenty-five miles from Cincinnati, Ohio. He had been a Hamilton City Prosecutor, Butler County Prosecutor, and for a brief time an acting judge on the Hamilton Municipal Court. In 1983 he was in the private practice of law in Hamilton. He was also a candidate for the position of Municipal Judge in Hamilton. In Ohio judges are elected by the voters, not, as in many states, appointed by governors. Connaughton was running against the incumbent judge, the Hon. James Dolan, who had served as Municipal Judge for one six-year term. The race was, by all appearances, deadly boring, at least until September 1983. Then it became a close, hard-fought race, marked by emerging scandal, even becoming a bit dirty.

Early in September 1983, amid increasing rumors about misconduct in Judge Dolan's court, Connaughton's wife, Martha, was informed by the president of the local chapter of Mothers Against Drunk Driving that some people had received preferential treatment for driving under the influence (DUI) and other traffic charges in Judge Dolan's municipal court. Martha Connaughton was specifically advised that Patsy Stephens was willing to talk about the many times she had visited the office of Dolan's Court Administrator, Billy Joe New, and paid cash to dispose of DUI and minor criminal charges brought against her former husband and other relatives and friends.

A week later, on September 15, Martha Connaughton met with Patsy Stephens to hear her story. The meeting lasted about thirty minutes and was attended by Alice Thompson, Stephens's younger sister. After hearing Stephens's story, Connaughton told her that she wanted to arrange for her to speak with her husband, Daniel. Stephens wanted to think it over. It was a big decision for her.

On Friday, September 16, Stephens had her mother call Martha Connaughton and arrange for the meeting. The meeting was set for the night of the seventeenth, after Stephens and her sister returned from work. Accordingly, shortly before midnight on September 16, 1983, Stephens and her sister were picked up at their home and were driven to the Connaughton home by Dave Berry, Martha's brother, and Joe Cox, Daniel's campaign manager. They arrived at 12:30 A.M. and were met by Daniel and Martha Connaughton and two of their neighbors, Jeanette and Ernest Barnes. All eight people were present during the ensuing tape-recorded interview, which lasted until

4:30 A.M. During the interview Stephens detailed her allegations, recounting "how, on 40 or 50 occasions, she had visited with the Court Administrator, Billy Joe New, in his office and made cash payments to dispose of DUI and other minor criminal charges against her former husband and various other relatives and acquaintances." Among the instances Stephens described was a shoplifting charge against her sister Alice Thompson.

Following the taped interview, Daniel Connaughton contacted the county prosecutor, who suggested that Patsy Stephens be given a lie detector test. Connaughton contacted Stephens, who said she was willing to take the test, which he then scheduled for September 22. Alice Thompson was also asked to take a test, but she declined. On the same day, September 22, Billy Joe New resigned. He had been asked by Judge Dolan to do so, in light of the growing chorus of rumors.

Five days later, after being informed that Stephens had passed the test, Connaughton delivered the tapes of the interviews to the Hamilton Public Safety Director and to the Chief of Police. He also filed a written complaint against Billy Joe New, who was arrested on October 3, following a brief police investigation. New was charged with three counts of bribery, which, of course, were made public and caused quite a stir. Judge Dolan described them dismissively as just dirty politics on Connaughton's part. A grand jury was thereafter empaneled and was considering an indictment of New in early November, on the eve of the election.

New's resignation and the charges brought against him became a central focus of the campaign and the subject of intense interest in the press. Hamilton, Ohio, was, it turns out, a hard-fought newspaper battleground. The contestants were the *Journal News*, whose principal market was Hamilton, and the *Cincinnati Enquirer*, a large metropolitan newspaper. At the time of the election, the two newspapers were engaged in a bitter rivalry for domination of the greater Hamilton circulation market.

The two papers took opposite editorial positions on the Dolan-Connaughton election and, as a general matter, manifested differing sympathies in their news coverage of the election. The *Enquirer* tended to favor Connaughton, especially in light of the controversy surrounding Billy Joe New and the possibility that Judge Dolan had been directly involved, or at least negligent in his administrative oversight. The *Journal News*, in contrast, favored Dolan, who it claimed had not been personally implicated in the Billy Joe New scandal, and strongly opposed Connaughton. The *Enquirer* had been the first paper to disclose the allegations about bribes in Judge Dolan's municipal court and had thus "scooped" the *Journal News* on the most important story of the campaign. It therefore had a certain stake in the controversy and its impact on the election. On the other hand, the *Journal News* editorial director, Jim Blount, had a "confidential personal relationship" with Judge Dolan. The *Journal News* had been scooped by the *Enquirer,* and any efforts it made to discredit Connaughton would effectively impugn the *Enquirer's* credibility and strengthen its competitive position in the Hamilton market.

Late in October, over a month after the allegations against Billy Joe New and Judge Dolan's court first surfaced, Henry Masana, New's lawyer, met with Blount and Joe Cocozzo, the *Journal News* publisher. Masana was representing New against the criminal charges that had been filed and that were at the time before the grand jury. Masana indicated to Blount and Cocozzo that Alice Thompson, Patsy Stephens's younger sister, wanted to be interviewed about Connaughton and the "dirty tricks" he was using in his campaign. She would make some significant allegations about the interview Connaughton conducted with Stephens, which Thompson had witnessed. Blount was aware of Thompson's prior criminal record, reported psychological problems, and the "treatment she had received for her mental condition."[1] He was aware, in short, that although she had been a witness to the Connaughton interview, Thompson's credibility might be doubted. Blount and Cocozzo agreed to have the *Journal News* interview Thompson on October 27.

The interview was in two sittings, both of which occurred in Masana's office. They were conducted for the *Journal News* by Blount and by Pam Long, a news reporter, and lasted nearly one and a half hours. While substantial portions of the tapes turned out to be "inaudible or incoherent," Thompson made a number of specific charges, all concerning Daniel Connaughton's September interview with Patsy Stephens.

The first allegation involved Connaughton's motive in interviewing Stephens.

Alice Thompson: They started asking me a bunch of questions so I asked Dan Connaughton . . . why are you doing this . . . ? And of course, he turned off the tape recorder. And he said, I'll tell you the truth. He said, all I want is to get enough evidence on Billy . . . and have Billy resign. And he said, of course, if Billy resigns, Dolan will resign, and he said, then I can just step up on the bench. . . . But he said right out of his own mouth, all I want to do is to get a story in evidence on them, to meet them face to face, and show them what evidence he had against him, or whatever, to get them to resign, and no more would be said about it.

---

1. Quoted material is taken from transcripts of tapes, depositions, and testimony in the record of the judicial proceedings.

Question: Okay. So in other words, based on what he said to you, you believed him?

Alice Thompson: Blackmail. I mean, you know, the way he phrased it, the way he said it, you know. He said all he wanted to do was get enough evidence on Billy, and he also used Dolan's name, which I don't know what he was going to get on Dolan—to scare them into resigning. I said "What happens when they resign?" Nothing more will be said about anything, he said, when I take the bench nothing will be said.

The second allegation concerned inducements Connaughton had offered to Stephens and Thompson in exchange for Stephens's story about Billy Joe New.

Alice Thompson: . . . I asked them what I was going to get out of it.

Question: What did they promise you? Or what did they say when you asked them?

Alice Thompson: They said my help would be deeply appreciated. And they went on to talk about the three weeks vacation they was planning on taking when the election was . . .

Question: He was planning to take three weeks vacation?

Alice Thompson: Yes, the family—Dave Berry and Martha, and Dan.

Question (by Blount): They wanted you to go along?

Alice Thompson: Me and my sister would be welcome to go along with Dave . . .

Question: Did they say they would pay your expenses?

Alice Thompson: Yeah. I made it clear to them that I couldn't afford a trip to Florida.

Question (by Blount): Was the tape recorder on at that time?

Alice Thompson: Oh, no.

Question: Now where were they going to go?

Alice Thompson: Three weeks in Florida.

Question: And they added Disneyworld?

Alice Thompson: (Inaudible) a three weeks trip to Florida. And they had a friend in Florida that wouldn't be home at the time, that we could stay at their condominium.

Alice Thompson: . . . [Connaughton] said he was thinking about putting a restaurant in [a building he owned], and he was wanting to know if my mother and father would run it for him. And I said, Oh, yeah, my mother would love to get back into the restaurant business. He said good, when the lease is up . . . , we'll tear the inside out and put a restaurant in there, and he said, your mother and father can run it, and he said that way, he said you girls can help run it too, and put your sisters in there working too. He said just . . . he even made up a name, Breedlove's Lunch or something like that. [Thompson's mother's name was Breedlove.] Ma Breedlove's Cooking, you know. He had the names figured out and everything. He offered to buy us a restaurant, you know, and put us in that building.

Question: Okay. So it would just be your parents being a manager, they wouldn't have to buy—did you understand him that they wouldn't have to—

Alice Thompson: Oh, they was going to do everything, you know. They was just going to put us in there to work, or to run it. They wanted my mother to run the business for them.

Question: Did he promise to find you a job?

Alice Thompson: Yeah.

Question: Why did he offer to find you a job?

Alice Thompson: Because the day at the house, going back to the first time I met them, Martha was asking me did I work, or anything, and I was telling her I was looking for work. I had been out of a job. Evidently she must have talked to her husband about it, and that night over at his home, he said are you employed now, you know . . . , and I said no. So he said, we'll see if we can't do something about that. I told him I wanted away from bartending and stuff. He said we'll see if we can't so something about it. You know, a decent job.

Mr. Masana: I'm going to interject. What about the job you were promised?

Alice Thompson: Oh, when they promised me, you know, the secure job and everything, they also promised—they promised Patsy a job too.

Question: That she would be in with Breedlove's Lunch, or café?

Alice Thompson: No, they promised Patsy a decent job, you know.

Question: That she would be (inaudible).

Alice Thompson: That she would be good up in Court. That come out of his own mouth. That come out of Dan's mouth. He said we need somebody like you up at the courthouse.

Alice Thompson: And he said . . . for a victory dinner he wanted to take me and Patsy to dinner at the Maisonette.

Question: This would be after he wins the election?

Alice Thompson: Ummm-hmmm.

Finally, Thompson claimed that Connaughton had assured her and her sister confidentiality.

Alice Thompson: But as far as anybody else, the public, or anything like that— or going to court, we wouldn't have to worry about it. We wouldn't have to go to court and our names wouldn't be on there. . . . [T]hey had already promised that our names wouldn't be mentioned, that nobody would know about us. . . .

Thompson explained that she had come to the *Journal News* because after word of her sister's interview with Daniel Connaughton and of Thompson's cooperation in the Billy Joe New investigation had become public, her friends had accused her of "being a snitch and a rat." She was speaking to the newspaper in order to "get that cleared up." Thompson indicated that she had already told her story to the *Cincinnati Enquirer* and to the police. "I explained to them the whole story, how I got offered this and that, you know. They wasn't interested in this, evidently." Thompson also stated that during the interview with Stephens, the recorder was frequently turned off, and the tape contained none of the statements Connaughton was claimed to have made.

Alice Thompson: I said, what's the whole deal? And of course, he turned off the tape recorder. . . .

Question (by Blount): Was being questioned by the Connaughtons tougher than going to court?

Alice Thompson: Ummm-hmmm. They turned that tape recorder on and off so many times, you know, left out what they wanted to.

Question (by Blount): Was the tape recorder on at that time [when Connaughton discussed confronting Dolan with the evidence on the tape and forcing his resignation]?

Alice Thompson: Oh, no.

Question (by Blount): They had it on when you were talking and off when they were talking?

Alice Thompson: I don't think Dan Connaughton's voice is on it.

Question (by Blount): Was it Dan Connaughton himself who talked about the trip?

Alice Thompson: Yeah. He did most of the talking in the living room. Like I said though, the tape recorder was off when Dan spoke.

At the end of the interview, after announcing to Thompson and Masana that "Pam will, of course, write the story," Blount asked Thompson, "what would happen if we called your sister?"

Alice Thompson: I think she's scared right now to talk to anyone, because the *Cincinnati Enquirer* has been trying to get her to talk to them. She's getting scared now since this is all reality. My sister is . . . she's kind of weak-minded when it comes to anything like that. She won't do nothing for nobody unless she thinks she's benefitting from it. And she honestly thought she was . . . getting a job out of this. And the Connaughtons just used her all the way. And now since she's seeing that it's coming down to where she ain't going to get nothing out of it, she's brought up in the middle of all this and everything, she's scared.

Question (by Blount): Obviously, we can't quote your sister from you (inaudible). What's your sister's position in this, would she support you or would she support him? In other words, if somebody said to her, who's telling the truth here?

Alice Thompson: She'll tell you about the trips, the dinner at the Maisonette, the jobs and everything. She'll tell you that's the truth, because they was offered to her, too.

Following the interviews with Thompson, on October 27, the *Journal News* managing editor assigned a group of reporters to interview the witnesses to the Connaughton-Stephens conversation. Connaughton and Thompson had of course already been interviewed, so the remaining witnesses were Patsy Stephens; Martha Connaughton; her brother Dave Berry; Joe Cox, the campaign manager; and neighbors Jeanette and Ernest Barnes. All but Stephens were assigned for interviews. The interviews were to take place on Monday, October 31.

Three days after the interview with Thompson, on Sunday, October 30, an editorial written by Blount appeared in the *Journal News*. The editorial referred to the charges against Billy Joe New and the effect they were having on the Dolan campaign but indicated that the race was far from over. The editorial quoted an anonymous voter saying, "I resent voting for a person who I later find has been deceitful or dishonest in campaigning." This was an unmistakable, though implicit, reference to Connaughton, an innuendo that was unexplained. The editorial also challenged the *Cincinnati Enquirer*'s coverage of the race and suggested that "the Connaughton forces have a wealthy, influential link to *Enquirer* decision makers." The paper made no endorsement in the editorial.

On Monday, October 31, Daniel Connaughton was invited by a *Journal News* reporter to meet with Blount. "[T]he endorsement may hang in the balance," Connaughton was told. On the afternoon of October 31, Connaughton met with Blount and Cocozzo, the *Journal News* publisher. He was asked about the rumor that he had an "influential link" to the *Enquirer*. He denied the rumor. Connaughton also explained his involvement in the investigation of Billy Joe New, claiming that he had had an obligation as a lawyer to report New's crimes.

Connaughton next met with Blount and Pam Long. He was told that Blount and Long had interviewed Alice Thompson and that they wanted to find out "how much of her statement was true." Portions of the transcript of the interview reveal Connaughton's responses to each of Thompson's allegations.

The first allegation was that Connaughton wanted only to confront Dolan with the tapes and force him to pull out of the race.

Connaughton: I think it would be fair to say, sometime during those three or four hours that they were there, that I probably made a remark along the lines that I just can't believe what I'm hearing, they would probably resign. I mean, I thought the allegation was that serious. But to tell her that—to answer that—and if she's saying that was my announced purpose of what I had them there for and what we were going to do with the information, my answer would be no.

Blount: You didn't tell her you were going to take the tapes to him? And play them for him?

Connaughton: No. No. What I might have said is, boy, I'd sure like to let them hear these tapes and see what they've got to say for themselves, you know, in a fashion such as that.

Blount: In an expression of shock.

Connaughton: Yeah. Yeah, as I almost fell off of the fireplace. Right.

The second set of allegations concerned offers of jobs, trips, dinner, and the promise of anonymity.

Question: Did you ever promise Alice Thompson anonymity?

Connaughton: That question was discussed, and I was hoping to her, and I told her it would be my intention and hope that she could remain anonymous, yes. But I did not promise her anonymity, the answer would be no. Did we discuss it? We sure did, and I expressed to her my desire as well as her desire that she could remain anonymous.

Question: Did you ever talk to Alice about getting a job for her in appreciation for her help with your investigation of New and Dolan?

Connaughton: No.

Question: Not a waitress job?

Connaughton: No.

Question: Did you promise a municipal court job for her sister Patsy Stephens?

Connaughton: No.

Question: Did you offer to have the sisters go on a post election trip to Florida with you and your family to stay in a condominium?

Connaughton: No.

Question: Did you offer to set up Thompson's parents, the Breedloves, in what is now Walt's Chambers, which you own and lease?

Connaughton: Absolutely not.

Question: Why would she say this to us?

Connaughton: What was discussed in an off-handed way, the people who own that bar, who we're not very pleased with, their lease expires next September. My wife has the idea that she wants to open an ice cream type shop like Graeters, or some such thing as that, and I heard her discussing with them that maybe, since Patsy had run this Homette Restaurant or something of that nature, that maybe she would help out and participate in the operation of this—whatever you want to call it—deli-shop or gourmet ice cream shop. Yes, and I was present when that took place.

Question: And when was that?

Connaughton: Well, I don't think it was that night. As I recall, this was a later time that we had seen them.

Question: But that would only be for Patsy (unclear)?

Connaughton: I guess Alice was there, and the offer may have been extended to her in that fashion, that she could work there or something—I wouldn't be surprised if that was said.

* * *

Question (by Blount): What about this post election trip to Florida? Did you talk about anything like that?

Connaughton: Ummm-hmmm. After getting over the initial shock it became a little clearer to me of—kind of how scary this thing was with the information they gave to us, as far as, if their personal safety was at stake. . . . I do remember in an off-handed way it being discussed . . . they could go down to Hilton Head or Florida, or something like that, or maybe hide out or something like that, I don't know. But I own no property and have nothing to offer them.

Question: But there was talk about a friend that had a condominium that would be vacant and it was in terms of a full blown trip, you know, you, the Berrys, the whole group going down to Florida and they were welcome to go along. . . .

Connaughton: No. The only conversation I remember along those lines was in connection with, if their personal safety might be in question because of going out on the line and making these serious allegations. . . .

Question: One last statement. At lunch Thompson said that you promised to take her and her sister out to a post election victory dinner at the Maisonette?

Connaughton: I promised to take them to the Maisonette? Hell, I haven't been to the Maisonette for years.

Question (by Blount): Was it discussed?

Connaughton: It may have been. It may have been. I won't deny that some loose discussion in a kidding way was . . . If she says that I made a firm statement that we were going to definitely plan a party at the Maisonette, that's not true. . . .

Question: So her sister Patsy, again getting back and going over the promises—pardon me for going back to them but that seems to be a hefty charge against you.

Connaughton: That's alright.

Question: Her sister Patsy is not going to get a job in the municipal court if you're elected?

Connaughton: Not that I know of.

Question: And she's not going to be disappointed to find that out, right?

Connaughton: She's not going to be disappointed at that. Right.

The other witnesses to the meeting, with the exception of Stephens (who had made the allegations in the first place), were also interviewed by various *Journal News* reporters on the thirty-first. Each denied Thompson's charges against Connaughton and corroborated Connaughton's account of the meeting. One reporter who had known the Barneses for several years and considered them credible said that Jeanette and Ernest Barnes denied that any promises, offers, or inducements were made. Dave Berry told another reporter that absolutely no promises or offers were made.

No effort was made, however, to contact and interview Patsy Stephens. Jim Blount and Pam Long would later claim that Connaughton had volunteered on the thirty-first to have Stephens get in touch with them. Connaughton denied it. But Blount and Long later retracted the claim and agreed that there was no contact, and no attempt at contact, with Stephens on October 31 or at any other time before November 1. Moreover, no one at the *Journal News* listened to the tapes Connaughton made of the interview with Stephens and Thompson. Blount and Long had asked to hear the tapes when they interviewed Connaughton on the thirty-first, and Connaughton had given the tapes to them. But no one listened to them. Blount later explained that he did not think listening to the tapes was necessary, "because we had from several sources what was on the tape, there was several sources including Mr. Connaughton, that there was no mention of things we were exploring at this time." When asked whether the tapes would help confirm or deny Thompson's claim, for example, that Connaughton's voice was not recorded, Blount again said the tapes were unnecessary "because we had been told from other sources that this matter . . . was not on the tape. This was not discussed on the tape. We had been told by other persons that the tape was junk as far as evidence."

Based on the interviews with Alice Thompson, Daniel Connaughton, and six of the witnesses to the meeting in which Patsy Stephens reported on the fixing of DUI and other charges by Billy Joe New, and without the benefit of an interview with Stephens or a review of the tapes Connaughton had provided, the *Journal News* published a lead story on Thompson's allegations on November 1, just a few days before the election. The headline was "Bribery Case Witness Claims Jobs, Trips Offered." The story, written by Long, began, "A woman called to testify before the . . . Grand Jury in the Billy Joe New bribery case claims that Dan Connaughton, candidate for Hamilton Municipal Judge, offered her and her sister jobs and a trip to Florida in appreciation for their help." Each of Thompson's allegations were accurately set out. Connaughton's denial was also included, and his different version of the events was accurately reported.

Five days later, on November 6, 1983, the *Journal News* endorsed Judge Dolan.

* * *

Daniel Connaughton lost the election. Judge Dolan was elected to another six-year term. Shortly thereafter the grand jury reported an indictment of Billy Joe New. He was later tried and found guilty of bribery.

Connaughton was not finished, however. He sued the *Journal News* for libel. He claimed that the November 1 article "was defamatory in its implication that Connaughton was an unethical lawyer and an undesirable candidate for the Hamilton Municipal judgeship who was capable of extortion, who was a liar and an opportunist not fit to hold public office, particularly a judgeship." The libel arose from the implication that a newspaper reader would draw about Connaughton from the appearance of the Thompson allegations in the *Journal News.* Newspapers don't publish just anything, and so there must be something there, and where there's smoke, there's fire.

Because he was a candidate for office, Connaughton had to prove not only that the libelous statements were false and damaging to his reputation but also that they were made with "actual malice." He had to show that Long, Blount, and the *Journal News* had published the Thompson allegations (and their implications about Connaughton's character) *knowing them to be false or had published them despite actually having serious doubts about their truth* and in the face of obvious steps that could have been taken to confirm or deny their truth.

It would be nearly impossible to prove that Long and Blount *knew* the allegations were false. They were unlikely to admit as much, and in any event the falsity of the allegations was, in a real sense, unknowable, for it depended on whose account one believed, Thompson's or Connaughton's. A jury might be persuaded by a preponderance of the evidence placed before them that the allegations were false, but that is a very different question from whether Long or Blount, in their own minds, were convinced of it and were morally certain of their own views. It is also a very different question from whether, in truth, the allegations were true or false. Courts of law are not places where actual truth is to be found.

So Connaughton had to take the alternative route, proving that Long and Blount had entertained serious doubts about the allegations and had published recklessly in view of those doubts. Here Connaughton had two powerful weapons. First, Blount and Long had *consciously* steered clear of speaking with Patsy Stephens and had purposefully decided not to listen to the tapes of Connaughton's original interview of Stephens and Thompson. Both Long and Blount had made excuses or explanations for each of these decisions. But they had later been forced to back down and recant the excuses. This combination of a conscious choice to learn no more, especially from the two most credible and direct sources, and the suspicious motives implicit in Long's and Blount's ill-fated excuses could lead a jury to conclude that they had entertained serious doubts about the truth of the allegations. Why else go to such lengths to avoid further information that would resolve the doubts? Why else *make up* excuses for the otherwise journalistically inexcusable failure to hear the tapes and interview Stephens? Why else do these things but to cover the tracks of your purposeful scheme?

The second weapon Connaughton had was proof of recklessness. Happily, the same circumstances could do double duty on the recklessness question. Assuming that Blount and Long actually had entertained serious doubts about the truth of the Thompson allegations, their failure to listen to the tape and to interview Stephens was, by any standard of journalism, objectively reckless. Stephens's account and the tapes were directly relevant to the truth of the allegations; they were perhaps the most credible information available, certainly more credible than the statements of Thompson and Connaughton and Connaughton's wife and brother-in-law and campaign manager and neighbors. Ignoring them in any circumstances would have been irresponsible; doing so in light of serious doubts actually entertained about the allegations was simply wanton behavior.

It was on this theory of the evidence and the case that Connaughton's libel suit proceeded to trial and then to judgment. Unsurprisingly, Connaughton won the case. The jury found, specifically and separately, that (1) the November 1 article defamed Connaughton, damaging his reputation in the community; (2) the Thompson allegations and the implications of extortion, suborning perjury, and dishonesty were false; and (3) the statements were published with actual malice. The first two conclusions were based on a preponderance of the evidence (i.e., 51 percent will do). The third was based on "clear and convincing" evidence, a rather strict standard of evidence required by the First Amendment on questions of fact bearing directly on liability or privilege, such as actual malice. In light of its findings, the jury awarded Connaughton $5,000 in compensatory damages and $195,000 in punitive damages.

The jury verdict was appealed to the Court of Appeals, which upheld the verdict and the damage award. The court concluded that "Connaughton proved, by clear and convincing evidence, that the *Journal News* demonstrated its actual malice when it published the November 1, 1983, article despite the existence of serious doubt which attached to Thompson's veracity and the accuracy of her reports."

The owner of the *Journal News*, Harte-Hanks Communications, Inc., then appealed the decision to the United States Supreme Court. The Court heard oral argument in the case on March 20, 1989, and issued its decision on June 22, 1989. The Supreme Court's decision, written by Justice Stevens, unanimously upheld the jury's verdict and concluded, also unanimously, that the *Journal News*—and Blount and Long—had published the November 1 story with actual malice. The Court's explanation is worth quoting:

> It is . . . undisputed that Connaughton made the tapes of the Stephens interview available to the *Journal News* and that no one at the newspaper took the time to listen to them. Similarly, there is no question that the *Journal News* was aware that Patsy Stephens was a key witness and that they failed to make any effort to interview her. Accepting the jury's determination that [Blount's and Long's] explanations for these omissions were not credible, it is likely that

the newspaper's inaction was a product of a deliberate decision not to acquire knowledge of facts that might confirm the probable falsity of Thompson's charges. Although failure to investigate will not alone support a finding of actual malice, the *purposeful avoidance of the truth* is in a different category.

* * *

What is to be made of the *Connaughton* case and the Court's decision? What role did truth play in the *Connaughton* case, and what role should it play in libel law? What about falsity? Can libel law be defended if it permits a newspaper to be held liable even when what it publishes might be true—when its publication can't be proven to be actually false? If the answer is yes—if newspapers should be held liable even if the publication might be true—how can this result be squared with freedom of the press guaranteed by the First Amendment? We will briefly explore each of these three questions—truth, falsity, and journalism—in the pages that follow.

We start with truth. The fact of the matter is that despite the questionable motives of virtually all of the characters in the story, despite their sloppiness and arrogance, and despite the jury's decision that the damaging allegations from the Thompson interview were false, we have no way to determine whether, in fact, the allegations are true or false. In the end the case is a "he said, she said" one, much like the Clinton scandal. Patsy Stephens, of course, was there, thus making it a "we said, he said" question, but in fact Stephens would later testify at trial that her sister Alice Thompson had made it all up. Then, toward the end of the trial, Stephens would file an affidavit recanting the testimony and saying that her sister was right and that Connaughton had promised her 10 percent of the judgment for her help. Finally, she would change her story one last time under cross-examination, denying the promise and claiming that her sister had lied. With this track record, we can legitimately doubt Thompson's account, but we can't really rely on any version of Stephens's story for corroboration.

There is, indeed, a certain respect in which our dilemma about Stephens is not unlike that faced by the *Journal News*. Blount and Long's claim that they believed Thompson's story to be true is pretty hard to swallow. The jury found it indigestible. But their claim that they did not know it to be false—indeed that they did not know what the truth was—is perfectly understandable. Like them, we might conclude in light of Stephens's shifting testimony at trial that, in the end, we don't really know what the truth is.

In Connaughton's case the likely truth is even a bit more uncertain. As incredible as Thompson's allegations might be, given her own record for veracity, Connaughton confirmed part of her story: prospects of jobs, dining at a fine restaurant after the election, and traveling to Florida had come up. Was Thompson overinterpreting what Connaughton had said, drawing conclusions that she wanted to hear, or was she just lying? Was Connaughton such an honest, naive, and straight-shooting person that he talked about jobs and meals and trips without appreciating how his words might sound, and on the assumption that everyone was trustworthy, honest, and would always speak the truth? And when asked about what he said by Blount and Long, was he so naive as to think there was nothing untoward in his admission that he or his wife, Martha, "may have" talked about the restaurant, and Martha may—no, probably did—suggest excitedly that Stephens could "help out"? Did he think Blount and Long would print nothing about such admissions? Was he unaware that they might cause controversy? Was he, in other words, something of a dupe?

Or was Connaughton, a young and successful attorney in Hamilton, a former Hamilton City Prosecutor, Butler County Prosecutor, and acting judge of the Hamilton Municipal Court, instead a savvy, experienced, and accomplished lawyer who knew his way around government and politics? Might his admissions about the subjects touched on at the meeting with Stephens and Thompson have been made with a view to the tapes that Connaughton himself had made? He couldn't deny something that was on the tapes. The police had the tapes, and Blount and Long would surely ask for them, as they did. Might his admitted references in the interview to jobs, meals, and a trip have been carefully crafted implications made in a way that would preserve his deniability? Might Thompson, in other words, have interpreted Connaughton correctly, though not literally?

All of this and more might lead a reasonable person, even a reasonable journalist, to conclude that the truth of the matter is unknowable. One version might seem to fit better than another; one person might seem more trustworthy or reliable. If the journalist were forced to come to a conclusion, he or she might be prepared to do so (claiming later, of course, that he or she had no doubt about the truth, perhaps on the advice of counsel). But in a quiet and confidential setting, the journalist would likely admit that the real truth was unknowable, and that in the end, he or she had just used the best judgment possible.

Perhaps Blount and Long would say something like this—if they could speak with candor. They might say: "We know something happened. The story was just too important, even with the uncertainty surrounding truth, to bury it. So we published the allegations and Connaughton's denial. We let the public decide, although in all frankness we knew that once published the allegations would take on some credibility simply from the fact of our publishing them, and they would hurt Connaughton more than Thompson. But what could we do?"

Let us assume, for present purposes, that this is exactly what happened. It no doubt bears a family resemblance to the real events and motives. Should the law ever be permitted to punish the publication of truth? It is, of course, possible that the allegations against Connaughton were, in fact, true. That possibility, standing alone, requires that we ask about punishment of truth, for a rule that stops short of requiring that truth be known makes it inevitable that some of the speech it punishes will have been true, just like a jury's decision that a person committed a capital crime "beyond a reasonable doubt" makes it inevitable, though hopefully rare, that an innocent person will be put to death. In any event, the *Journal News* article was, in a literal sense, true. Its account of the allegations and Connaughton's denials and explanations was accurate, even if its implications and innuendos were not. The tapes of both interviews bear that out.

What about falsity? Isn't falsity but the perfect opposite of truth? If the law punishes published falsity, then isn't that acceptable, since that which is false cannot, by definition, be true? In a perfect world of absolute knowledge of facts and motives and intentions, this conclusion would be logically unexceptionable. Thompson's allegations were false, therefore, by definition not true, so the law is not, by imposing liability on the *Journal News*, punishing truth. But the matter is more complicated than this. If falsity is the logical opposite of truth, and if we cannot know truth, how then can we know falsity? The circle cannot be closed so easily.

But the real problem is a more practical and earthly one. The Thompson allegations were, indeed, found to be false. But this conclusion was made by a jury—even a unanimous one—in answer to a specific question: "Do you find, by a preponderance of the evidence before you, that the statements were false?" The jurors' decision, in short, was based only on the evidence before them: the two tapes; the testimony of witnesses; the innuendos about motive; and the character and credibility of the witnesses, especially Thompson and Connaughton, whom the jury could judge only on the basis of their demeanor in the artificial atmosphere of trial and cross-examination by good lawyers. More fundamentally, the jury did not have to decide truth or falsity in any absolute sense but merely whether the balance of the evidence—51 percent versus 49 percent the other way—supported a conclusion that the statements were false. The jury, in short, did not decide that the statements were false but instead that the statements were *probably* false in light of the information available to them. This falls far short of the mark of truth.

The question whether the law, and the First Amendment in particular, should ever impose liability on truth cannot, therefore, be escaped. To many, the idea of punishing truth is anathema to the First Amendment. But there are at least two responses to this view. The first is practical: imposing liability on truth cannot be escaped in a theoretical sense, but the law makes do with the tools it has at its disposal—rules of evidence, juries, and the like. Thus, although the jury's decision is not perfect, it is as close to correct as is practically possible, and therefore, it is a good enough justification for imposing liability even though, in some metaphysical sense, truth might occasionally be the victim.

The second response is that there is nothing in legal tradition or in the First Amendment that makes truth especially sacrosanct. The First Amendment is about free speech, not truth, and speech is protected under the Constitution whether it is true or not. Indeed, Justice Oliver Wendell Holmes Jr. was of the view that the First Amendment was based on the distinctly skeptical, even cynical, premise that there is no absolute or enduring truth. Thus truth can never be used as a justification for prohibiting contrary speech. The point of the First Amendment, Holmes believed, was to assure that differing views—both opinion and fact—could compete with one another in the hope that, at some point, *a truth* (itself contingent and subject to further discussion and reflection and experience) might emerge.

Moreover, there is little basis in the history of the law or the Constitution to support the claim that truth should be absolutely protected. Many acts of speech that are deemed criminal, such as extortion, bribery, or blackmail, are based on spoken truth. The blackmailer truthfully tells the victim that his or her sordid secrets will be disclosed unless a price is paid. This is truth. The sordid secrets that would be disclosed without payment are also true (or at least this is often the case). Yet the law does not hesitate to punish the speech as a crime. Someone who copies the copyrighted words or music (or news story) of another and publishes it (whether for a price or not) will be punished by the law in the form of money damages or even, if the act is repeated, in the form of incarceration for contempt. But the music or words published are true, or at least not false.

The goal of the First Amendment, of course, may be truth—*contingent* truth, as Holmes put it. But this sense of truth—the quest for truth—cannot be achieved by protecting truth from liability and punishing only falsehood. Instead, and paradoxically, it can be achieved by protecting expression that is considered false or not provably true, on the ground that ideas of truth may some day change. Truth, like opinion, must be the subject of open debate. A First Amendment governed by an idea of real truth would be a dangerous instrument of suppression. Freedom of speech is therefore about speech, not truth.

If this is what free speech is about, what about freedom of the press? Free speech may be about speech, but isn't the question different for the press? If freedom of the press is about the press, isn't the press about truth? Do we not expect the press to be devoted to truth, to adopt truth as its central purpose and justification? Don't people need the press in order to get the truth—indeed the unvarnished, independently judged truth? There will be errors, of course, but they should, for constitutional purposes, be seen as errors, not valuable falsehoods.

There is much substance to this view of the press. Its justification is not open and uninhibited debate, as such, but the independent publication of information and opinion about people and events. But while the press's function must in some sense be related to truth, the *Connaughton* case illustrates the problem with taking truth too seriously as a measure of press freedom. With most events and people, truth is hard to ascertain in any absolute, or even "beyond a reasonable doubt," sense. The difficulty is even greater for the press. The press is always looking at events after the fact. The press is rarely a witness or participant, and therefore, its judgment of fact and truth must always be filtered through the eyes of others—their views of fact and truth. And the press lacks perfect access even to all of the people who themselves witnessed or participated in an event. Many simply will not talk to the press. Others talk, but selectively. Others color what they say by their own interests and purposes. Some lie. This would make the press's obligation to publish truth difficult enough, but we must add to the mix that the reporters and editors are generalists, not knowledgeable about banking when a banking scandal arises or about nuclear energy when a question of risk is voiced. The press, in other words, doesn't even start on an even playing field.

So we can't demand truth from the press. Does this mean, however, that truth plays no role? People do, after all, rely on the press for information that, at a minimum, reflects the newspaper's best judgment about what's true and what's not, what's important and what's not. People excuse the press's errors—especially if it admits them. But people would not want to read a newspaper whose motto is "All the Falsehood Fit to Titillate." For people who rely on the press, truth is important; indeed, it was important for those who drafted the Constitution and placed reliance on the press serving as an independent check on government abuse and misconduct. But it was important as an aspiration, not as an accomplished fact. What is important, in other words, is the *search* for truth, not truth itself. For the press, and for journalism, truth is a means, not an end. Truth must be its object, though not necessarily its accomplishment.

How might this relate to the *Connaughton* case—to the law's punishment of a story that may have been true? The Supreme Court's explanation of the case rested on the phrase "purposeful avoidance of the truth." What is important to the First Amendment, the Court said, is not truth but instead whether the decision to publish is animated by an effort to speak the truth—a truth-seeking purpose. The press and journalism must seek truth, not falsehood. *Purposeful* avoidance of the truth, by definition, is not a seeking of the truth. It therefore does not qualify as journalism. And this is so, ironically, despite the fact that a story may inadvertently—indeed unintentionally—end up being true. It is the *process* that counts with journalism and the press.

The *Journal News's* conduct in the *Connaughton* case was not truth seeking. Neither Blount nor Long—nor for that matter anyone else employed by the *Journal News*—listened to the tape of the original interview of Stephens and Thompson by Connaughton. The *Journal News* had the tape, as did the police and prosecutors pursuing Billy Joe New's case. A truth-seeking journalist might have inadvertently forgotten to listen or been prevented from doing so by serious deadline pressure. But neither excuse is available in the *Connaughton* case. The decision not to review the tape was premeditated. The tape, Blount said, was "junk," or so some sources (undisclosed, but including Thompson) said. How could Blount know? Or didn't he want to know?

Blount did not order anyone at the *Journal News* to interview Patsy Stephens, the main character in the drama and the only person who might be able, firsthand, to confirm Thompson's account of the interviews. A truth-seeking journalist would not have missed this step. It was too obvious for inadvertence and too critical to sacrifice to deadline pressure. Blount claimed at first that Connaughton had volunteered to have Stephens call Blount. Even if this were true, it wouldn't have excused Blount's failure to follow up. But it was not true. It was instead an attempt to shift blame and explain away a fact that otherwise could only be explained in one way: Blount did not want to know what Stephens would say, for that might prevent publication of Long's story, avert the damage to Connaughton, and sacrifice a chance to thoroughly discredit the stories about the Dolan scandal that had been published first and prominently in the *Enquirer.*

This, at any rate, is what the jury found, as a matter of fact, based on the evidence presented to it. For the Supreme Court of the United States, the jury's factual findings must stand if they represent reasonable conclusions drawn from the evidence. They did. Indeed, it is hard to imagine any other conclusion than that Blount (and through him the *Journal News*) was consciously indifferent to the truth and acted in ways that safeguarded his ignorance. Blount—and with him Long and the *Journal News*—was not a truth seeker, but a truth concealer.

Can the law live comfortably with a definition of journalism and a standard for libel that rest not on truth but on truth seeking? If, for example, a story published in conscious disregard of the truth turns out, in hindsight, actually to be true, what is to be done? Do we offer truth some protection under the First Amendment, as truth, but deny it any protection as journalism or press? Or do we protect it as journalism *because it is true,* even though nothing resembling a truth-seeking process of judgment existed at the time of the statement's publication? We can't do the latter for two reasons. First, such an approach would require courts to determine *actual* truth in all cases, something that, as we have seen, cannot be done and that juries cannot be expected to do. Second, such an approach would treat all truth as journalism or press, a result difficult to square with the text of the Constitution and with common experience. It would throw open all expression claimed true—television ads, campaign statements, all information on databases and available over the Internet—to the protection of the free press clause. *Press* would become a meaningless and vacuous term.

But the press—and its practice, journalism—is a special calling with special objects, historically understood when the First Amendment was drafted and ratified. Journalism is what we today would call a "filter" in the technological world of communications, a world of raw data, of unlimited information. In this world we need a "press," or journalism, filter perhaps more than at any other time. The press does not give us the "quality" or "highbrow" filter, not the "well-educated" filter, not the "everything you want to see" filter. The press instead gives us the independent, truth-seeking filter. It does not claim truth but claims to have sought truth pursuant to generally known and respected protocols we think of as journalism: gathering as much relevant information as possible; judging its public importance; corroborating it; disclosing its sources; separating fact from opinion; exercising independence of judgments about what is believed true; basing judgments about truth on empirical information—from sources, from documents—not simply on personal ideology or preference; being honest with the reader and user of information.

The jury in the *Connaughton* case decided that the *Journal News* could make none of these assurances to its readers. It had breached its covenant with them and in the course of doing so had breached its covenant with journalism and with the Constitution. The *Journal News* decided to step out of its role as the press. It can't do so and at the same time claim the press's freedom simply because it is convenient (or profitable). For better or worse, the United States Supreme Court agreed.

Additional Reading

Anderson, David. "Is Libel Law Worth Reforming?" *University of Pennsylvania Law Review* 140 (1991): 487ff.

Bezanson, R., G. Cranberg, and J. Soloski. *Libel Law and the Press: Myth and Reality.* New York: The Free Press, 1987.

Smolla, Rodney. "Let the Author Beware: The Rejuvenation of the American Law of Libel." *University of Pennsylvania Law Review* 132 (1983): 1ff.

Soloski, J., and R. Bezanson, eds. *Reforming Libel Law.* New York: The Guilford Press, 1992.

3. News

When we think of the "press," we ordinarily think of "news"—current information and opinion on matters of government, politics, economics, and social affairs. This intuitive definition pretty well captures the term used in England as the press was struggling to emerge from beneath the heavy hand of control by the Crown, enforced through the hated stamp. There the battle cry was for independent information on matters of "politics and political economy."[1]

Most people would likely agree that news is a medium of nonfiction consisting of information and opinion focused on current events and issues or relevant to understanding them. This is a very broad definition. On its face it excludes fiction and literature and history and philosophy. Or does it? History and literature and philosophy surely bear on our understanding of current events and issues; art and fiction, also, can claim relevance to the world we perceive and the problems with which we cope—the "exigencies" of modern society, as Justice Brennan put it in the famous 1964 Supreme Court decision in *New York Times v. Sullivan.*

Yet no matter how murky and potentially expansive the boundaries of news, the press consists of a *constitutionally* special subset of all publishers, a part of a broader universe that also includes humorists, novelists, historians, playwrights, poets, film producers, even pornographers. And the press's special place is marked, among other things, by what it publishes. In mod-

---

1. Collet Dobson Collet, *History of the Taxes on Knowledge: Their Origin and Repeal* (Ann Arbor, Mich.: Gryphon Books, 1971), 45.

ern parlance, the shorthand term we use to describe what the press publishes is *news*.

Just what is news? What qualities does it possess that other forms or genres of expression lack? How should a court interpreting the First Amendment go about placing boundaries on news, distinguishing news from other genres, such as entertainment or advertising? The stories that follow will illustrate just how difficult, yet essential, such an undertaking can be.

STORY 4

News and Entertainment
Zacchini v. Scripps-Howard Broadcasting Company
433 U.S. 562 (1977)

The Supreme Court's first, and apparently only, experience with what the law calls the appropriation, or "right of publicity" tort, occurred in 1977 in the case of *Zacchini v. Scripps-Howard Broadcasting Company.* As with many first efforts, the Court's attempt to square the tort with the First Amendment was sketchy, even a bit ungainly. But this can perhaps be forgiven, for the task before the Court in the *Zacchini* case was nothing less than to define *news,* a term freighted with ambiguity, a term with deeply embedded cultural and sociological meaning, a term that is perhaps impossible to capture in the principled terminology of the law.

Hugo Zacchini was born to the circus. His father and uncle were circus performers of considerable fame. The Zacchinis were known widely as inventors, trapeze artists, and riders. Hugo's father and uncle invented, among other things, a mechanism by which a person could be propelled over one hundred feet out of a cannon, a distance well beyond the sixty-feet mark set by P. T. Barnum's human cannonball act. It was Hugo who was first shot from the Zacchini cannon by his father. He achieved a distance of one hundred feet, to much acclaim, and made it his life's work. He became the Human Cannonball, shot from a cannon several hundred feet into the air and falling, after nearly fifteen airborne seconds, safely into a net. His livelihood consisted of traveling around the country, making a living by selling his act to circuses from coast to coast.

In August and September 1972, Hugo Zacchini's act was performed at the Ceauga County Fair in Burton, Ohio, a town of 1,349 people located just east of Cleveland. On August 30, 1972, George J. Masaur, a freelance reporter for Channel 5, the local television station owned by Scripps-Howard Broadcasting Company, attended the fair and witnessed Zacchini's human cannonball act. Spectators were not permitted to have cameras in the big tent. But having seen the act, Masaur spoke with Zacchini and asked whether he could film it. Zacchini declined.

The next day Masaur consulted with the producer of Channel 5's *Eyewitness News,* informing him of Zacchini's refusal to be filmed. The producer nevertheless instructed Masaur to return to the fair and film the act for use on the 11 o'clock news program. Masaur returned to the fair, this time with a handheld camera, and filmed Zacchini's act from start to finish. The film of the act, unedited, was broadcast on Channel 5's news program at 11 o'clock on September 1, 1972, all fifteen seconds of it, showing Hugo Zacchini propelled from the cannon, flying two hundred feet into the air, and falling safely into a net. The footage was accompanied by a script read by David F. Patterson, coanchor of the news, recounting the excitement and suspense of the act and its enthusiastic reception by the audience: "This now is the story of a *true spectator* sport, the sport of human cannonballing. . . . In fact, the great *Zacchini* is about the only human cannonball around, these days. [It] just happens that, *where* he is, is the Great Ceauga County Fair, in Burton and believe me, although it's not a long act, it's a thriller and you really need to see it in person to appreciate it." The news story was not *about* Zacchini's act. It *was* Zacchini's act.

Zacchini was surely upset to see his act broadcast on the nightly news, available to everyone in the county, everyone who might have been attracted to the circus or to his show just to see it happen. He was also worried, we can assume, by the possession of the full fifteen-second tape in the hands of the local television station and by his inability to control its possible sale to other stations in other counties and cities to which his act would travel. His livelihood was at stake. And we might surmise that he was angry that the station had filmed the act without permission, indeed, in the face of his request that it not be filmed, angry also at the arrogance with which the station claimed its right to do what it wanted in the name of news. All these and perhaps other reasons led Zacchini to commence a lawsuit against the station and its owner, Scripps-Howard Broadcasting. He alleged in his lawsuit that Channel 5 had "showed and commercialized the film of his act without his consent," that the act was "invented by his father and . . . performed only by his family for the last fifty years," and that by its broadcast Channel 5 had engaged in an "unlawful appropriation of [his] professional property." In the terminology of the law, Channel 5 had "appropriated" Zacchini's act.

The appropriation tort, as it is often called, is a common-law tort. It is largely a creature of judicial imagination, not the product of a law enacted by the legislature. The tort gives each of us a legal interest, akin to a property interest, in controlling the use of our name or likeness or performances to prevent commercial use of them by another person. The interest is much like a copyright enjoyed by a songwriter or an author, or a trademark granted to a product. But it is much wider in scope: it applies to the use of a person's name or photograph or likeness; and it prohibits the use by someone else for their benefit, whether commercial or not. It prohibits, for example, anyone from using Elvis Presley's photo on their own T-shirt.

Such uses are of course only prohibited if they harm the commercial value of the name or likeness. Two things should be said about this. First, commercial value goes to the harm caused by a use, not to the character of a use. Thus, in many states, including the state of Ohio, any harmful use, even use as a part of news reporting, can be a wrongful appropriation. In states with such an open-ended rule, privileges are recognized that protect certain socially valuable uses against liability. News is one such privileged use. In other states the tort applies only to commercial uses, a rule that arrives at the same end point by deeming uses in the reporting of news to be noncommercial. How news is defined, then, can be the critical question in many cases. It was *the* critical question in Zacchini's case.

The second point to emphasize is that the tort's protection extends only to a name or likeness or performance that has commercial value. Since most people's name or likeness, or even their performances at the piano, for example, have no commercial value, the tort's utility is largely restricted to the famous or infamous, such as Elvis Presley or Martin Luther King Jr. Both made generous use of the tort to protect their commercial interests against other users during their lives; and their heirs have used the tort after their deaths, since the right to control use of name, likeness, or performance becomes part of the estate and continues after death. The tort's protection is also available to the less famous, persons not widely known but who have unique talents or features upon which they rely for their livelihood. Hugo Zacchini was such a person.

Zacchini's lawsuit was initially dismissed in the trial court on the ground that Ohio courts did not recognize, and had not created, the appropriation tort. He appealed to the Ohio Court of Appeals, which reversed the trial court, concluding that the Ohio courts had, indeed, recognized the tort of appropriation, and thus individuals were permitted to sue for damages resulting from the appropriation of their "right of publicity." The appeals court also concluded that Channel 5's broadcast was not privileged as news, for the broadcast of the entire fifteen-second performance did not qualify as publication of news but, instead, was entertainment. Channel 5 and Scripps-Howard Broadcasting appealed the case to the Ohio Supreme Court, which agreed that the tort of appropriation was recognized in Ohio, but the court concluded that appropriation of one's name or likeness or performance in the course of a news broadcast was privileged by the First Amendment's guarantee of freedom of the press. Channel 5's broadcast, the Ohio Supreme Court said, was news.

Feeling like something of a ping-pong ball, perhaps, having lost, then won, then lost again, Zacchini decided to pursue the last and only remaining avenue of appeal. He appealed his case to the United States Supreme Court. In early 1977, almost five years after the date of the broadcast, the Supreme Court agreed to hear his case. Oral argument was scheduled for April 25, 1977.

Oral argument in the *Zacchini* case was a rather desultory affair, with long series of questions bearing on some rather technical and jurisdictional questions that need not detain us. But the heart of the case was definitional: did Channel 5's broadcast of the act qualify as news and thus deserve special protection under the free press guarantee of the First Amendment? The Court was firmly aware of this central question, exploring it through a number of hypothetical questions designed to reveal just where, and how, the line between news and entertainment might be drawn.

Hugo Zacchini's lawyer was John C. Lancione, of Cleveland, Ohio. He began his argument by emphasizing two points. First, he said that Zacchini's claim was based on a property right, a "proprietary interest" recognized in Ohio law. The right was a "right of publicity that inheres in a professional entertainer's act, that [gives the entertainer] a property right to govern how, when, and where his performance is published." Second, he argued that Channel 5's broadcast of the act was not an instance of reporting, but "a verbatim reproduction." By this he meant, implicitly, that because the act was entertainment, its broadcast unaccompanied by anything more was entertainment, as well. If, he suggested later in the argument, something more than the performance had happened—if, for example, Zacchini had "miss[ed] the net and [broken] his legs," using the act to report that additional matter would be to report "something different than his professional act" and would present an altogether different case.

The Court did not seriously challenge Lancione's first point. Once he had established to the Court's satisfaction that the state of Ohio did indeed grant Zacchini a propertylike right to control the use of his act, that was the end of the matter. The only question that remained was whether, since Channel 5 had violated Zacchini's right by broadcasting the act on the evening news, the First Amendment prohibited Zacchini from enforcing his right against the station. This, in turn, was a question of freedom of speech and press, a question that did not turn on the nature of Zacchini's property interest, but instead on the kind of use made of the act and its value in the larger constitutional scheme of things. If Zacchini was to prevail, therefore, the Court would have to distinguish some uses of an entertainer's act, which could be prohibited, from others, which could not. And more specifically, the Court would have to decide whether Channel 5's use was a news use and thus a specially protected one. Where does the line between news and non-news lie? The Court's hypotheticals represented efforts to explore and chart this previously uncharted territory.

Justice Blackmun posed the first hypothetical to Zacchini's lawyer.

Question: Let me pose a hypothetical to you, and I am going to ask your friend [Scripps-Howard's lawyer] to comment on the same hypothetical later on when his turn comes. When Muhammad Ali engages in one of his professional exhibitions of prize fighting, I understand that the ratio [of broadcast to gate] is about ten-to-one or more; that the TV rights are many, many times the income he receives from the persons who are present at the arena.

Suppose . . . either one of the networks or an outlaw group . . . surreptitiously . . . filmed the entire fight and then tried to put it on the air. Do you analogize your client's situation to what that would be with Muhammad Ali? . . . I assume that your client has TV rights? Muhammad Ali does.

Mr. Lancione: I don't know that for a fact, Your Honor. I am sure that Muhammad Ali does. In fact, as a legal proposition he does [just as, implicitly and legally, Zacchini does under Ohio law.]

I do [think that the two situations are analogous], Your Honor. [And] I think that it would be the very same situation if on a program on fine arts the media would go into the concert hall and tape Beethoven's Eighth Symphony, which . . . doesn't take more than half an hour, and play the entire symphony.

[Indeed,] our case is stronger because Hugo Zacchini only has one performance. He doesn't play a different tune like a violinist. He has one 15-second act, and [Channel 5] captured that . . . over his specific objection.

Question: Do you think the Supreme Court of Ohio would have reached a different result in your example of the taping of the Eighth Symphony played at Kennedy Center?

Mr. Lancione: The Ohio Supreme Court would not have.

Question: Even though [it] were put on an educational television station, not billed as news but [instead] said, "here is a brand new performance of Beethoven's Eighth?"

Mr. Lancione: Well, I think if it were outside of a news showing, the Supreme Court of Ohio may very well have come to a different conclusion. But what they said relates to news programs . . . , and the only exception [they made] was [for] non-news use, which seems to me to be a non sequitur. You can't [gain] a First Amendment right . . . [simply] by putting [otherwise unprotected material] on your news if [the material] is a non-news use.

Lancione's argument has a weakness. He treats the distinction between news and non-news as resting on the thing—the item broadcast—as if certain items or facts or events are inherently news. But this is surely incorrect, or at least incomplete, for facts have contexts that give them meaning. A Marlboro Man ad in 1960 was a very different thing from its status today as a cultural icon, even as a piece of cultural history. A fact reported by Peter Jennings is likely quite different in meaning from the same fact reported by Jay Leno in his monologue.

But the problem was lost, at least for the moment, as the Court turned the questioning to other matters.

Question: If Mr. Zacchini had just done this for the fun of it in a county park or in a public square, just like they do it every now and then . . .
(Laughter)
   and if a TV news camera had gone out there and reported that as news, there would be no proprietary right that had been appropriated, would there, because there was certainly no monetary right?
Mr. Lancione: I don't think that you would be able to establish any damages under the Ohio law because he would have no commercial value if he did not perform as a professional entertainer.
Question: It was a property right for which he was paid?
Mr. Lancione: That's correct.
Question: Under contract. And that is critical, isn't it?
Mr. Lancione: Yes, it is. He is a professional entertainer and that is to whom the right applies, the right of publicity applies to an entertainer or to a professional athlete or to anyone who has developed some commercial value in the use of their name and their image and their success.

Lancione is on uncertain ground here, as his answer makes clear. The fact is that the right of publicity is not restricted to professional entertainers under contract. Lancione, of course, would be very happy to have the issue so limited, for then the more perplexing and broad applications of the right would not get in Zacchini's way. A right limited to professionals under contract would be easier to defend, although it would not, in reality, be a "property" right, but rather one that stems from private contract, and the tortious behavior of Channel 5 would be more like intentional interference with a contract rather than a tortious invasion of property such as trespass or theft.

But the fact is that the right of publicity, as Lancione explains, applies not only to professionals or entertainers but also to any name or likeness or performance that has commercial value. And its existence is not dependent on a contract but instead inheres in the performance or likeness or name, just as if it were property. Its violation by a use by another for commercial purposes is not contingent on denial of consent by the owner or even on a requirement that the owner post notice that it cannot be used. Like a trespass on private land, the wrong occurs by the entry, for the right of exclusive use by an owner inheres in the property itself. So although in Zacchini's case, the facts of a contract and paid performance were perhaps helpful in making his claim appear more compelling or sympathetic, those facts were actually legally irrelevant.

The Justices understood this, as evidenced by the next question.

Question: Suppose [Zacchini] had performed in the square in front of the TV station for the general public to see? . . . Can the TV station photograph it and put it on the news program?

Mr. Lancione: I don't think they could film [or broadcast] his entire act.

Question: If he was doing it right in their front yard [so to speak]?

Mr. Lancione: If he was doing it as a commercial act and TV cameras were there—

Question: If he was doing it and he was being paid because as he got shot out of the cannon he had "Buy Blatz Beer" on his back, could they publish that?

Mr. Lancione: No, I don't think they could publish his entire act under any circumstances. . . . [Of course, if they shot him] missing the net and breaking his legs, then I think it becomes something different than his professional act. . . . That would be a different situation.

Question: He doesn't have to take the trouble to exclude people, on the theory of your case . . . ?

Mr. Lancione: To film the entire act I believe he would have to give permission.

With this, Lancione and the Court seem to have reached a clear understanding of the breadth and true nature of the appropriation, or right of publicity, tort. Zacchini possessed a property right in his performance, just as Elvis Presley possessed a property right in his performances as well as his likeness or image, and just as Martin Luther King Jr. later would be found to possess a property right in his presentation of the "I Have a Dream" speech in Washington, D.C. The performance did not have to be paid for or be under contract to possess this exclusive property value. And Zacchini did not have to warn people or refuse consent or post a notice in order to have an enforceable property claim against commercial use by another. All a person had to do was sit back and perform—or give a speech or be Elvis—comforted by the fact that his or her rights in the act were secure against any and all subsequent commercial uses.

The commercial use here, however, was claimed to be news. This would come to be the heart of the case. In a few closing remarks, Lancione alluded, almost offhandedly, to this question, saying "I don't think there is any similarity to capturing an entire entertainer's performance and putting it on a news program." For him, use of the entire performance, by itself, excluded Channel 5's broadcast from the definition of news.

The Court did not pursue the matter with Lancione, as his time was up. But the news versus entertainment question would be the central focus of the argument by Channel 5's lawyer.

The lawyer representing Scripps-Howard Broadcasting Company, the owner of Channel 5, was Ezra K. Bryan, of Cleveland, Ohio. His burden in the argument was to cast the case as a conflict between a dangerously broad and ambiguous, judge-made right of publicity, on the one hand, and the press's freedom to report on facts and events of the day, on the other. He thus began—unwisely, perhaps, in retrospect, and with more than a hint of arrogance—by belittling Zacchini's claimed right. And in the process he belittled the Court for hearing the case at all.

"I still am perplexed," he began, "after hearing my eminent opponent . . . , as to how we got here. When I first heard that [the Court had decided to hear this case,] I was at least seriously puzzled and, as a matter of fact, [I] had the apocryphal thought that perhaps we had slipped back of the looking glass with Lewis Carroll [and] Alice."

He then turned to Zacchini's act, belittling it, too. He acknowledged that the Zacchinis were a noted circus family and that they had invented a "better mechanism for a cannon to project a human being. . . . But," he added, "P. T. Barnum shot Mademoiselle Harzelle out of a cannon for sixty feet back in 1879 and called it the human cannonball act." Zacchini's act, in short, was hardly unique; indeed, he implied, it was simply a copy of one begun fifty years earlier.

Bryan had unknowingly set a trap for himself, and the Court caught him in it. Justice Stewart began the questions.

Question: There is nothing very original about the performance of the Eighth Symphony, but do you suggest that if someone came in and covered it in the Kennedy Center without the consent of the performers, the conductor, and the members of the orchestra, they could put it on television?

Mr. Bryan: No, sir, and I don't think that this—

Question: Then what does the history of the act have to do with it?

Mr. Bryan: I don't see how this theory of a unique little situation of a 15-

second act can apply on any broad principle to the kind of question that you are raising, sir.

Question: Well, what is the difference whether it takes 15 seconds or 30 minutes for the performance of Mr. Zacchini?

Bryan is now on very, very thin ice. Demeaning Zacchini hadn't worked. And as to his argument about the need for a broad principle, it hardly follows that a distinction between a fifteen-second act and a thirty-minute act is principled in any way. Perhaps sensing this, he tried to shift ground to the press's freedom.

Mr. Bryan: [The time distinction] would make a serious difference under the definition of the [First Amendment] media privilege by the Ohio Supreme Court. They have said that the media may use [Zacchini's 15-second act] for news contents but they may not appropriate the benefit of the publicity for some non-privileged [*and implicitly non-news*] private use. You can't make a news program, in my judgment, . . . out of a full symphony.

Question: Well, that wouldn't be a non-privileged private use, it would be a use on the news program, precisely the same use that was made of the cannonball act here, wouldn't it?

Mr. Bryan: Mr. Justice Stewart, . . . those people [symphonies] are protecting themselves. They are protected by notice on the ticket, there are contract arrangements . . . which limit the right of anybody to come in and take it. . . . [And] as to Muhammad Ali, there isn't any possibility in my judgment that that would get by the Ohio courts. [They are] not saying that you can go in any steal things and break contracts.

Bryan, it should be noted, has evaded the time-period question, and now also the definition of news issue, by shifting the topic to the presence of contract restrictions and clear notice to those in attendance, including the press, that no pictures could be taken or used without express permission. This, of course, would have the effect of defining Zacchini's claim as one of interference with commercial contract rights, a very different claim from the property-type right of freedom from commercial exploitation of name or likeness or performance. The narrower contract claim also made the factual question of consent and notice critical. These issues, as it turned out, would not help Bryan.

Question: Well, some of Muhammad Ali's performances last only about fifteen seconds.

(Laughter)

Does that mean that the performance would be open to any surreptitious coverage by a television camera?

Mr. Bryan: This was not surreptitious. The TV people, along with others, were invited free in order to do this. . . .

Question: Not by Mr. Zacchini, though?

Mr. Bryan: No, but he contracted to put on a performance for some promoters who did invite these people and he did not have an agreement with them that would prevent the taking of pictures. As a matter of fact, the only facts in this record do not support my eminent [opposing] counsel's position with respect to the [claim that] Zacchini sought out the photographer and objected.

At this point the argument shifts to a different topic, but Bryan comes back to the point later in the argument, clarifying what he had intimated.

Mr. Bryan: There was no condition imposed by Zacchini in a way in which he could prohibit anyone from taking pictures. The fact is that . . . the only evidence before the Ohio courts . . . was . . . that Zacchini, seeing a cameraman with a television-type camera, approached him and told him he did not want it done. There was no seeking out of Zacchini to obtain consent or permission.

The point Bryan is making is pretty unclear. Can there really be a distinction between a case in which the TV station sought permission and was denied it (in which case it could not film), and a case in which the station was told by someone who saw the camera that they couldn't use it? The distinction hardly seems persuasive. In any event, the factual argument is beside the point, for there had as yet been no trial in Zacchini's case—a trial was what he was seeking—and the time for evidence supporting the allegations in Zacchini's lawsuit was at trial. Until then, all factual doubts should be resolved in Zacchini's favor as a matter of law.

The express refusal question, however, raised another issue: was Zacchini's claim based on property rights or on contract rights? If property, no refusal by Zacchini was needed; absent express consent, the TV station was barred from converting Zacchini's property to its own use. If contract, advance notice of the contract and express refusal by Zacchini might be required. It was to the nature of the claim that the Court next turned.

Question: Don't you think that the performer has something to say about whether they have a right to coverage or not?

Mr. Bryan: No sir, I do not. I would have to argue very strenuously that our—

Question: Then you argue with the Eighth Symphony illustration, too? You said that if the Eighth Symphony is being performed by—

Mr. Bryan: I'm sorry, sir . . . you are referring to the question of the full "entire performance"?

Question: I am talking about the performance, whether it is 10 seconds, 15 seconds, or 30 minutes or two hours. Does the performer not have something to say about whether it is going to be covered by television?

Mr. Bryan: Your Honor, in my judgment if there is a legitimate news use . . . , then the performers must rely on agreements and contracts.

Question: Well, I thought it was quite the contrary. Your opponent feels that . . . the Ohio Court [said that there] was a property right, [but held that it] is struck down by the First Amendment.

Mr. Bryan: Mr. Justice Rehnquist, I do not think that our court looked at this in any sense as a property right.

This is a subtle and difficult argument for Bryan to make. Whether the right of publicity was a property right or some other form of right turned only on the Ohio court's definition of state law, and the Supreme Court could do nothing about it except try to interpret what the Ohio Supreme Court said. The fact is, moreover, that while the exact nature of the right was left somewhat ambiguous by the Ohio court, it was perfectly clear from the Ohio court's opinion that the right was not a contract right. If not strictly speaking a right to property, the right of publicity was at least a propertylike legal claim that did not depend on a prior contract. Elvis Presley had no contract reserving the right to restrict use of his photograph or likeness by others for commercial purposes. Martin Luther King Jr. had entered into no such contract before giving his "I Have a Dream" speech. But both were found to have a right to control commercialization of their likenesses and performances by virtue of the right of publicity, or the appropriation tort. After a brief diversion into the language used by the Ohio Supreme Court to define the right, the questions returned to Bryan's earlier argument that the First Amendment protected news organizations against liability when the performances were used as part of the news.

Question: Let's begin with the proposition . . . that the Ohio court has said there is in Ohio a common law right of publicity. . . . So you begin with this proprietary right that is protected against acquisition [whether it is strictly called property or not].

What if there were a brand new hit record . . . in which there is of course the same kind of proprietary right, and a news program on television said there is a brand new hit record, it leads all the lists everywhere in the country, and as a matter of news we are now going to play it in its entirety. Would [the station] be immune from paying for copyright infringement, paying the usual fee for playing the record just because it is on a news program? Would there be anything in the First Amendment that would make it immune from paying the royalty?

Mr. Bryan: Well, I don't think we are arguing that far, Mr. Justice Stewart, that the First Amendment immunizes . . . a news broadcaster . . . from things that are covered by specific kinds of property law.

Question: This is a specific kind of property law, created by the common law of Ohio.

Mr. Bryan: I respectfully disagree, Your Honor. They say this is a personal right because it is part of the right of privacy.

Question: No, publicity. Publicity!

Mr. Bryan: Yes, but it grows out of privacy—

Question: Whose right of privacy?

Mr. Bryan: Ohio's.

Question: No, No! Whose, your client's or [Zacchini's] right of privacy? The [Ohio courts] are talking here about the right of publicity.

Mr. Bryan: Right, but the right of publicity is an outgrowth of the right of privacy. . . .

Question: Well, the Ohio court has ruled the opposite, hasn't it?

Mr. Bryan: Of course it sounds that way, but in the State of Ohio the fact is that it is specifically recognized—

Question: As a property right.

Mr. Bryan: I'm sorry, sir, they did not use that—

Question: As a right when one is liable for acquiring with compensation.

Bryan is in serious danger here. He has made his case rise or fall on the nature of the legal interest reflected in Ohio's right of publicity. He has done this by saying that the station could play the record as long as it was not protected as a property interest of the musicians. The case thus depends on the Court's reading of the Ohio Supreme Court decision. But more fundamentally, Bryan has drawn a distinction between the right of publicity—not a property kind of interest, he says—and copyright, which he treats as a property right. But the right of publicity is a state law counterpart of federal copyright protection. And copyright is not itself a property right—certainly no more than the right of publicity. It is instead an interest in control of uses of a performance that is granted the performer by statute, just as the publicity right is a right to control performances granted to the performer by judicial legislation, also called "common law." And that is precisely what the last question observed.

Following the brief, but unhelpful (to Bryan), foray into the nature of the interest claimed by Zacchini, the questioning returned to the hit record hypothetical.

Question: Well, what is your answer? Do you think, under the law of Ohio, that a news broadcaster could with impunity play a hit record in its entirety on the basis of its leading all the lists, and this is the news of tonight in the entertainment field?

Mr. Bryan [trying desperately to hold his head above water by hanging to the contract thread, which had been effectively severed earlier]: I think those are all covered by contract and I don't think that [the Ohio] court is granting immunity to [breach of] contract rights [by broadcasters].

Question: But the court doesn't have to stick to just the strictly contract approach. It can say the thing arises out of a common law property concept, can't it?

Little more was to be gained from repeating the same arguments and interpretations once again. And so, with just a brief summary statement, Bryan concludes his argument. He has been bloodied and beaten, though it was not, in all candor, entirely his fault. His client had asked him to make the best argument justifying what it had done. The only really good argument that Bryan could have made was an absolutist one: if an act, a symphony, a boxing match, a record, or whatever is broadcast as news (with the news outlet having total and unreviewable power to so characterize it), there may be no liability, whether there was a contract restriction, a property right, a copyright or trademark, or anything else. Freedom of the press means that the press and no one else decides what to publish, when, how, and why. This is an argument that can be made. It even has respectable justifications to support it and a certain pedigree. It's what many good newspeople would say if asked.

The problem, though, is that it would never win in the United States Supreme Court, and it would be suicidal to make the argument there. Bryan knew this. So he was stuck with a messy, middle-of-the-road argument that had to be couched in terms of distinctions—such as amounts of time, contract rights versus property rights versus other personal proprietary rights, and notice and consent—that could not be persuasively linked up to the First Amendment as a matter of general principle.

The oral argument in Zacchini's case was gaveled to a close by Chief Justice Burger at 1:11 P.M., and the case was submitted for decision by the Supreme Court. On Friday the Justices would gather, alone, in the Justices' conference room, discuss the cases heard during the week, including Zacchini's, and vote. The senior Justice in the majority would then assign the writing of an opinion to one of the other Justices in the majority or to himself or herself. Over the course of the following two months, a draft opinion in the *Zacchini* case would be written, circulated for approval or dissent to the other Justices, and modified as needed to gather at least five votes to make it an opinion of the Court. At the same time, another Justice—or perhaps more than one—who voted in the minority would draft a dissent, circulating it in hopes of gathering enough votes to change the outcome, but in the absence of that, at least gathering the support of other dissenters. Once the majority and dissenting opinions come to rest, the Court would decide that the case is ready for announcement, and it would set a day, usually the following Monday, for release of its decision to the parties and to the public at large.

On June 28, 1977, at the very end of the Court's Term, the Zacchini decision was announced. The Court issued an opinion written by Justice White, and in which Chief Justice Burger and Justices Stewart, Blackmun, and Rehnquist joined, reversing the Ohio Supreme Court's decision, declaring that Hugo Zacchini did in fact have a legally enforceable right to control publication of his act, that the First Amendment did not shield Channel 5 from liability for its broadcast, and that therefore Zacchini's case should proceed to trial. Four Justices dissented: Justices Powell, Brennan, Marshall, and Stevens. It was a 5-4 decision, the narrowest of margins. But Zacchini had won.

The Supreme Court's opinion in the *Zacchini* case was hardly a model of judicial clarity, and the same can be said for the dissenting opinions. The Court focused on whether the broadcast of the act as news, in and of itself, compelled a finding that it was immune from any form of liability, and if so, whether broadcast of the "entire act" somehow disqualified it from being treated as news. As the Court put it: "It is evident . . . that petitioner's state-law right of publicity would not serve to prevent [the television station] from reporting the newsworthy facts about [Zacchini's] act. Wherever the line in particular situations is to be drawn between media reports that are protected and those that are not, we are quite sure that the First and Fourteenth Amendments do not immunize the media when they broadcast a performer's entire act without his consent."

The Court's approach, while resting on none-too-clear premises about news and newsworthiness, actually reflects a common-sense view of the genre of news. The question presented in the case was whether the act's broadcast on television represented a different genre of communication from its performance at the fair, and if so, whether its broadcast satisfied the technical requirements that precondition any claim that a distinct genre was employed. Was it, for example, like Jay Leno's use of a quote from President Bill Clinton in a joke, converting the President's statement from a formal declaration to a humorous instance of satire or irony?

If a distinct genre claim could be made out, and assuming that the new genre was substantially distinct from the genre of Zacchini's performance, the broadcast should be treated as transformative—as transforming Zacchini's communication into another—and its degree of First Amendment protection should rest on the value of that transformation to the aims of the First Amendment.

The application of this analysis, which bears a striking resemblance to the reasoning employed in copyright cases, would look something like the following. Zacchini's genre was the dramatic performance of an act for an audience. This definition of genre is not restricted to a place (such as performance at a fair) or a time or, most importantly, to a live setting (such as a performance before a live audience). Such narrow limits would not capture the full aesthetic content of the act. They would not reflect the commercially feasible settings in which the act might, without substantial modification, be communicated. And such place or time limits would defeat the very policy interests being served by the tort.

The genre claimed by the television station, in contrast, was news. This, of course, is a distinct genre with its own qualities, such as usefulness to an audience, interest, accuracy of representation, and value to the community as judged editorially. The question in the case, then, is whether the station's claim that it had transformed the segment of Zacchini's act into a new and valuable genre of news is persuasive.

One could pose this question by asking, as the Justices did, whether the "entire act" had been broadcast and, therefore, whether the station's claim should be disbelieved because the act is entertainment pure and simple, not news. But it might better to approach the question from the other end, measuring the segment broadcast, including the pictures as well as the surrounding text, against the elemental characteristics of news as a genre. This would require that the station first identify the broadcast's news content and news function. Assuming that the function was simply to report the occurrence of a notable event—assuming, in other words, that the act's presentation was not part of a larger story, such as how people do silly things that risk their lives for money—the question would then become whether depiction of the entire act was necessary to serve that news function (utility to the audience, value to the community) or whether that function could be performed as well, if not more effectively, without broadcasting the effective heart of the performance. To put the question a bit differently, the issue would be whether the act was transformed into something new through its use in the news broadcast—whether the station had added value through its use for news—or whether its significance remained the same, with its venue simply having been changed.

By rejecting any broad First Amendment privilege for news broadcasts, this is effectively the analysis that the Court required the Ohio courts to apply in trying the case. The fact that the broadcast was of "legitimate public interest," as the Ohio Supreme Court had declared, was not enough to warrant First Amendment immunity. Virtually anything can be clothed in such sweeping garb, whether it is news, entertainment, theater, music, or most any other genre. News, the Court necessarily implied, is more than that. Precisely what the "more" consists of, however, was a question on which the Court only gave intimations, reserving such a difficult inquiry for further reflection at a later time and in a different case.

For Hugo Zacchini, the outcome of the case was surely satisfying, though he had achieved only the opportunity to start his lawsuit all over again, this time with the chance to have it presented before a sympathetic jury. For him, winning his case was all that mattered. Scripps-Howard Broadcasting, on the other hand, lost in the Supreme Court. But for Scripps-Howard, Zacchini's case was not the main question. The larger concern was the line that would be drawn between its news activities and other stories that would not receive the full protection of the First Amendment. This was the deeper question Zacchini's claim raised. The Supreme Court only offered slight hints at the ultimate answer to this question. To begin probing it, we must get past the narrow confines of the *Zacchini* case.

For Hugo Zacchini, what Channel 5 did was nothing more nor less than theft. It stole his act, his creative property, and in doing so threatened his livelihood. What he asked was hardly different from what every book author receives: legally enforceable copyright protection against anyone else—even the press—publishing his or her words. Indeed, even newspapers claim such protection in their own stories, prohibiting other papers from simply copying their stories without permission and, usually, payment. Muhammad Ali is likewise able, through exclusive television contracts and copyright interests, to protect himself from the Channel 5s of the world. Martin Luther King Jr. was able to obtain a copyright in the film of his "I Have a Dream" speech, thus blocking unauthorized and uncompensated rebroadcasts of the speech by CBS in its documentaries and public affairs programs—a right enforceable even after his death. In view of this, is it too much to give Hugo Zacchini, circus performer and the Human Cannonball, a similar right to protect the filmed broadcast of his fifteen-second performance, the product of his efforts and talents, and the basis for his livelihood? His act, unlike Dr. King's, does not bear on broad public policy, only simple, local entertainment. His act, like an author's book, is available to the public, but only if they pay to see it.

For Scripps-Howard, and more generally for the press, facts cannot be owned. The idea that people can have a property right to information is anathema. The press deals in information—hopefully real and true information. Hugo Zacchini's act, his vaulting through the air and into the net, is a real and true fact. How can the press be made subject to a regime by which certain facts, certain events, when judged interesting or useful or valuable—even when judged to be of interest to the viewers and no more—are nevertheless placed beyond reach, their publication punished by the law? If the idea of information as privately controlled property is cast too wide, the press's ability to report on the events and people and facts of the day will be compromised. Can the press live up to its obligation to serve as an independent source of information and opinion if, for much information and opinion, it cannot serve as a source—if, in other words, many facts and events are placed off limits? This is particularly troublesome with privately controlled information, in which the sources are persons, companies, or government agencies, whose disclosure judgments reflect only their own interests, not the interest of an informed public.

Is a fear of too much private control of facts and events and opinions an exaggerated one voiced only by the press, which has its own interests at stake? Perhaps it is not, when one thinks of Elvis Presley, of Muhammad Ali, of Martin Luther King Jr.—certainly not when one thinks of the Internet and the new communications environment in which information is made the subject of commerce, commerce whose conduct is utterly dependent on the firms engaging in it having a property interest in the information they provide. Indeed, even the press is in on the act: access to the archives of the *New York Times* is available only upon payment of a fee. The *Times* owns its version of history, even though that history was written and reported by it under the wing of the First Amendment, which protected the *Times* because it served as an independent source of information and opinion to the public. Database companies, such as Westlaw and Lexis in the legal world, charge people very high prices for access to their vast accumulations of information. And what is the information? It is the text of laws and regulations enacted by governments and the text of judicial opinions written by judges. To be sure,

Westlaw users pay for the technology by which access to the information is obtained, but can technology of access, any more than technology of storage, such as print, the newspaper, the book, the written page of text, be easily separated from the fact or idea or message itself? It is clear that government itself can claim a property right in its own information. When it does it may sell that information to private concerns that then parcel it out to willing bidders only. State motor vehicle departments have successfully asserted "ownership" of the information they require each and every license holder to divulge, claiming a right to sell it to the highest private bidder rather than to make it available to the general public.

The press's claim is that information is power and that if facts and events and even opinions become subjects of private and even government control, the press's ability to function will be seriously compromised. This is surely correct.

Hugo Zacchini, however, would likely respond that his claim has little if anything to do with the press's function or, for that matter, with the First Amendment. He claims no property interest over information. He claims no right to prevent the evening news from doing a story about his act, even from taking a picture of the cannon, with him standing on it before entering its maw. Fact and information and event are all fair game. Instead, his claim goes to the press's broadcast of his whole performance, something that exceeds "mere" fact and event. Zacchini's act is part of—indeed a very large part of—his very identity: his livelihood, to be sure, but also who he is, what he stands for, his talents, personality, goals. All fact is not and cannot be made common public property. In a free society people must be able to protect and preserve facts about themselves and even to control when and the ways in which those facts may be released, and to whom. Disclosure of personal information may undermine a person's identity and his or her personal and social relationships.

A line must, therefore, be drawn. The press's claimed right to publish fact and event and opinion can be accepted, but not as to all facts and events and opinions. If the line is not drawn, the insatiable appetite of the occasionally salacious press, of debasing editorial judgments, would tear a rip in the social fabric of families and communities and would divest individuals of their presumptive right to create their own persons and personalities, a central ingredient of individuality and freedom. The law protects against the press publishing certain highly personal and embarrassing facts about individuals. It protects individuals' right to maintain control of personal financial, medical, and employment information, for example, in order that they can conduct their social and business affairs without public intrusion. Isn't Zacchini's claim of this sort? Need the prying eye of the press intrude on these matters in order to preserve its constitutional function?

Scripps-Howard would respond that the law should not be governed by our sympathy with Hugo Zacchini. Larger issues are at stake. No dividing line can be drawn to separate some fact from other fact. Drawing such a line would inevitably involve government imposing its preferred social or political values or its standards of taste on the press. Requiring the press to subordinate its judgment to a value—entertainment versus literature, international versus national news, personalized angles versus "just the facts, Ma'am"—would be to undermine by definition the press's editorial freedom of judgment, a freedom that is in turn definitionally necessary to the press's independence. So fact must be fact, no exceptions made. Which facts are to be published, and how, must be the press's independent call to make. Any other line must by necessity prejudge the values of the society about which the press is to render its own account, and any other line must by necessity also be enforced against the press by law, and thus by government.

In any event, giving the press untrammeled discretion about publication of fact and event is unlikely to do great harm, unlikely to tear a rip in the social fabric. After all, the threat to privacy—to a person's control over facts about himself or herself—can hardly be traced to the press and to the reporting of news. With but a few rare exceptions—the photo of a child falling from a burning apartment, the reporting of a person's medical history, and the like—the press has not been the source of privacy invasions. The source has instead been other, nonpress actors, such as companies that collect and sell information to others for advertising and marketing, and even more so the gossip and rumor that seem as inherent in the human character as the instinct to protect one's privacy. To the extent that salaciousness is on the rise and tastelessness rampant, blame cannot be placed at the feet of the press. It is instead a manifestation of broader social, political, economic, and cultural conditions, conditions not caused by the press and over which the press has no control. The public's interest in the President's sexual habits or private parts, for example, is not created from whole cloth by the press. The press is simply an actor in a larger drama here.

But Hugo Zacchini's point, he would claim, is a different one. And the difference, he would argue, is central to his legal claim. Zacchini might admit all that has been said above, even to the extreme of accepting, for argument's sake, the proposition that fact must be fact, whatever its character, and that the press must, with news, be left with the final say, for better or worse. But Zacchini's case involves the press only in the most nominal sense, only because the fifteen-second film was broadcast on the evening news and was thus denominated, impliedly, as news. Surely a thirty-minute surreptitious-ly filmed performance by the Cleveland Symphony would not be news, sim-ply because it was broadcast in a program called *Evening News*. Its qualifica-tion as news as opposed to some other form of broadcast—perhaps entertainment—should be made dependent on whether the point of the broadcast was simply the performance or was instead something more, and of which the performance was but a part. Announcing as news the fact of the performance wouldn't, of course, require broadcasting the full perfor-mance. Describing an event that occurred during the performance—perhaps a remarkable audience reaction or an accident—wouldn't require airing the full performance. News, in short, requires that the journalist either stick to the reporting of facts as they occurred, a rather bleak enterprise, or put the fact into some narrative form, some perspective in relation to other events. It requires a transformation of the facts into the journalist's own account, an exercise of judgment that reflects, only implicitly to be sure, the reasons why, as a news organization or entity, the publisher concluded that this fact, from among all others, should be published in the way that it was.

Channel 5, Zacchini would argue, did no transforming. It exercised no judgment entitled to the name "editorial" news judgment. Instead, Channel 5 simply broadcast the entire fifteen-second act, valuable in that form sim-ply as a substitute for the entertainment enjoyed by those who actually went to the fair and paid to see the act in person. Nothing was said about the his-tory of the act, the science of its accomplishment, the social or cultural set-ting it occupied, or the reaction of the audience. The news story, if it was that, was simply the act. It wasn't quite as bald an act as putting the Cleveland Symphony performance on the news or broadcasting an entire movie in the news program and then trying to call it the product of editorial news judg-ment. But this is only because Zacchini's act, otherwise indistinguishable from the symphony or a movie, was unfortunately only fifteen seconds long. It thus fit nicely into the typical news slot, easily placed in clever disguise. But that did not make it news.

The press's response is equally telling, and ultimately equally indetermi-nate. The "entire performance" standard, the press would say, simply can't work as a general rule and thus can't be permitted to determine the result in Zacchini's case. The press often reports entire performances and does so in ways that treat the performance as itself "news." A candidate's speech at a political convention, for example, might be broadcast as news, a description that the press may surely claim for such current information even though it does not fit within, or bear the name *Evening News*. Is CBS's live coverage of a space shuttle taking off not an instance of news reporting? Must CBS somehow add a scientific angle or comment on the event's cultural significance to qualify the broadcast as news? Must CBS do more than respond to the public's interest—even its occasionally salacious interest in a scandal, a crash, or an explosion—in order for its broadcast to be news? Of course not. Zacchini's act was no different. Its broadcast cannot be said inherently to constitute something other than news. The fact that the decision to broadcast the act was largely, even wholly, based on Channel 5's judgment about what the viewers would enjoy seeing, even though they would not be particularly edified by it, cannot make any difference. If the answer were different, what would come of the publication of the Kennedy assassination photos or the tape of Los Angeles police officers beating Rodney King? Would the Kennedy family or Rodney King be able to control their use?

Transformation as news is not a function of literalism: whether the police log published in a newspaper has been edited for style or punch or whether a story taken from the Associated Press wire has been refashioned. It is instead, Scripps-Howard would argue, a function of selection and of endorsement of that selection as the news publisher's judgment about what it considers relevant and important. News, as Walter Lippmann said, "signalizes" an event. It need not alter the event to do so.[2]

This is a point well taken, Zacchini might admit, but there are two serious problems raised by it. First, if news is simply choice and "signalization," then the genre question becomes entirely circular. If a news broadcast showed the act, that fact alone proves its "transformation" through endorsement. There is no limit to what is news under this view, as long as the publisher calls itself a news publisher.

Second, the illustrations offered up by Scripps-Howard about the Kennedy assassination and Rodney King also make a quite different point. Perhaps the whole performance standard is not the best. Perhaps news must be a product, in part, of judgments about what facts and events and opinions and angles the audience wants, rather than just what an editor believes the audience needs. But it is nevertheless true that in all of the illustrations just given, the press was not free to publish the event. In the case of the space shuttle, the press's ability to get close enough for its cameras was completely dependent on NASA's wishes. In the Rodney King case, the film was shot on a private camera, and the press was made to pay for it, whether in still form or in the form of a broadcast video. In the Kennedy assassination example, the film is, of course, the famous Zapruder film, bearing the name of the photographer, and Zapruder was able to control use of the photos for years

---

2. Walter Lippmann, *Public Opinion* (1922; reprint, New York: The Free Press, 1965), 358.

until the federal government paid him for the rights to it. Control is now not in the public's, but in the public's government's, hands. Use of the film can still be purchased. In view of this, Zacchini would say, his claim of control over use of the entire act should be equally respected.

But in relying on these examples, defenders of Zacchini would have implicitly accepted the press's claims to its own freedom in significant respect, resorting instead to an idea of a property interest. For him it's property. For Channel 5 it's news. The argument, in short, has come full circle, arriving at no end other than its beginning. And there is still no answer to the central question, which is, what is news?

How should we judge the Supreme Court's decision in Zacchini's case? More importantly, how well did the Court answer the questions that the case raised? The short answers are, not terribly well, and certainly not clearly. But one thing is clear. The Court chose to define the case as one requiring that in certain contexts a line must drawn between news and non-news, the very question that ultimately led us, above, into a circle. The Court did not find a way out of the circle. It will ultimately have to—if not in Hugo Zacchini's case, then in others that will surely follow.

Additional Reading

Altschull, J. Herbert. *From Milton to McLuhan: The Ideas behind American Journalism.* New York: Longman, 1990.

Roshco, Bernard. *Newsmaking.* Chicago: University of Chicago Press, 1975.

Schudson, Michael. *Discovering the News.* New York: Basic Books, 1978.

Story 5

News and Commerce
Pittsburgh Press Co. v. Pittsburgh Commission
   on Human Relations
413 U.S. 376 (1973)

From the beginning of the American republic, the press has been private and, at least in aspiration, profit making. Indeed, its private character is essential to its freedom and thus to the freedom of the press as we know it. News is commerce in America, and newspapers and other press entities are commercial enterprises.

The press is, however, a private organization performing public tasks. At least this is so with news, the fact and opinion of public and private life upon which people rely in conducting their lives. If the press must be private to perform its public duty, must the press's freedom extend to its private and largely commercial activities? Should its freedom extend to decisions about the organization and layout of a newspaper, to the advertisements that are run, to the classified sections? Should the labor laws or the minimum-wage laws be suspended for the press in order that profitability can be assured?

Our story involves these very questions. The newspaper is the *Pittsburgh Press,* a respected newspaper in Pittsburgh, Pennsylvania. The setting is the classified-advertisement section of the paper and, more specifically, the ads that the paper carries and the column headings the paper chooses to use. The issue is whether the *Press* should be subject to a law against sex discrimination. The conflict is between the private imperatives of commerce and the public duty of equality. The questions are the following:

1. Whether editorial decisions about advertisements, their location, and the layout of the pages on which they appear are legally distinguishable from editorial decisions about news, editorial opinion, and related layout or compositional matters
2. Whether a newspaper should be liable for publishing material that facilitates illegal acts by others
3. Whether the press's public task of disseminating information and opinion should be performed only through its news reports and editorial opinions, and not through choices of layout and arrangement, by symbol or metaphor, or even through conduct in defiance of the law (civil disobedience)

In our case, as we will see, the *Pittsburgh Press* claims that its decisions about which advertisements to run and how to present them are editorial choices no different in character from decisions about news. It further claims that presenting classified job advertisements under sex-identified column headings communicates a view on a question of social policy—sex discrimination in employment or intrusive government regulation—just as an editorial would: indeed perhaps more powerfully because it is a conscious act of objection to the dictates of law.

* * *

In February 1967 the City Council of Pittsburgh, Pennsylvania, enacted a Human Relations Ordinance prohibiting discrimination on grounds of "race, color, religion, ancestry, national origin or place of birth" in employment, housing, and public accommodations. The Commission on Human Relations was created to enforce the new law. On July 3, 1969, the city council extended the ordinance to also prohibit discrimination on the basis of sex. The 1969 amendment also made it illegal for "any person, whether or not an employer . . . , *to aid* . . . in the doing of any act declared to be an unlawful employment practice," including discrimination in employment based on sex.

At the time the amendment was passed, the *Pittsburgh Press* followed a longstanding, and not uncommon, practice of presenting help-wanted advertisements under sex-designated column headings: "Male Help Wanted," "Female Help Wanted," and "Male-Female Help Wanted." In October 1969, in apparent response to the amendment, the *Press* modified its help-wanted column headings to "Jobs—Male Interest," "Jobs—Female Interest," and "Male-Female." The following illustrative advertisements were included in an appendix to the United States Supreme Court's opinion:

> Among the advertisements carried in the Sunday *Pittsburgh Press* on January 4, 1970, were the following:

JOBS—MALE INTEREST		JOBS—FEMALE INTEREST	
ACAD. INSTRUCTORS	$13,000	ACAD. INSTRUCTORS	$13,000
ACCOUNTANTS	10,000	ACCOUNTANTS	6,000
ADM. ASS'T, CPA	15,000	AUTO-INS. UNDERWRITER	OPEN
ADVERTISING MGR	10,000	BOOKKEEPER-INS	5,000
BOOKKEEPER F-C	9,000	CLERK-TYPIST	4,200
FINANCIAL CONSULTANT	12,000	DRAFTSMAN	6,000
MARKETING MANAGER	15,000	KEYPUNCH D. T.	6,720
MGMT. TRAINEE	8,400	KEYPUNCH BEGINNER	4,500
OFFICE MGR. TRAINEE	7,200	PROOFREADER	4,900

LAND DEVELOPMENT 30,000	RECEPTIONIST—Mature D. T. ...... OPEN
PRODUCT. MANAGER 18,000	EXEC. SEC. 6,300
PERSONNEL MANAGER .... OPEN	SECRETARY 4,800
SALES-ADVERTISING 8,400	SECRETARY, Equal Oppor. 6,000
SALES-CONSUMER 9,600	SECRETARY D. T. 5,400
SALES-INDUSTRIAL 12,000	TEACHERS-Pt. Time .... day 33
SALES-MACHINERY 8,400	TYPIST-Statistical 5,000
RETAIL MGR 15,000	

In 1969 the newspaper ran nearly 250,000 help-wanted advertisements under its sex-designated headings, largely deferring to the advertiser's preference on the column placement of any particular ad. The continuation of the column-heading policy, the *Press* claimed, was an editorial decision based on advertiser and reader preference and convenience, and on the judgment that the headings reflected "the cultural and biological differences . . . in general patterns of job preference by" men and women. The *Press* also published a "disclaimer" at the beginning of the help-wanted ads, which read:

Notice to job seekers.

Jobs are arranged under male and female classifications for the convenience of our readers. This is done because most jobs generally appeal more to persons of one sex than the other. Various laws and ordinances—local, state, and federal—prohibit discrimination in employment because of sex, unless sex is a bona fide occupational requirement. Unless the advertisement itself specifies one sex or the other, job seekers should assume that the advertiser will consider applicants of either sex in compliance with the laws against discrimination.

The *Pittsburgh Press*'s new help-wanted policy was challenged almost immediately. In early October 1969 a complaint was filed against the *Press* by the National Organization for Women (NOW), charging the *Press* "with deliberate and constant violations" of the ordinance by aiding employers' illegal sex discrimination. Specifically, the complaint alleged that the gender-based column headings assisted classified-job advertisers' unlawful discrimination against women by discouraging women from applying for the systematically higher-paying "Male Interest" listings, thus facilitating the unlawful gender preferences of the employers. Following a hearing on the complaint, the commission decided that the *Press* had violated the ordinance because the gender-based column headings facilitated the publication of gender-based advertisements by employers, and thus they facilitated, or "aided," the employers' discriminatory employment decisions. The First Amendment's guarantee of freedom of the press, the commission said, had nothing to do with classified help-wanted column headings.

The *Pittsburgh Press*, joined by the American Newspaper Publishers Association (ANPA), appealed the commission's decision to the Supreme Court
of Pennsylvania, losing at every stage. On September 12, 1972, the *Press* filed
its final appeal with the United States Supreme Court. The Supreme Court
accepted the appeal on December 4, 1972, and scheduled the case for oral
argument. At that point, the case assumed momentous proportions. Amicus (or friend of the court) briefs were filed in support of the Commission
on Human Relations by a wide array of organizations and interests, including the United States government, many state governments, the American
Civil Liberties Union (ACLU), the American Veterans Committee, the Wom-
en's Law Fund, and the International Association of Official Human Rights
Agencies. The American Newspaper Publishers Association was the only
organization to support the *Pittsburgh Press*. The *Press* may have begun to
feel a bit lonely by comparison.

The Supreme Court that heard the oral argument on March 20, 1973, was
a Court in transition from the Warren Court of the 1950s and 1960s to the
Burger Court of the 1970s and 1980s. It was, by most standards, a strong Court
marked by clear divisions. The Chief Justice was Warren Burger, appointed
by President Nixon. The other Nixon appointees were William Rehnquist
(who would later become Chief Justice), Lewis Powell, and Harry Blackmun.
Remaining from the Warren Court were William O. Douglas, the most senior Justice on the Court; William Brennan; Thurgood Marshall; Byron
White; and Potter Stewart. Conventional wisdom described Burger, Blackmun, and Rehnquist as conservatives and Douglas, Brennan, and Marshall
as liberals. Byron White, Potter Stewart, and Lewis Powell Jr. were moderates,
often serving wild-card roles. Time would undermine this conventional wisdom. The liberal/conservative labels are not particularly revealing when applied to the Supreme Court, and in the First Amendment field they are downright misleading. Indeed, the *Pittsburgh Press* case itself would undermine any
such distinction, for the case would ultimately be decided by a closely divided 5-4 vote with "liberals" and "conservatives" forming unexpected, indeed
somewhat strange, alliances. To some extent, this outcome was foretold in
the wide-ranging and exacting questions posed by the Justices in oral argument.

Three lawyers participated in the oral argument. Representing the *Pittsburgh Press* was Charles R. Volk, a partner in a Pittsburgh law firm. Volk had
represented the *Press* when its help-wanted column policy was changed following the 1969 amendment to the ordinance. He also drafted the disclaimer. The Commission on Human Rights was represented by Eugene Strassburger, Assistant City Solicitor in Pittsburgh. Finally, NOW, which brought

the case originally and, after winning, joined the commission in defending the commission's decision on appeal, was represented by Marjorie H. Matson, a Pittsburgh lawyer.

At 11:23 A.M. Chief Justice Burger opened the oral argument, announcing, "We will hear oral arguments next in [case number] 72-419, Pittsburgh Press Company against The Pittsburgh Commission on Human Relations. Mr. Volk."

Mr. Volk: Mr. Chief Justice, and may it please the Court: The Pittsburgh Press Company has, as most newspapers in the country have, a system of classifying its Help Wanted advertisements under either Male or Female.

Some time after [federal law was changed to bar sex discrimination in employment], the *Pittsburgh Press* went to a system of Male Interest and Female Interest and a third column heading, Male-Female. Appropriately and prominently displayed . . . in the want ads themselves, at the heads of the columns, was a rather large disclaimer box, entitled "Notice to Job Seekers," which pointed out that the classification was for reader interest only and should not be construed as being a limitation, since . . . laws in most jurisdictions . . . proscribe discrimination on the basis of sex.

Question: Who made the decision, just as a matter of fact, as to which column heading each ad went in?

Mr. Volk: The record is fairly complete on that, Mr. Justice White. The system is that the advertiser calls up and in essence says where he wants it. If he does not express a preference for placement of the ad, the newspaper will help him [decide] where most ads of the type, [say] Secretaries-Female, would appear.

Question: So in this case there are instances, I suppose we're talking ads, part of which the newspaper made the decision as to which column it went in?

Mr. Volk: Yes, the newspaper will help.

Question: Will help—where it's the one that makes the decision as to which column to put it in?

Mr. Volk: [The newspaper] reserves for itself the final determination. But [it] would be . . . untrue if I told this Court that that's the way it happens in actual practice. In actual practice, the advertiser who is seeking an employee calls in—

Question: Invariably, then, the advertiser is the one who finally says to the newspaper, "Well, now that I've talked to you, I suggest it go into this column?"

Mr. Volk: Yes. Yes, sir, that's essentially the way it works.

Question: So this isn't an independent judgment of the newspaper as to which—it isn't its judgment as to whether this job is more attractive to males or females?

Mr. Volk: It isn't its judgment in any specific case, no. I would be fatuous if I said that. However, we do contend that the newspaper gets into the act by making an editorial decision that there are jobs—[that] there is a large body of differing interests between males and females as they relate to the job market. And it is the decision of the newspaper to run column headings appealing to this real interest and permitting advertisers to place jobs in that column.

Question: Yes, but if the advertiser said—if in each case the advertiser said to put it in the other column, the newspaper would put it in the other column?

Mr. Volk: Yes, it would. In this particular case—

Question: But it's not its judgment in any case as to which—as to whether the job is more fitting for males or females?

Mr. Volk: Not on the record. There could be, of course, occasions where the newspaper would nudge it into one, or refuse to carry it—refuse to carry, perhaps, a Go-Go dancer in the Male section. But we can search throughout the record and not find any reference to that.

Question: But . . . again, as a matter of fact, is there any question but what the decision to set up the classified ads, the Help Wanted ads, under this format was exclusively the decision of your client, the newspaper?

Mr. Volk: Absolutely, sir. That's why we're here.

Question: That's what I thought.

The Justices are intensely interested in exactly how the help-wanted-ad policy works. This is not an idle curiosity. It has much to do with defining the precise First Amendment claim that the *Press* is making. That claim could take two forms.

The first claim the *Press* might make is that the *Press* reserves to itself the sole power to decide whether and where to run any particular ad. Because each advertisement embodies an exercise of the newspaper's editorial judgment, it should be protected by the First Amendment. Such an argument would require Volk to explain why advertising decisions, as opposed to news decisions, should be constitutionally protected or, more broadly, why all decisions a newspaper makes about material it publishes should be equally protected by the First Amendment. Both of these arguments are tricky for reasons that will become evident as the oral argument unfolds.

It would thus be tempting for Volk to evade the difficulties of the ad-specific claim by relying instead on an alternative theory. Under this approach

Volk would concede that the *Pittsburgh Press* exercises no independent editorial judgment whatsoever as to specific ads, but he would claim that general editorial decisions concerning the layout of the paper—in this case the column headings—are instances of editorial judgment protected by the First Amendment. In many respects Volk seems inclined to place primary emphasis on this more general claim of editorial judgment—a claim of freedom in compositional choices and policies. Shouldn't decisions about the sequence of material and sections in a newspaper be protected? How about the titles a paper gives its sections: Op Ed, Autos, National News, Leisure? Framing the *Press*'s argument on general, or compositional, rather than on ad-specific grounds also has the virtue of blunting the commission's argument that by making a decision about a specific ad the *Press* was not acting as a disinterested party but instead was party to employers' discriminatory hiring decisions—that the *Press*'s decision about an ad was part and parcel of the employment discrimination.

But Volk also knows, both as a matter of fact and of legal strategy, that he cannot simply dismiss the argument that the *Press* was also exercising editorial judgments with respect to the specific ads. This is because to do so would play directly into his opponents' hands. The commission would be likely to argue that placement of ads under the column headings involves no editorial decision whatsoever by the *Press* but instead involves nothing more than the *Press* deferring to the preference of the advertiser. If no editorial judgment by the newspaper is involved, no First Amendment claim may be lodged by the newspaper. If, for example, a newspaper simply gives away a page to other parties, retaining no say whatsoever in what is printed on it, the most the newspaper could claim is that the decision to give the page away is somehow protected editorial judgment. As to material actually placed on the page, the newspaper would be hard pressed to say that it in any way reflected the newspaper's publication decision or that it was an exercise of the paper's protected editorial judgment.

Thus, Volk must straddle the fence in a very delicate way, arguing that the decision is virtually always the advertiser's, but the *Press* retains the final say in each case. The Justices' questions attempt to force him to pick one side or the other. Having set himself firmly on both sides of the fence, Volk now tries to shift the argument from the ad-specific level to the more general question of editorial policy and newspaper composition. He wants to elevate the plane of the compositional decision about the column headings, to rest it on responsiveness to readers and serious editorial judgments about why readers prefer the *Press*'s way, indeed, even to inject a note of philosophy and social policy.

But at least one Justice—we don't know who, because the Court does not give the questioner's name—will have none of Volk's higher plane of justification, and he lowers the boom.

Mr. Volk: It is the very strongly held opinion of Scripps-Howard Newspapers, who have the controlling interest in the *Pittsburgh Press,* and of the *Pittsburgh Press* that this does serve a legitimate reader and advertiser function in providing a—well, [like] playing Twenty Questions, the first question is always, "Is it animal, vegetable, or mineral?" And this makes a gross categorization from which you take off.

    We feel that the cultural patterns, or biological [ones]—we won't get into that debate, I trust—for some reason men and women in this country prefer different types of jobs and it is a legitimate newspaper function to cater to these differences by putting the ads in, by providing differing columns wherein advertisers can place these ads.

Question: And the proof is that the advertisers utilize them?

Mr. Volk: Yes. If one reads . . . the allegations . . . in this case, one would assume that these are placed there solely for the purposes of invidious discrimination. . . . On the contrary, . . . the average advertiser is merely seeking an employee, and the idea of discrimination, one way or the other, doesn't come into his mind. He's looking for an employee. If he advertises for a truck driver, the odds of him getting a female truck driver are relatively limited, no matter where he puts the ad. . . .

    [F]or the advertiser it is a service which permits maximum reader response. The complainants in this case and the city have made much that this is a service for the advertisers. It is a service for the advertiser, it is a service for the reader. It is an intention, a device to get maximum response to an ad.

Question: [T]hese were all ads for help wanted. How about ads for Positions Wanted, Jobs Wanted? That is, job seekers' advertising.

Mr. Volk: Job seekers are neutered. There aren't very many of this in regard to number, and they are merely placed in the . . . Situations Wanted ad.

It is the advertisers, in short, who are calling the tune. For the Justice, the stuff about reader responsiveness, cultural preferences, and biologically driven habits doesn't ring true. If the policy were a reflection of these factors, the sex-designated columns should be used for job seekers as well as for job advertisers.

    Volk, however, feels that he must not let go of the claim that the *Press*'s freedom rests in part on its ability to make ad-specific decisions and thus that the advertisements themselves reflect in part the *Press*'s choice of material to publish. This form of claim has a strong pedigree in earlier Supreme Court decisions. But if he must explain the ad-specific claim in much detail, he must also identify the kinds of decisions the *Press* makes, what those decisions are based on, and why they should be deemed valuable or worthy of protection under the First Amendment. Volk is having great difficulty explaining the decisions, much less making them appear coherent, other than as a raw deference to advertiser preference.

This, it should be said, is not Volk's fault. He is not in control of the direction the questions are taking. Nor is he in control of the facts. If the actual facts of what the *Press* does turn out to be problematic, even ugly, that's the *Press*'s problem.

Question: All just neutered, indiscriminately?
Mr. Volk: Yes, sir. Now—
Question: Would you reject an ad if it said, "Middle-aged woman wants housekeeping job?"
Mr. Volk: Yes, they do that. They don't feel, necessarily, that they're compelled to, but the *Press* does, in cooperation with the Pittsburgh Human Relations Commission, engage in a voluntary screening process on these ads. It's part of our contention here that the First Amendment does not require them to do so.

Volk must be very careful here. It is evident that the refusal of the middle-aged woman's ad on sex discrimination grounds is, to put it mildly, silly. If that silly decision is the *Press*'s own decision, the strength of the *Press*'s claim that it must be free to make such decisions will lose credibility. It is one thing to declare in broad turn of phrase that the press's freedom includes the freedom to err or do silly things. It is an altogether different matter, however, when the focus is turned on a particular newspaper and particular decisions that can only be described as incoherent.

On the other hand, if the silly result is required by the Commission on Human Relations, nothing but good can come from that fact for Volk and his client.

Question: If it is a middle-aged woman who wants a job, isn't she—and she wants to say she is a middle-aged woman who wants a job—you wouldn't reject her ad because of that, because she didn't say she was a man, would you?

Mr. Volk: I believe the city would attempt to get her—to dissuade her from placing it—

Question: Really?

Mr. Volk: —because of their agreement with the Human Relations Commission. Of course we reject all kinds of ads. . . .

Mr. Volk: We do censor ad content voluntarily, based on the editorial judgment of the newspaper.

Question: But you see no First Amendment problem in either rejecting or trying to control an ad, "Middle-aged woman wants housekeeping job?"

Mr. Volk: Yes, sir. I see a First Amendment problem in forcing a newspaper to do it. I think they've got the right to censor it if they wish.

But I see a First Amendment problem if the newspaper [were compelled to censor the ad and] wished to resist, which is precisely the case [here].

Volk has managed, for the moment at least, to escape the trap laid for him. And he has finally escaped the Court's nettlesome questions about who decides what, how, and why. He has been bloodied a bit but has survived. But a larger question remains unexplored: what, precisely, is the purpose or function of the newspaper under the First Amendment, and how do classified advertisements—whether for jobs or for used Chevy trucks—fit in? It is to this question that the Court now turns its attention.

Question: Mr. Volk, sometime in the last two or three weeks I remember seeing some sort of a statement from some paper that it was going to start publishing want ads for nothing, without charging people for them. And that led me to wonder whether want ads, from the newspaper's point of view, are an inducement to buy the paper to the readers as well as a way of raising revenue, so far as the newspaper is concerned.

Mr. Volk: Yes. It's part of our contention . . . that a newspaper, Mr. Justice Rehnquist, is a forum, and country marketplace, if you will, a Roman forum [for] the flow of information and ideas. And a very significant part of this is the want ad columns. . . . They are an interchange of people who have a right to a job, seeking a job, and people who wish to hire people, trying to find these people who are seeking jobs. It provides a very major community service.

Now, I'm not prepared to answer whether the company makes money on them or not. I suspect it does. They charge for want ads, and they do make a lot of their revenue in the newspaper through advertising, of course. And I suspect it is profitable. The *Pittsburgh Press* has a massive organization, editing and setting up classified ads.

But it is a major community service. And we further contend . . . that the complainants find this to be a major throat through which the job applications flow . . . , and if they can control . . . what they feel to be a discriminatory aspect of this, at the throat, then they can take a big step forward in eliminating discrimination without the difficulty of proving any individual act of discrimination or any individual intent [by an employer] to discriminate.

They can get what they culturally seek, which is broader job opportunities for women—something which we don't necessarily disagree with editorially—but we feel that the place to battle this is not in the want-ad pages of the newspaper, particularly as it relates to the judgment of the newspaper as to how they're going to run those ads.

Two noteworthy points are being introduced here. The first is Volk's attempt to define the newspaper, including its want-ad section, as a community or public forum, an independent and private source of information on the full range of public and personal, political and economic, information and opinion—information, as the Court had put it just a few years earlier, about the "exigencies of life" in a free society. Precisely what the contours of this public function are under the First Amendment will be the subject of increasing attention by the Court.

But Volk also makes a second point. He argues that if government wishes to stop sex discrimination in employment, it should do so directly by bringing complaints against employers who discriminate rather than against a newspaper whose actions do not in themselves constitute job discrimination. The First Amendment has long been read to prohibit the regulation of speech even when it supports or encourages illegal action by those to whom the speech is directed. Without such a rule, free speech would be greatly reduced, for every time government is concerned about illegal acts by individuals, it could simply prohibit anyone from publishing material that supports or encourages such acts. If the government wished to prohibit teenage smoking, for example, it could simply adopt the expedient of prohibiting all cigarette advertisements and any speech that supports smoking or portrays it as sophisticated and smart—even speech that criticizes the government's own policy. It is much easier—and therefore much more dangerous to freedom—for the government to censor speech rather than to do the hard work of prosecuting teens who smoke and stores that sell tobacco to teens, or of taking on the politically powerful tobacco interests. Volk's argument fits squarely within this First Amendment tradition: government should go after the employers who discriminate, not those whose speech might support or even encourage discrimination. To do otherwise would stand the First Amendment on its head, making it an authorization for government censorship rather than a protection against it.

But Volk has carefully read the briefs written by NOW and the commission. They argue that this First Amendment tradition applies to the news and editorial content of a newspaper—political and social and economic information of a public character—but not to classified advertising and want ads. They claim that the advertising material is not really the newspaper's own speech but the advertiser's, and in any event it involves purely commercial transactions that need no protection and have no public value under the First Amendment. Casting a vote in an election is a far cry from buying a pizza, they argue.

And there is another argument that can be made about the newspaper's role in discrimination. NOW and the commission will argue that many employers want to discriminate (surely true in the late 1960s and probably still true today), but they can't afford to be open about it for fear of being charged with violating the law. For these employers, a very attractive alternative would be a system by which few, if any, women applied for jobs, because without any female applications the employers couldn't be charged with discrimination for hiring men. Happily, the *Pittsburgh Press,* an independent newspaper in town, is willing to provide that system (as a service to advertisers) and indeed to structure it in such a way—through column headings—that the employers *have no choice,* for the newspaper *requires* that they place their ads in a sex-designated category. Under this view of the case, the *Pittsburgh Press,* willingly or not, is much more than an incidental player in employment discrimination; it is instead providing a necessary instrument for discrimination, without which much of the discrimination could not occur.

There are thus two images of the *Pittsburgh Press*'s actions, and of the First Amendment, that compete with each other in the case. Volk is well aware of the image that NOW and the commission will try to convey when they present their oral arguments. So he is trying his best to paint his own picture in a persuasive way while he has a chance.

Mr. Volk, continuing: The *Pittsburgh Press* was . . . found guilty of aiding an employer in the act of discrimination. It is important to note that no . . . act of discrimination on the part of any employer was found as a fact. There was minimal testimony presented at the hearing [about] one potential discriminatee, but no proof was ever [presented] that this particular job situation was covered by the ordinance. The ordinance has many exceptions, [including] a bona fide occupational qualification exemption. It applied only to employers of five or more, and it is limited to the city of Pittsburgh itself, and does not apply to domestic help. . . . [T]he Commission did not . . . find [discrimination].

Volk now turns from the lack of actual discrimination point to the argument that NOW and the commission will make, which is that want ads are simply commercial speech and thus are entitled to no First Amendment protection as free speech or freedom of the press. In arguing that the *Press*'s ads are protected speech, Volk must grapple with a much earlier Supreme Court decision, *Valentine v. Chrestensen*, 316 U.S. 52 (1942), in which the Court dismissed a sidewalk vendor's free speech claim on the ground that his sign, although containing a snippet of political expression, was in essence just a ruse to sell his goods and therefore was a commercial message entitled to no protection under the First Amendment.

Mr. Volk, continuing: [W]e are here today to ask this Court to extend . . . First Amendment rights [to the] commercial context. As Mr. Justice Douglas has said . . . , speaking of *Valentine v. Chrestensen,* "The ruling was casual, almost offhand. And it has not survived reflection." He also said that the press in its historic connotation comprehends every sort of publication which affords a vehicle of information and opinion, which is precisely what we're talking about in this free flow of [job] information here.

Question: Well, I thought a major part of your argument perhaps was that even if commercial speech isn't protected, there's more to this speech here than commerce.

Mr. Volk: Oh, there certainly is. There is an editorial—

Question: Well, forget about that part of it. . . . I suppose you say that we could decide the case in your favor without overruling *Valentine* at all?

Mr. Volk: Yes, you could. . . . You've already said in *New York Times v. Sullivan*[1] that merely because a matter is commercial, newspapers are bought and sold, wages are paid, money changes hands—

Question: Well, the advertisement in [*Sullivan*] was distinguished from *Valentine,* wasn't it?

Mr. Volk: Yes, it was.

---

1. *New York Times v. Sullivan,* 376 U.S. 254 (1964), is a famous case in which the Court granted full First Amendment protection to an advertisement placed in the *New York Times* criticizing the Montgomery, Alabama, police commissioner's handling of civil rights protests and the police's repeated jailing of Rev. Martin Luther King Jr.

Question: That was an advertisement in *New York Times v. Sullivan.*
Mr. Volk: Yes, it was a political—
Question: It was an advertisement.
Question: It was paid.
Mr. Volk: An advertisement.

A number of Justices are jumping into the questioning here, trying, perhaps, to find a way around the *Valentine* case without overruling it.

Question: And it was said [in *Sullivan*] that . . . *Valentine v. Chrestensen* had nothing to do with the First Amendment questions raised by the advertisement [in *Sullivan*]. That's what *Times v. Sullivan* held, wasn't it?
Mr. Volk: Yes. . . .
Question: And are you suggesting you may make the same argument, perhaps for different reasons, as to this, as to these arguments?
Mr. Volk: Yes. . . .

Volk is being carried along by the tide of the arguments here, and the Justices are trying to steer him to the issue he needs to address, which is what, if any, free speech value inheres in the job ads.

Question: I just wonder, then, if the question Justice White put to you is one you ought to address yourself to; namely, assuming that *Valentine v. Chrestensen* is not overruled, [then] like the advertisement in *New York Times v. Sullivan,* ought we to agree that these [job ads], too, should be distinguished?
Mr. Volk: We certainly think that you should, sir.
Question: Why?
Mr. Volk: We feel that the help wanted arrangement . . . is a statement . . . of the editor's opinion as to how best to service the readers and best appeal to the readers, just the way he arranges his paper vis-a-vis placing of . . . the television section, the sports pages, and where the editorial page is versus the front page where the average reader wouldn't be too enthused . . . to buy the paper [if] he puts it in the middle.

One may make a social commentary that maybe should be on the front page. We say how he arranges his newspaper is an editorial judgment, and that this is not commercial.

And secondly, if it is, it is a mixed editorial and commercial policy. Now, want ads . . . are a basic community service, they are like a community billboard. And we feel that this is a forum that should be intruded upon only with great caution. [The First Amendment's concept of speech related to self-government or] governing interest is very broad, indeed, including those forms of thought and expression within the range of human communication from which the voter derives the knowledge, intelligence, sensitivity to human values, required to sanely and objectively judge the power and duty of government.

Volk has taken a very broad, theoretical, and perhaps unexpected turn here. Instead of focusing on the value of jobs and job advertisements for the average American and the average employer, he has waxed eloquent about self-government and the information people need in order to vote and make public choices. The argument is an interesting and quite subtle one; it is also treacherous. If he loses it, he is left with little more than an advertisement written by someone other than the newspaper, which the newspaper is paid to publish. But if he succeeds in raising the argument to a different plane, one focused on the relationship of want-ad headings to issues being debated in the political and public arena, he will end up squarely within the most protected core of First Amendment speech.

How does he connect the help-wanted ad to democratic self-government? He tries to portray the newspaper's policy as an act of civil disobedience—objection by action, not simply words—to a controversial social policy of legally guaranteeing gender equality in jobs and to the burgeoning of big government and intrusive regulations. These are wholly uncharted legal waters.

Question: There's a great difference between somebody using its expertise and its political thought and its editorial policy as to Vietnam and as to somebody getting a job as a plumber.

Mr. Volk: That argument has been made and has attractive merit, until we realize that we are in a law explosion. . . . Those of us who labor in this vineyard out there see that [with] every passage of every new Act of Congress, we have new guidelines, new regulations, and new rules that are imposed upon business. And we find that the newspaper business—

Question: Well, business is not protected by the First Amendment.

Mr. Volk: Well, I'd like to think that business has some protections under the First Amendment, Mr. Justice Marshall. I think a newspaper—

Question: Well, I don't think the plumbing business has any protection under the First Amendment.

Mr. Volk: Well, I think the plumbing business, if [it] places a commercial advertisement in a newspaper, has certain First Amendment rights to express his—to put his ad in. I think that's what our case is, to some degree, all about; that the commercial context is not totally devoid of First Amendment protection.

[This case involves not the plumber, but] the right of a newspaper. . . . The First Amendment [isn't just about] freedom of speech, it mentions the press separately. It says Freedom of Speech and of the Press. The press has been a particular institution in this country since the days of the Framers of the Constitution. The press is a major, complex business, which provides a basic interflow of communication and ideas, and one of them is want ads.

One of the aspects here is the placement of the want ads. And it may be a small chip [in the system of government regulation]; I like to refer to it as the Lilliputians tying down Gulliver. He's a big giant, and every little rope that they put across him is no bigger than a sewing thread, [but they] eventually tied him with girth.

And that's what we have with the newspapers, as these guidelines proliferate and the newspapers become the enforcement arm of agencies seeking to produce meritorious or non-meritorious [ends]—we don't pass judgment on that here. I'm not trying to redraft the ordinance. But as these agencies attempt to use the newspapers of the country as enforcement arms, as they have here, making them a screening agency, this impinges on the freedom of that newspaper to control its pages.

Volk has woven an interesting argument, tying together the claim that the First Amendment should prohibit government from restricting speech in order to prohibit conduct, with the claim that the newspaper's want-ad column headings were a form of voiced protest over what the paper considered a flawed and unconstitutional policy. But making the argument was a far cry from supporting it and convincing the Justices. For one thing, granting for sake of argument that the editors really intended to use the columns as a political statement, is there any reason to think that anyone reading the paper would have understood them that way? More fundamentally, the argument that the newspaper actually intended the want-ad columns to serve as a form of political protest was met with skepticism by some Justices.

Question: Does the newspaper retain the right to take whatever regulations they like and reject those they don't like, as witness the fact that you said the middle-aged woman couldn't put the ad in? So you take what regulations you like and discard what you don't like. Is that your position?

Mr. Volk: Our position . . . on that one . . . is that . . . voluntary cooperation with the Human Relations Commission I don't think obligates us to take the whole law, if it impinges on us in some way we wish to challenge in court. The Pittsburgh Press Company decided that it had a commitment to civil rights and to certain social change, and did indeed work with the city's Human Relations Commission and with the State commission on the content of the ads. But it did not do so under compulsion of law, where [it was] forced to do something which [it], in [its] best judgment, did not think was proper, it fought, and here we are.

Now, I say that we can't pick and choose those regulations which we find meritorious, but most certainly, sir, we have the right to challenge those regulations which, in our opinion, impinge on the freedom to run the newspaper in an efficient matter in conducting the interflow of information in the way we see fit.

Newspapers are being impinged on [in] some significant degree. [This ordinance] may be an idea whose time has come. But we ask that it should be let come through the free interchange of ideas and through the interchange of advertisers and readers, and through cultural change, if you will. Let it not come through government fiat and the cultural predilections of local special interest groups or government officials.

And with this, Volk's argument is over. He has experienced some rough spots, but he has managed to hold to his basic theory of the case: distancing the *Press* from the *text* of the specific ads and thus from any job discrimination that likely followed an employer's placement of an ad in the newspaper, yet maintaining that the editorial judgment involved in the *selection* of the specific ads as well as the compositional judgment reflected in the column headings should both be protected as part of the *Press*'s freedom under the First Amendment. And Volk has also managed to present a fairly bold argument, claiming that the column headings were, in effect, a form of protest that voiced objection to government power, excessive regulation, and intrusion into the editorial freedom of newspapers. Some Justices expressed disdain for this line of argument, to be sure. But is it really that much different from newspapers protesting payment of the hated Stamp Tax in England by handing out newspapers without the required stamp?

Should the fact that nothing more than a classified ad was involved make a difference to the ultimate decision? The Commission on Human Relations and NOW argue that it should. But just two years after the *Pittsburgh Press* case, the Supreme Court would strike down a Virginia law prohibiting classified advertisements for abortions in other states on the ground that the advertisement concerned an issue of great public controversy: abortion. Can one distinguish on principled, constitutional grounds, rather than on grounds of political preference or personal value, the issue of abortion from the issues of sexual equality, intrusive government regulation, and use of speech as an instrument for regulating conduct?

With these and other questions now hanging in the air, the Chief Justice called on Strassburger to present the commission's argument.

Mr. Strassburger: I represent the City of Pittsburgh and its Human Relations Commission. The Commission . . . was created in an attempt to eliminate discrimination, including employment discrimination.

The National Organization for Women filed a complaint [with the Commission in 1969] alleging that the *Press* had [aided discrimination by] permitting advertisers to advertise in sex-segregated columns. The Commission, after a hearing, held that there were violations of the ordinance and that no constitutional rights of [the *Press*] had been denied.

[The city and the Commission] believe that there is no First Amendment violation in this case. This Court has continually held that [the] Constitution['s protection of] speech is less than absolute. The [*Press's*] activity in this case, we believe, fails to qualify for First Amendment protection. . . .

First of all, it's commercial speech, and this is one of the contexts where this Court has held [in *Valentine v. Chrestensen*] that the First Amendment does not apply. We believe that *Valentine* is good law today. Non-protection of commercial speech . . . makes a great deal of sense. [It concerns] a separate sector of economic activity, an area that involves economic interests—the production of goods and services—rather than the interests of free expression. We're not dealing with any essential part of the exposition of ideas.

[The *Press's*] response to this is to say that the ads themselves may not be ideas, but that the column headings are different, that they are abbreviated editorial comment that certain jobs are of more interest to men than to women. However, this argument corresponds neither to the facts nor the law. . . . [T]he paper does not give the slightest thought to whether the advertised job interests men or women. It goes wherever the advertiser wants it to go, regardless of whether the newspaper might have thought that this is a female type job or a male type job.

Question: But the newspaper has, in setting up its help wanted pages, given advance thought to the proposition that some jobs may be of more interest to women, and other jobs of more interest to men. It has given thought to the basic idea, and has conceptualized that idea in the setup of its

classified advertising, hasn't it? And that was the *newspaper*'s decision, at
least that's what counsel answered to me.

Mr. Strassburger: Your Honor, I don't think that this is any more an idea than,
say, that a violator of the antitrust laws says that, well, his violation of the
antitrust laws shows his idea that monopoly is beneficial to society.

Strassburger is taking on Volk's civil disobedience point directly, arguing
that what's involved here is commerce, pure and simple, and that the *Press*'s
claim that it is violating the ordinance in order to editorialize against it is an
argument that would permit lawbreakers to escape punishment by claiming
that their illegal acts were simply protests against laws they disliked, as illus-
trated by the monopolist example. But the example doesn't exactly fit, for
the monopolist is not using speech to express its views; it is simply acting in
violation of the law. In contrast, the *Press*'s expression of dissent is accomplished by speech—words in a column heading—and the *Press* is not alleged
to have discriminated but rather to have aided others in discriminating by
means of its speech.

The Justice, perhaps vaguely sensing that the illustration isn't quite on
point, nevertheless drops the matter and moves on.

Question: Well, but that doesn't involve—perhaps you're quite right. But
you're not contending here that it's the advertisers who have forced the
newspaper to do this, or have persuaded the newspaper to do this, or that
it's the advertiser's idea for the newspaper to set it up this way, are you?
Because I understood the facts were otherwise.

Mr. Strassburger: No. The newspaper sets up the framework, but the advertiser, by placing an advertisement in this sex-segregated column, is discriminating. I think Mrs. Matson [co-counsel representing NOW] will get into
this in more detail, but the ordinance defines discrimination as any difference on the basis of sex. And by placing an ad in this sex-segregated column, the advertiser is discriminating and the newspaper is aiding that.

Strassburger is attempting to portray the discriminatory act as an employer's sex-identified advertisement, not the separate and later act of refusing
to hire on grounds of sex. By shifting the definition of what is illegal, Strassburger is trying to connect the *Press*'s actions more immediately and directly to an illegal act. The Justices raise no questions about this, perhaps because
they agree or perhaps because they already have determined that they disagree and that Strassburger's definition would rest the *Press*'s liability for
"aiding" discrimination on too shaky a foundation, especially given the Su-

preme Court's longstanding distaste for laws that would impose punishment
for speech that advocates or encourages illegal acts. Under the First Amendment, for example, advocating an illegal act, without directly intending to
produce it, cannot itself be made illegal. One cannot escape this rule by
making the advocacy itself a crime and then arguing that the advocate can
be held liable because he or she committed a crime. The harm that justifies
prohibition of speech must be the resultant conduct, not the words. Thus,
the city of Pittsburgh can't avoid the tenuous link between the *Press*'s want-
ad columns and job discrimination by employers by the expedient of making advocacy of discrimination or aiding discrimination by speech the crime.

But the Justices fail to explore this question. Instead, they move on to that
now familiar middle-aged woman housekeeper.

Question: What about the hypothetical situation I put to your friend, about
   the woman who is middle-aged and has no skill except she knows how to
   take care of a house, putting an ad in the paper: "Middle-aged woman
   wishes housekeeping job, living in." No problem with that?
Mr. Strassburger: I completely disagree with the answer that Mr. Volk gave.
Question: What would yours be?
Mr. Strassburger: Well, first of all, it's not covered by the ordinance. We're
   talking about help wanted, not jobs wanted. The ordinance speaks of an
   employer, an employment agency, or a labor union placing an ad indicating discrimination.

This is a bit of a sleight of hand. Wouldn't someone who hired the woman be guilty of discrimination under the ordinance, and if so, wouldn't the
woman who placed the ad be guilty, as the *Press* was alleged to be, of "aiding" that discrimination—indeed more directly than the *Press* did? But the
Justice lets this point pass.

Question: All right. Then turn it around the other way now. Now we have a
   man who has a wife who is a semi-invalid and two small, at least adoles-
   cent, children, and he wants a housekeeper who is a woman, and he'd like
   some stable, middle-aged woman. Can he specify all of that in the ad?
Mr. Strassburger: He can do that because . . . he's not covered by the ordinance, [since] the ordinance excludes situations of five or fewer employees.
Question [perhaps exhibiting a little impatience with Strassburger's evasion
   of the question]: All right. Let's move over. Now it's an employment agency
   doing this.

Mr. Strassburger: If the job is certified as having a bona fide occupational qualification, then either the employer or an employment agency can place this type of ad.

This is why the screening argument [by the *Press*—that the *Press* is given the government's task of making judgments about justifications for ads—] is a complete red herring. . . . [I]t's perfectly clear to the newspaper whether this job has a bona fide occupational qualification. [The *Press*] doesn't have to guess. [The] ordinance . . . provides that if the employer wants a bona fide occupation exemption, it can apply to the Commission and get that exemption.

Question: But the Commission isn't required to give that exemption. Isn't that judgment left with the Commission as to whether or not it will give such an exemption?

Mr. Strassburger: Well, certainly there is a judgment involved . . . I don't know what the Commission would do with that sort of case, but as far as the *Pittsburgh Press* is concerned, it doesn't have any problem as far as screening the advertisements. It knows, because there either is an exemption or there isn't.

Question: Who has to get the exemption, the employment agency or the newspaper?

Mr. Strassburger: The advertiser, whomever that may be.

Now, [the fact that the *Press*'s headings] were created so as to cater to the reader preferences [does not] excuse . . . violation of the [Ordinance]. [In a recent circuit court case], involving a stewardess, the employer argued: Well, my customers prefer women as performing this job on airplanes. And the court said that doesn't excuse discrimination, what your customers prefer.

Question: Did that case involve a newspaper?

Mr. Strassburger: No, Your Honor, it didn't.

Question: Well, that's the big difference here. I mean that at least one of the two issues here is the First Amendment, and the First Amendment doesn't protect airline companies, unless they want to speak.

The Justice is returning to the earlier monopoly hypothetical Strassburger used, now probing the difference between a business claiming to speak by its illegal action—sex discrimination—and a company (here a newspaper) whose only action is itself speech, not illegal conduct. This is the difference between the *Press* itself discriminating in its own hiring (for which it could not easily make an argument that its hiring decision was speech in opposition to the law) and the *Press* employing column headings, which are indisputably speech, and claiming that those headings, themselves not illegal, convey a message of objection to the law. The *Press*'s claim is therefore like the claim accepted by the Court two years later in the abortion advertisement case: the ad for out-of-state abortions, though published in a state in which abortions were illegal, was speech only, and it conveyed a message (pro-abortion) on a controversial legal question (regulation of abortion).

Mr. Strassburger: Well, Your Honor, [our] contention is that these [ads] are non-ideas and these column headings can't raise non-ideas to the level of ideas. And I'd like to point out that [many lower courts have upheld] the [federal] Civil Rights Act of 1964, which . . . prohibits an employer from placing a want ad in a sex-segregated column.

Question: It's one thing, it would occur to me, to prohibit *an employer* . . . from advertising that would indicate any discrimination. But that's quite another thing from government putting a restriction on the newspaper as to what it can print, in advance.

The question poses a serious problem for NOW and the commission. Why didn't the commission make it illegal for the employer to place its ads in a sex-segregated column, rather than leaving the employer free to do so but trying to regulate the *Press* on grounds that it was aiding discrimination by using such columns?

Indeed, if the employer's use of the columns is not prohibited under the ordinance, how can the *Press*'s use of the column headings be viewed as "aiding" anything illegal at all? The Justices, perhaps seeing the defect in Strassburger's argument, dropped the matter. Oral argument is not an occasion to drive points home and debate with or embarrass counsel; it is supposed to assist the Justices' understanding of the facts and the issues.

So the Justices moved Strassburger on to the commercial speech question and the *Valentine v. Chrestensen* case. If the column headings were not considered speech protected at all by the First Amendment, the weakness in Strassburger's argument wouldn't matter, for the commercial speech, treated not as speech but simply as conduct for constitutional purposes, could be regulated for just about any reason the city chose, without any First Amendment limitations whatever.

Question: That all gets us back to *Valentine v. Chrestensen*, doesn't it?

Mr. Strassburger: No Your Honor, it doesn't necessarily. First of all, we [do] feel that this falls directly within *Valentine v. Chrestensen*. Commercial speech is not protected [by the First Amendment]. But in addition to this, even if we are dealing with speech that is . . . protected, this Court has also held that general regulatory statutes which incidentally affect speech are permissible if there's a valid societal interest involved.

Strassburger is referring to statutes that, for example, prohibit littering or draft card burning or trespass on property, the enforcement of which might affect some speech activity. But those statutes are all directed toward conduct—throwing litter, trespassing—not speech; their aim is to restrict conduct, not speech. All conduct, like the acts of the monopolist, may consist in part of speech: the litter may be a political flyer; the trespass may be part of a demonstration. But as long as it is the conduct the government is after, not any possible speech (such as burning one's draft card in protest of the Vietnam War), the regulation will generally be upheld, and the First Amendment will play only a muted role in determining the regulation's constitutionality.

The validity of Strassburger's reliance on this line of reasoning, therefore, depends on whether we should view Pittsburgh's prohibition of "aiding" discrimination as primarily directed toward speech or as primarily directed toward conduct. If toward conduct, what would that conduct be? It would not be job discrimination, as that is separately prohibited. It would instead have to be acts that facilitate others' discrimination, a category of acts that may, indeed, consist largely of speech, such as the *Press*'s column headings. In any event, the commission's decision to apply the aiding provision to publishers such as the *Press* was clearly intended to focus on speech. Under this reasoning, Strassburger's reasoning once again falls short of the mark, taking us full circle to the vexing *Valentine* case, which says that commercial speech is conduct, not speech, for purposes of the First Amendment.

And this is precisely where the Justices' questions take Strassburger.

Question: Yes, but [those cases] didn't . . . involve the government telling a newspaper what it could and could not put in its newspaper.

Mr. Strassburger: Well, it's our feeling that what the petitioner says here is that we're entitled to special protection because we're a newspaper. But in this economic area, [a newspaper] is not entitled to more protection just because it has editorial functions, [any more] than the ad in *Valentine* was entitled to protection because it was appended to the back of a political protest.

Question: But you seem to separate the First Amendment completely from the economic aspect, but could a newspaper survive if it just sold the newspapers to readers without any advertising?

Mr. Strassburger: Your Honor, we're not saying that the newspaper can't have this advertising. All they have to do is put it in a single column. And here

it's a situation where there's a general anti-discrimination statute, a statute premised on an important governmental interest [of eliminating] the
vast amount of discrimination against women.

The burden on the press is absolutely minimal. If the press, if this newspaper, is expressing any kind of ideas here—

Strassburger is cut off here, in the midst of driving home his most important argument—an argument that until now he seems to have been reluctant
to make, perhaps because he doesn't want his case to stand or fall on the uncertain continuing vitality of the *Valentine* case. His argument is this: The purpose of the statute, of which the aiding provision is but a part (but an important one), is exceedingly important. Eliminating sex discrimination in jobs has
nothing to do with restricting speech. The burden on the *Press* of eliminating the silly columns, which serve only to satisfy the advertisers' interests, is
minimal; they could easily use headings based on the job type, allowing readers
to seek their own interests free of a gender referent. And the only speech here,
the only editorial judgment by the press, involves whether to publish and
where to place someone else's speech (the ad), and that speech concerns no
more than the buying and selling of goods and services. Newspapers needn't
be protected under the First Amendment for carrying commercial advertisements that on their face involve no message of public significance.

To the *Press*'s argument that the column-heading policy is a metaphor for
its objection to the law, there are two responses. First, put the objection in
the news and editorial parts of the paper and have the courage to express it
directly as your own editorial view rather than to disguise it in the column
headings, where few will perceive it. Second, in our complex society virtually any ad could be seen as a metaphor. A cigarette ad could be an implicit
objection to government regulation of tobacco or a symbol of the avarice of
tobacco companies. A Campbell's Soup can is a symbol of a commercialized
and advertising-driven society. The *Press*'s metaphorical argument knows no
limits and thus would eviscerate any distinctions among types of speech—
obscenity, fraud, libel—under the First Amendment.

After a brief diversion into a tangential matter, Strassburger is able to return to this argument.

Mr. Strassburger: I would just like to say one other thing with regard to the
fact that this Court, even the absolutists on this Court[2] have said that con-

---

2. The "absolutists" refers to the few Justices who would protect all speech equally and absolutely, drawing no distinctions among speech based on its subject matter and value, and thus
treating advertising and obscenity and libel the same as political statements.

duct can be regulated. And that's what we have here. The newspaper isn't prohibited from expressing its idea. If all it were doing was expressing an idea, it would be satisfied to express it in an editorial or a news column. But it says, well, we have to do it in the want-ad headings.

Question: What is the conduct?

Mr. Strassburger: The conduct is participating in this discriminatory scheme.

Question: Mr. Strassburger, in connection with the distinction you are drawing between editorial and commercial advertising, may I put this hypothetical? Suppose an employer, who profoundly disagreed with the social utility of the ordinance in question, went to the newspaper and said, "I want to buy a full-page ad in which to express my disapproval of the ordinance and include in it a statement to the effect that I want to engage women only (for whatever his business may be), and I want to state the reasons why I think they should be exempt from this law or that the law is invalid." Would that be something that, in your view, the newspaper would be prohibited from publishing?

Mr. Strassburger: Your Honor, if we're dealing with just the editorial type advertising, if they're not actually hiring people, then I think it's . . . protected speech under the First Amendment. They could [run] this editorial advertisement.

If, on the other hand, this is just a subterfuge, then I feel that there's no protection for this, and they're violating the ordinance.

At this point, Strassburger's time runs out. He has finally managed, though briefly, to make his central and most persuasive argument: this is advertising, commercial speech that has little constitutional value, so it should be treated as conduct and subject to broad government regulation. If the *Pittsburgh Press* wants to object to the ordinance, it is perfectly free to do so expressly in the news or editorial sections of the paper.

But Strassburger's answer to the last hypothetical left something to be desired. How can we know whether running the full-page ad is a subterfuge or not? Will we have to put the editors of the paper on the stand and ask them how and why they decided to run it, and what they knew about the intentions of the person paying for it? Perhaps an easier answer could have been given. The hypothetical full-page ad, whatever hidden purposes it might have had, was explicit in expressing objection to the ordinance. Readers, in other words, would understand the message being conveyed. In sharp contrast, the column headings themselves say nothing explicit about the ordinance or the paper's objection to it. Therefore, the Court shouldn't credit them as expressing any other message than the one they actually carried: "We're interested in hiring you for a job opening we have, but we're less interested if you are a woman."

The ad contains an explicit message about the buying and selling of specific services, not one that concerns matters of public interest or general interest to the newspaper's readers. That message is the advertiser's message, the advertiser's speech, not the speech of the *Press*. The *Press* should not receive protection under the First Amendment for someone else's speech unless it has had the courage to adopt it as its own. But the *Press* disclaims that message, arguing that its message is instead one of civil disobedience to the ordinance, a message that, in all likelihood, no one but the editors of the classified section even saw.

The *Press,* in short, wants to have its cake and eat it too: to sell space for someone else to speak, and also to claim protection as if the speech were its own, even while disclaiming any exercise of editorial judgment in publishing it. The First Amendment neither requires nor permits such a result.

Strassburger's co-counsel Marjorie H. Matson, representing NOW, then came to the podium to argue on behalf of her client. Her time was limited and much of her presentation involved matters not bearing on the First Amendment issues, such as evidence of sex discrimination on a national level and the negative impact of the column headings on women's willingness to actually apply for "Male Interest" jobs. But she did relate these matters to the First Amendment issues in response to a number of questions raised by the Justices.

Question: Why wouldn't it be enough for the State to move against the employer and forbid the employer from indicating to the paper any preference whatsoever, unless he had a certificate?
Mrs. Matson: Well, Your Honor, the ordinance itself provides for the people to get a certificate if there is a bona fide occupational qualification.
Question: I understand that.
Mrs. Matson: But we are trying to break down the classification system.

In saying this, Matson is coming close to acknowledging that the column headings express a distinct and a general message or idea, apart from the employee-wanted message. She must be careful not to unwittingly accept the *Press*'s civil disobedience argument, which goes to the classification system, not to the particular ad.

Question: Do you think the *Press* would continue this if the employer was forbidden [to answer] when the paper asked him to specify a column? Let's for the moment assume that no employer would ever break the law if it was forbidden to indicate a preference, and that whenever they were asked, they'd say: "Awfully sorry, we just couldn't care less." Do you think the *Press* itself would then go on with this scheme?

Mrs. Matson [hoping to avoid the issue being raised]: Well, that question, I guess, would have to be addressed to the *Press*.

Question: Well, don't you have to answer that question . . . before you can justify putting a prohibition on the *Press* itself?

The question goes back to part of Volk's argument and to the traditional First Amendment rule. Freedom of speech and of the press requires that government regulate conduct initially, and only if that doesn't work may the government justify regulating speech as a means of prohibiting or preventing conduct. Government may not regulate speech about smoking in order to prevent smoking, at least unless it can prove that it has first tried to control smoking directly (making it illegal, prohibiting its sale) *and* that such direct regulations have failed, whereas speech regulation will not. In light of this rule, Matson must, indeed, answer the question.

Mrs. Matson: Well, Your Honor, the thing is that we could knock off one employment agency after another and go through all of those . . . get each of them enjoined from carrying the—

Question: All right. So it's a conservation of resources. There's only one newspaper.

Mrs. Matson: But what we're trying to do is to get at the advertising, which is the thing—the advertising headings which are the message which is being conveyed to women that they should stay away from applying for a particular job. . . . It's not anything that's said in the ad itself, rather, it is the headings under which the ads appear which deters women from applying for jobs for which they may very well be qualified.

Question: Well, I take it that you concede, don't you, that if you could get an injunction against the press you could also get an injunction against the employer from communicating with the press as to what column to put [the ad] in?

Mrs. Matson: Well, then, you see, you would—

Question: Well, could you or couldn't you?

Mrs. Matson: I don't know that you could, as a communication of that kind, I shouldn't think that we could reach that very readily, Your Honor.

Question: Well, not readily but legally, could you?

Mrs. Matson: It seems to me that you would have to enjoin the individual

employment agency or employer from advertising under a Male Help
Wanted column, or a female, as the case may be. . . . So that you would have
an immensely difficult problem of reaching each of the employers, and it
is a job which really is not forced upon us when we have the ordinance
which says that anyone who aids in discrimination . . . can be reached
directly.

With all due respect, Matson's final statement is wholly unresponsive, for
the Justice's question was, "Why go after the *Press* when you can forbid the
employers directly from using sex-designated columns for their ads?" Matson's answer is, "Because the ordinance lets us go after the *Press* instead." But
as Matson well understands, the point of the question was whether there was
any justification *under the First Amendment* for going after the *Press* and its
speech rather than dealing directly with the employer's conduct. Matson simply ducks the question—indeed the many and increasingly frustrated questions of the Justice—and thus fails to explain why, in this case, the First
Amendment should permit government to regulate speech in the first instance as a means of controlling conduct, rather than the other way around.
She does say that regulating the conduct directly—regulating the actions of
each employer—would be inconvenient and costly, but this is not a fully sat-
isfactory answer, for the very point of the First Amendment is to make regulation of speech inconvenient and costly in order to assure the individual's
and the press's freedom to say what they want. As Justices Holmes and Brandeis said in some of the earliest free speech cases decided by the Court, it is
always easier and cheaper, and often politically more palatable, to regulate
speech instead of conduct. But the First Amendment's protection was intended to safeguard against this very tendency.

But it was Matson's lucky day. She didn't have to face the Justice's next
question. Her time was up, and the Chief Justice thanked her and invited her
to return to her seat. Time limits for oral argument before the Supreme Court
are strictly enforced—sometimes to the point of cutting counsel off in mid-
sentence.

After a brief rebuttal argument by Volk, which dwelled only on a technical matter, the Chief Justice banged his gavel, thanked the three counsel, and
at 1:30 P.M. announced, "The case is submitted."

At the end of a week in which oral arguments are heard, the Justices gather in the Supreme Court Conference room, a room tucked at the back of the
Supreme Court building, across from the courtroom, and behind the Justices'
robing chamber. The room is large enough for a conference table that can
accommodate the nine Justices, with a fireplace at one end, bookshelves along

the two sides running the length of the conference table, and a door to the robing room and the main hallway at the back of the building. When the Justices retire there for their conference, the door is closed and no one but the Justices is permitted to enter. Messages are occasionally brought to the Justices, delivered by a messenger who knocks at the door and is met by the junior Justice, serving as doorkeeper, who takes the message without permitting the messenger to enter.

In this inner sanctum the Justices discuss, one at a time, the twelve or so cases argued on Monday, Tuesday, and Wednesday of the week, following a ritual by which the Justices, from junior to senior, make any points they wish to make about their views of a case, and then in reverse order the Justices cast their votes, starting with the Chief Justice and ending with the most junior Justice. If there are enough votes to decide the case, the senior Justice in the majority assumes responsibility for assigning the opinion to himself or herself or one of the other Justices in the majority. Opinion assignment is often strategic. If the vote is close, say 5-4, the opinion will often be assigned to a Justice whose vote is most uncertain, thus hopefully locking the Justice in to the majority. In the alternative (or in addition), the assignment in such cases may go to the Justice who is least likely to strike out and break new ground in his or her opinion, for if a Justice's proposed opinion takes too extreme a position, there is risk that one of the other Justices in the majority will shift to the other side or will feel compelled to write his or her own, more modest, opinion, depriving the majority of an opinion in which at least a majority of the Justices concur and thus depriving the Court of a legally governing rationale.

The molding of consensus can occur in other ways, too. The Justice writing an opinion will prepare a draft and circulate it to all of the other Justices. If the reasoning in the draft is unacceptable to one of the other Justices in the majority, that Justice will often express his or her concerns and make suggestions as to more agreeable language or reasoning, and the author of the draft will frequently demur in order to "hold a Court," or an opinion in which at least five Justices concur.

We can't know, of course, exactly what transpired in the Justices' conference on the *Pittsburgh Press* case. Judging by the final outcome of the case and the author of the Court's opinion, however, we can surmise the course of events. The vote in conference was likely the same 5-4 vote that is reflected in the reported opinion. In the five-Justice majority were Justice Powell, the author of the Court's opinion, and Justices Brennan, White, Marshall, and Rehnquist. The four who dissented were Chief Justice Burger and Justices Douglas, Stewart, and Blackmun. By most popular accounts of the Justices' ideological leanings, this would seem a strange set of combinations. But for those more familiar with the Justices' attitudes toward freedom of the press, it is a bit less surprising. Justice Douglas was a First Amendment absolutist, believing that the Constitution prohibited any law restricting the press's freedom to decide what to publish. Justice Stewart, while not an absolutist, had a record sympathetic to free press claims, believing that the press's near absolute freedom served as an essential check on government power in a democratic state. Justice Blackmun was still relatively new to the Court, but he had displayed an independent streak, and more importantly, he would lead the Court, just a few years later, in overruling the *Valentine* case and declaring that commercial speech, like political speech, is entitled to protection under the First Amendment. The Chief Justice's dissenting vote might surprise some, although he, too, had a tendency toward independence and often resisted philosophical stereotypes.

It was the composition of the majority block, however, that was most intriguing. Justice Powell wrote the opinion. He was the principal "swing vote" on the Court during his tenure, a distinctly moderate and practical jurist. His opinion would be most likely to hold the majority together and attract all five needed votes, for he would decide the case on the narrowest and least activist grounds. Justices Brennan and Marshall were the liberals on the Court. They had both written stirring opinions on freedom of the press. They would also agree, in time, that *Valentine* should be overruled. But the constitutional imperative of equality and the elimination of pervasive sex discrimination were also central tenets of their constitutional belief systems. Justice White was a consummate pragmatist, oriented to the specific facts of cases and loathe to indulge in broad theorizing. For him the column headings likely were seen to serve commercial interests only, and the civil disobedience rationale presented by Volk surely found no welcoming audience in his sharply practical mind. Finally, Justice Rehnquist would prove, over time, to have surprisingly little patience with free speech claims by corporations or businesses—which, he would say, had no mind or will of their own and therefore had little claim to individual liberty.

After the Justice's conference and following assignment of the majority opinion to Justice Powell, the opinion writing began, followed by the back and forth of qualifications, comments, concerns, and suggestions from various Justices, all in an attempt to pin down the case and reduce it to a coherent explanation in the Court's published opinion. In uncomplicated and uncontroversial cases, this process can move along quickly. In the complex and controversial cases, it can take considerable time, often delaying the issuance of an opinion until late June, just before the Court's Term ends, on June 30. In the *Pittsburgh Press* case, this process took three months, which suggests that it was not easy to arrive at an opinion and a rationale that explains the decision in light of First Amendment principles, yet avoids producing unintended consequences in future cases. In the *Pittsburgh Press* case, this was surely a delicate task, for if the *Press* was to be held subject to the ordinance, the reasoning that supported such a result would have to be carefully crafted and limited, lest a signal be sent that even broader government control of the press would be tolerated.

In this respect Justice Powell's opinion did an admirable job, closely limiting its focus to the specific facts surrounding the *Press*'s actions and thus confining its rationale to a very narrow set of circumstances. The opinion first addressed the important and general purpose of the ordinance, noting also its negligible impact on the *Press*: "[N]o suggestion is made in this case that the Ordinance was passed with any purpose of muzzling or curbing the press. Nor does *Pittsburgh Press* argue that the Ordinance threatens its financial viability or impairs in any significant way its ability to publish and distribute a newspaper."

Justice Powell then turned to the content of the ads and the commercial nature of the column headings, giving no credence whatever to the *Press*'s claim that it was voicing objection to the law through the column-heading policy.

> In . . . crucial respects, the advertisements in the present record resemble the *Valentine v. Chrestensen* . . . advertisement. None expresses a position on whether, as a matter of social policy, certain positions ought to be filled by members of one or the other sex, nor does any of them criticize the Ordinance or the Commission's enforcement practices. Each is no more than a proposal of possible employment. The advertisements are thus classic examples of commercial speech. . . . [They] did no more than propose a commercial transaction.

Justice Powell next addressed the *Press*'s editorial freedom claim, concluding that whatever editorial judgment the *Press* exercised concerned commercial, not public, matters and was largely dictated by the advertiser, not the newspaper.

> [W]e are not persuaded that either the decision to accept a commercial advertisement which the advertiser directs to be placed in a sex-designated column or the actual placement there lifts the newspaper's actions from the category of commercial speech. By implication at least, an advertiser whose want ad appears in the "Jobs-Male Interest" column is likely to discriminate against

women in his hiring decisions. Nothing in a sex-designated column heading sufficiently dissociates the designation from the want ads placed beneath it to make the placement severable for First Amendment purposes.

Finally, Justice Powell concluded that reconsideration of its earlier *Valentine* decision was unnecessary, for an additional and limiting element was present in the *Pittsburgh Press* case.

> Whatever the merits of [reconsidering *Valentine*] may be in other contexts, it is unpersuasive in this case. Discrimination in employment is not only commercial activity, it is *illegal* commercial activity under the Ordinance. We have no doubt that a newspaper constitutionally could be forbidden to publish a want ad proposing a sale of narcotics or soliciting prostitutes. Nor would the result be different [if the paper used] columns captioned "Narcotics for Sale" and "Prostitutes Wanted."
>
> Any First Amendment interest which might be served by advertising an ordinary commercial proposal and which might arguably outweigh the government interest supporting the regulation is altogether absent when the commercial activity itself is illegal and the restriction on advertising is incidental to a valid limitation on economic activity.

So much for civil disobedience by the press. So much, perhaps, for an advertisement for the Boston Tea Party.

The dissenting Justices would have none of this. For Justices Douglas and Stewart, in particular, the ordinance was a camel's nose in the tent of a truly free press, a necessary and fiercely independent institution whose very purpose was to form its own judgments, however they might be manifested, whether, that is, by polite essay, news account, or civil disobedience. According to Justice Douglas:

> The First Amendment does not require the press to reflect any ideological or political creed reflecting the dominant philosophy, whether transient or not. It may use its pages and facilities to denounce a law and urge its repeal or, at the other extreme, denounce those who do not respect its letter and spirit. . . .
>
> [W]e have witnessed a growing tendency to cut down the literal requirements of First Amendment freedoms so that those in power can squelch someone out of step. Historically, the miscreant has usually been an unpopular minority. Today it is a newspaper that does not bow to the spreading bureaucracy that promises to engulf us. . . . But the First Amendment presupposed free-wheeling, independent people whose vagaries include ideas spread across the entire spectrum of thoughts and beliefs. I would let any expression in that broad spectrum flourish, unrestrained by Government, unless it was an integral part of action.

Justice Stewart wrote in a similar vein.

> Th[e] question, to put it simply, is whether any government agency—local, state, or federal—can tell a newspaper in advance what it can print and what it cannot. Under the First and Fourteenth Amendments I think no government agency in this Nation has any such power.
>
> So far as I know, this is the first case in this or any other American court that permits a government agency to enter a composing room of a newspaper and dictate to the publisher the layout and makeup of the newspaper's pages. This is the first such case, but I fear it may not be the last. The camel's nose is in the tent.
>
> It is said that the goal of the Pittsburgh ordinance is a laudable one, and so indeed it is. But, in the words of Mr. Justice Brandeis, "Experience should teach us to be most on our guard to protect liberty when the Government's purposes are beneficial. Men born to freedom are naturally alert to repel invasion of their liberty by evil-minded rules. The greatest dangers to liberty lurk in insidious encroachment by men of zeal, well-meaning but without understanding."

The *Pittsburgh Press* had lost its case; the commission and NOW had won. At a practical level the *Press*'s loss didn't really amount to much. It now had a legal excuse to reject its advertisers' entreaties. It had only to dispense with an inconsequential editorial policy on want-ad column headings.

But what about the other popular causes that might intrude themselves upon newspaper pages in the future? What about the drug wars? What about ads for illegal abortions? What about a paper's decision to run an ad for a product that turns out to be dangerous? Would the personal injury lawyers arrive at newspaper doorsteps? What about the Boston Tea Party or the in-your-face unstamped newspaper? Should the newspaper's editorial statements on matters of social policy be restricted to the polite conversation of the news and editorial pages?

These questions would lurk in the background of the case, worrying editors and news organizations. And they lurk today in cases such as one in which *Hustler* magazine was sued for a story about autoerotic asphyxiation, which led a young boy to his death while trying it himself; one in which a publication was sued for running a "gun for hire" advertisement because a reader hired the "gun" to kill his wife; or another in which a Web site was held to be liable for publishing a list of doctors who perform abortions and thus, in the expressly stated view of the site's authors, are murderers who should be punished.

On the other hand, the commission and NOW were surely happy. They could expunge a system of advertising that certainly proved convenient for employers who wished to discriminate. But the "system" of column head-ings did not, as Volk said, cause the discrimination; nor did it even represent the newspaper's aiding or abetting specific instances of discrimination. It's like guns, in the modern libertarian parlance: "Guns don't kill people, peo-ple do." Most gun owners are law abiding. So are most advertisers.

So what followed from the commission's victory? With the *Pittsburgh Press*'s pages now free of sex designation, would job discrimination fall dra-matically? There's reason to doubt it. Those who want to discriminate will find ways to do so. The only way for the law to change their habits is to chal-lenge them directly and impose costly consequences on their actions. The Pittsburgh ordinance failed in this. It did not punish the employers who dis-criminate but instead punished the newspaper. It restricted speech, not con-duct. Going after a newspaper may be efficient, but it is not a very effective way for the law to change the employers' habits.

And finally, on a related note, we should ask why the commission and the city council didn't make it illegal for the *employers* to use sex preferences in their ads. Was it because it's easier to pick on speech rather than on conduct, as long as it's for a good and popular cause, as Justice Brandeis said? Or was it political cowardice? Would it simply have been too unpopular in the busi-ness community to impose such restrictions on the employers themselves? Perhaps there is another reason. But if either or both of these accounted for the commission's decision, then the victory was indeed a hollow one.

Additional Reading

Baker, C. Edwin. *Advertising and a Democratic Press.* Princeton, N.J.: Princeton Universi-ty Press, 1994.

Commission on Freedom of Expression (The Hutchins Commission). *A Free and Respon-sible Press.* Chicago: University of Chicago Press, 1947.

Lippmann, Walter. *Public Opinion.* 1922. Reprint, New York: The Free Press, 1965.

Nerone, John, ed. *Last Rights: Revisiting "Four Theories of the Press."* Urbana: University of Illinois Press, 1995.

4. Privacy and Responsibility

The press is perhaps most widely and persistently reviled and feared for its power to invade personal privacy. Instances of outrageous publication are not hard to find: a photograph of a small child in midair as he falls to his death from a ten-story window, with his mother watching in stark terror from below; medical records and photographs of pitiful men confined against their will in a run-down mental hospital, hopeless and abused. There are many other examples, two of which we shall turn to in this chapter. What is interesting about press violations of privacy, however, is not that the violations are so rampant, but that they are comparatively rare.

What does privacy mean? Surprisingly, there is no clear answer to this question. Does privacy concern information the disclosure of which would be embarrassing or harmful to one's reputation; or does it protect and foster personal relationships or habits; or should it focus on an individual's ability to control her own identity in public? Is the law capable of controlling the press's disclosure of private matter? Protecting against publication of dangerous secrets, against theft of material, or against publication of false fact that harms an individual is, as we have already seen, far from an easy task. Privacy, in contrast, is an infinitely more pliable, elastic, and circumstantial concept. Is the risk that the law will discourage the publication of important and lawful news for fear of running afoul of ambiguous privacy restrictions simply too great a price to pay for privacy? Are there circumstances in which invasion of privacy is justified notwithstanding the harm it produces? Were the stories of personal tragedy following the World Trade Center and Pentagon attacks on September 11, 2001, deeply personal and private as they were, also valuable and cathartic to us all when reported by the press?

The two stories in this chapter will present us with distinct examples of privacy, one involving a claim of confidentiality and the right to control disclosure of information by the individual in a complex and technological world, the other involving the damage that can result when deeply personal and embarrassing private information is broadly disseminated. The cases will require us to think about the types of harm that justify the law stepping in, the difficulty of settling on an idea of privacy that the law should protect, the intractable problems presented in defining it, and the problems that are confronted in identifying those instances in which invasions of privacy are justified because the public value and importance of the private information clearly outweighs the harm done to the individual.

Most importantly, the cases force us to look at privacy claims as they arise in specific and unique circumstances and thus to see privacy as a concrete claim, not just as a theoretical construct. In the *Bartnicki* case, involving an illegally intercepted telephone conversation, we will see the privacy invasion as it arose from the actions and motives of the people involved; and then through the quite remarkable oral argument before the Supreme Court, we will witness the process by which new and untested legal ideas take shape in the medium of legal theory and doctrine. The second case, *Howard v. Des Moines Register,* which involves disclosure of intimate and embarrassing information in the news, will afford us another perspective. There we will examine privacy from within the case, not from without, trying in the process to understand the competing perspectives of the individual and the press at a human level. Supreme Court opinions rarely do that. Common-law privacy cases that arise in state courts more often do, and this is especially true with Robbin Woody Howard's case.

STORY 6

Protecting Privacy
Bartnicki v. Vopper
532 U.S. 514 (2001)

On a spring day in May 1993, Gloria Bartnicki was doing what she normally did, driving to and from meetings in Wilkes-Barre, Pennsylvania, and talking on her cell phone. Bartnicki was the chief negotiator for the teachers' union in the Wyoming Valley West School District. And she was busy. At the moment she was talking to Tony Kane, the president of the local teachers' union.

The union was in the midst of a prolonged negotiation that had begun nearly sixteen months earlier, in January 1992. There was little progress to show for the months of effort. The teachers were asking for a 6 percent pay raise, among other things. The school board was offering less than half that amount. The board's intransigence, if that's what it was, was assisted by an active, vocal, and determined taxpayers group headed by Jack Yocum, a local builder. The group was holding the school board's feet to the fire.

As might be expected, media attention to the negotiations had been ratcheting up, with stories almost every day. The union felt beleaguered. Someone close to the negotiations had been persistently leaking information favorable to the board. The union, according to Kane, was "dealing with a party that whenever we said anything [in the negotiations], it was reported in the press. . . . Conversation was being quoted in the paper. All our conversations. If we suggested something to someone, it was repeated. I mean, there was no confidentiality, no semblance of respect on the part of the Board to at least understand what was going on. That's what made it difficult. I don't know how you operate with that in effect."[1]

A second problem was the approaching end of the school year and the deadline it posed for arbitration of the dispute. Arbitration was only possible in two situations: if both parties agreed to it, or if there was a strike. The union wanted arbitration, but the board would not agree. That left the strike option. In the event of a strike, even a short one, arbitration would be required. But the strike option was only available when school was in session;

---

1. The material quoted in this story is from transcriptions, depositions, and other evidence in the record of the case.

therefore, the fast-approaching end of the school year put the union in a bind. It had to act quickly.

This was the background for the conversation that Gloria Bartnicki had with Tony Kane on that spring day in May 1993. The topic was the strike.[2]

Kane: . . . So there's no . . . no problem. [. . .] Tomorrow we're passing out information . . . You know that thing about moving [. . .] things up [. . .] the, uh, exams up?
Bartnicki: Yes.
Kane: That we can have a strike almost any time.

* * *

Kane: Ah, you were, you had the right intuition. But at this point [. . .] we may have to set a strike date, uh, ah early next week.
Bartnicki: Yea, we might Tony.

* * *

Kane: Andy [. . .] told me that they [school officials] called [the Department of Education] this afternoon [. . . about the effect of a possible strike at year's end].
Bartnicki: Yes.
Kane: And the department said yes, they [the schools] could move the date of the exams. [. . .] Now that has nothing to do with how short school is gonna be.
Bartnicki: That's right.

* * *

Kane: They still have to have a hundred and eighty days, but I don't think they can have exams tomorrow. I don't think the teachers would go through with it. [. . .] They haven't prepared the kids for it. They have to tell the kids to study. [. . .] At least get them going for it.
Bartnicki: Yeh . . .
Kane: That would be grossly unfair, too. . . . So what I'm saying, [the teachers in the union] thought there was some kind of a leak, because at a quarter of three the high school principal called and said there was a rumor going around that the teachers were talking about that [. . .] test date being moved back.
Bartnicki: Oh, really?

---

2. What follows is an edited and partial transcript of the call.

Kane: [. . .] I said to everybody, pass the word that we never know, but the principals were meeting this morning and they may be trying to move back [the test dates]. [. . .] [But] they were not! [. . .] They're meeting on Friday to discuss that . . . from what I understand.

* * *

Bartnicki: So, if they meet on Friday, Tony, the earliest they can tell the kids is Monday.
Kane: But [. . .] Monday there's no school.
Bartnicki: Oh, that's right. So Tuesday . . .
Kane: They'd have to tell the kids they're gonna have a test on Tuesday.
Bartnicki: If that happens, then we strike them Tuesday, Tony.

* * *

Bartnicki: Fumanti told me that Norm Namey called him today. [. . .] He was beside himself.
Kane: Yea, well I feel sorry for Norm.
Bartnicki: I know. I do, too.
Kane: Because I don't think this should be.
Bartnicki: No.
Kane: I don't think this should be . . . But this is again . . . its (undecipherable). If they're [the school board] not gonna move [from] three percent, we're gonna have to go to their, their homes . . . to blow off their front porches, we'll have to do some work on some of those guys. (Pauses) Really, uh, really and truthfully because this is, you know, this is bad news. (Undecipherable) The part that bothers me, they could still have kept to their three percent, but they're again negotiating in the paper. This newspaper report knew it was three percent. What they should have said [is] "We'll meet, we'll meet and discuss this." You don't discuss items in public.
Bartnicki: No.
Kane: You don't discuss this in public . . . Particularly with the press.
Bartnicki: Exactly. Well, but now, uh, all rules are off and they'll discuss anything they want.
Kane: Yeh, well if the rules are off, the rules are off for us, too.
Bartnicki: Exactly.
Kane: The rules are off for us, too. So, if you want to get beat over the head, [they,] too, get beat over the head.
Bartnicki: Yes.
Kane: But what they should have done is said, Look, we'll meet tomorrow and see if we can't resolve . . . But you don't discuss your position openly. [. . .]

But you know they're saying no and they, the taxpayers, love it. [. . .] You see the media goes and tries to talk to them in private, but they're doing everything in public. . . . So we have to talk about the humming that took place at the school [apparently by the taxpayers group at a board meeting]. . . . You know, we're going to buy him [perhaps Jack Yocum, head of the taxpayers group] a song sheet. [. . .] You know . . . and we can put words to his songs the next time instead of humming. Put some nice words to it.

Bartnicki: That's [. . .] that's how seriously he took this.

Kane: That's right. And that's how serious the whole question might be . . . They're, they're, they're nitwits. But, I'll tell you I think there's eight or nine of them. [. . .] That's the sad part.

Bartnicki: And you know, Tony, I'm gonna say this to you. I don't think George Dervinis is assertive enough with them. I just don't. [. . .] He's too nice a guy, Tony.

Kane: Yeh, I think he tells them, but then they say well the hell with you. . . . You've got the rabble rousers, like Jim Burns . . . See, if that were Vivian he'd fight with them [. . .] he'd argue with them. [. . .] But I don't think the others have the energy to do it. . . .

Bartnicki: No. No.

Kane: Yeh . . . so that's . . .

Bartnicki: Okay kiddo . . .

Kane: If I hear from the school tonight . . . I'll definitely call you.

Bartnicki: Okay [. . .] Bye.

Kane: Bye-bye.

What Bartnicki and Kane did not know was that their conversation had been intercepted and taped. To this day, the identity of the person who taped the conversation is unknown. But shortly after the conversation, the tape fell into the hands of Jack Yocum, the president of the Wyoming Valley West Taxpayers Association. According to Yocum's testimony, he had "no idea" where it came from. "It was in my mailbox . . . and I came home and found it." Yocum was at that time engaged in a "war . . . against a union that we view as being out of control." The union was out of control, he said, in "their aspirations for money and benefits" and "out of control in their behavior . . . the many threats I received at home . . . , having school board members tell me that you people had better start looking under the hoods of your cars before you start them in the morning."

Yocum immediately listened to the tape. He then made two critical decisions: he would inform some members of the school board; and he would give the tape to at least two media outlets, including WILK, a local radio station with a Rush Limbaugh–like local affairs talk show hosted by Fredrick Vopper (whose radio name was Fred Williams) for three hours each morning. "Hearing the tape," Yocum said, "I felt morally in a position where I had to make a decision . . . whether I should do something with that tape or not." Yocum informed the school board of the tape, playing it for at least two members.

He then decided not to inform the police but instead to make the tape public by giving it to WILK. "If I went to the police, I knew they would say . . . 'Well, Mr. Yocum. When someone's porch is blown off, or after something happens, we'll do something. We can't do anything before that.' So it was my position, which I felt strongly about, to make it public. And if WILK was willing to hear it, so be it. And that would at least provide protection in the best way that I could. I could not morally live with the fact that what if this did happen, if I did nothing." Yocum accordingly called Fred Williams (Vopper), brought him the tape, told him he believed Bartnicki and Kane were the persons on the tape, and Williams and a colleague listened to it.

Surprisingly, Williams and his colleagues at WILK, including the news director, listened again to the tape some days later, Williams testified, and "just put it in a drawer for a while. . . . I knew the ramifications of doing something that might be illegal." The tape remained in the drawer until September. In the meantime, Yocum "never said, when you going to play the tape? Never said, what's going on?" And then in September, when the contract negotiations had reached something of a fever pitch, Williams said, "we started to be concerned about maybe this is really a legitimate news item that should be looked at. . . . [W]e listened to it carefully again and Nancy (the news director) and I spoke to Gerald, the WILK general manager. I said, 'I think we ought to do this; I think we ought to broadcast this, but first, let's see if it's legal.'"

By September 1993 the negotiations had reached a critical stage. The union had held a two-day strike in June, so an arbitrator was called in. The arbitration was nonbinding: both sides had to agree with the recommendation before it took effect and settled the new contract. The arbitrator had recommended, among other things, a 6 percent pay increase for the teachers. The school board rejected the recommendation. Things were falling apart quickly.

On September 30 the entire tape was played on WILK as part of Williams's talk show. It continued to be played almost daily for weeks thereafter. Other radio, television, and newspaper media soon joined the fray. The tape was very damaging to the union. But it was even more devastating to Bartnicki and Kane; they were identified as the persons speaking on the tape who had "threatened to blow up front porches of school directors' houses."

"I thought it was sort of unfair," Kane later said. "[T]hat was the first thing that struck me. You know, self-concern, that type of thing. And I thought it was . . . totally taken out of context, out of the meaning of what it was supposed to be because I certainly am not a criminal. And people that know me know that. I mean, I certainly would not attempt to do such a thing." Kane had been frustrated at the board's unwillingness to follow the rules of negotiations. "I mean," he said, "they ran to the press constantly; they were doing things that were unorthodox in negotiations. They weren't following any rules at all, so we could do the same things as far as perhaps going to the press. . . . We would play rough in the negotiating game, too. We were calm up to that point, trying to get them to understand reason. We weren't, you know, having any strikes. . . . What I said, it was just a harmless thing, [hyperbole]. The experienced reporters knew what was going on." But the public understanding of the tape, Kane believed, was not so benign. "My friends, it didn't matter anything. But I don't know how it appears to other people that I don't know, strangers. [They] probably thought I was some type of gangster. . . . [But fortunately] I still have my job . . . and people that know me, even acquaintances in the community that—I'm associated with the United Way . . . —it has not affected my contacts with people like that."

"I've known Tony [Kane] for 24 years," Bartnicki would later testify. "I've heard him talk rough for 24 years and never once thought that he would hurt a fly. I do know that at that particular time—Tony didn't tell you this; Tony wouldn't tell you this—he was very upset about the possibility of a strike in Wyoming Valley West, and for a while before the strike took place, the team and I were trying to convince him that the strike had to take place. And he really hesitated at the time of the conversation. . . . When he talked like that, in my mind, I know that he had come to the conclusion that we were going to have to go ahead with the strike, and that's the only thing that I thought about when he said it."

* * *

On August 11, 1994, with the union contract finally settled by another round of arbitration, Gloria Bartnicki and Tony Kane filed a lawsuit in a Pennsylvania federal court against Fred Vopper (aka Fred Williams), WILK Radio and its corporate owners, and Jack Yocum, seeking money damages for the illegal disclosure of the tape. Federal and Pennsylvania law made it illegal to intercept electronic communications, and it also prohibited the disclosure and use of illegally intercepted communications by any other person, including a radio station or news organization, who knows or "has reason to know" the communication has been illegally intercepted. In November 1998 the

United States joined the lawsuit with Bartnicki and Kane. Vopper and the other defendants claimed that the law violated their First Amendment rights to publish the tape. The trial judge disagreed, but before the trial could begin, the defendants appealed the district court's decision; and in 1999 the United States Court of Appeals agreed with them, ruling that enforcement of the federal law's ban on WILK's disclosure of the intercepted tapes violated the First Amendment. The Court reasoned that because Yocum, Vopper, and WILK had not themselves illegally intercepted Bartnicki and Kane's conversation (though they clearly had reason to know the tape had been illegally intercepted), and because the contents of the tape—especially the threat of violence—qualified as a matter of utmost public interest, Yocum had a right to distribute the tape for publication, and the press (WILK) was free to publish it.

Beaten but not defeated, Bartnicki and Kane, joined by the United States government, asked the United States Supreme Court to accept the case for review. After reviewing the petition, the Court agreed to hear the case and scheduled oral argument for December 5, 2000. In the months leading up to oral argument, briefs would be filed by the parties, and amicus, or friend of the court, briefs would be filed by dozens of media companies, news organizations, and public interest groups such as the ACLU. All, of course, argued in support of Jack Yocum, Fred Vopper, and WILK.

* * *

The Supreme Court Justices who would preside over the oral argument were a combination of old and new. The Court was changing. It was a Court dominated by Reagan and Bush appointees, less inclined to expansive and ahistorical interpretations of the Constitution, but these judicially conservative attitudes were also leavened by a few recent Justices appointed by President Clinton. On First Amendment questions, however, the ordinary divisions between conservative and liberal don't generally hold up. Is the individual's freedom to speak a conservative, libertarian idea or a liberal one? Is the press's function of independently checking government power more consistent with a conservative philosophy or a liberal one?

The Chief Justice was William Rehnquist, appointed as an Associate Justice by President Nixon and elevated to Chief Justice in 1986 by President Ronald Reagan. Next in seniority was Justice John Paul Stevens, a moderate-to-liberal Justice appointed in 1975 by President Ford. The Reagan appointees were Justices Sandra Day O'Connor, the first woman Justice and a conservative, appointed in 1981; Antonin Scalia, a very conservative Justice known for his combative style of questioning in oral argument, appointed in 1986;

and Anthony Kennedy, a relatively moderate Justice, appointed also in 1986. Next in seniority were Justice David Souter, a moderate-to-liberal jurist appointed in 1990 by President George H. W. Bush, and Justice Clarence Thomas, a conservative jurist appointed amid great controversy by President Bush in 1991. The final two Justices were Ruth Bader Ginsburg, a former law professor and a liberal Justice, and Steven Breyer, a moderate-to-liberal Justice who had previously served as a federal judge. Both were appointed by President Clinton.

The lawyers arguing before the Court, in order of appearance, were Jeremiah Collins, an attorney in Washington, D.C., representing Bartnicki and Kane; Seth Waxman, the Solicitor General of the United States, representing the United States; Lee Levine, a lawyer in Washington, D.C., who regularly represents media clients and who represented Vopper, WILK, and its corporate owner; and Thomas Goldstein, of Washington, D.C., representing Yocum.

Before we turn to the oral argument in the Supreme Court, a few background principles and rules of First Amendment law must be understood. Constitutional law is heavily grounded in what lawyers call doctrine, which consists of the accumulated rules drawn from prior decisions. This is particularly so with the law of the First Amendment. The rules derived from prior cases tend to channel and constrain the Justices' decisions, forcing them to act consistently and limiting their discretion to simply decide a case based on their own personal predilections. With free speech, it is said, such limiting rules are essential: they allow Justices to decide difficult cases in unpopular ways, because the rules require them to do so; and the rules give both speakers and legislatures a measure of certainty or safe harbor—knowledge of what they may and may not do.

First Amendment law rests on a few elementary and fundamental rules. For purposes of our story, the First Amendment distinguishes among three basic types of regulation of speech. First are laws that regulate conduct but incidentally restrict speech. A city may have an ordinance against jaywalking, but its enforcement might fall upon a group that is demonstrating in the street. Such conduct-related laws are treated leniently under the First Amendment—they are modestly scrutinized, we might say—to ensure only that the law is really aimed at conduct and is not a pretext for regulating speech, and that the law is a reasonable method of controlling the conduct. A general law against jaywalking would survive this modest scrutiny. A law prohibiting jaywalking only during demonstrations would not, because it is really directed at speech and because it is hardly a reasonable way of restricting the conduct of jaywalking.

The second type of law is aimed expressly at speech and limits speech only on certain topics or those containing certain ideas. A law prohibiting speech that advocates the violent overthrow of the government is such a law. With this kind of law, the First Amendment guarantees the highest level of protection for speech, and the rules exact the highest level of scrutiny of the law, because the risk is that the government is censoring ideas, which should be free in a free society; targeting people who believe in "dangerous" ideas, such as communism or fundamentalism or any other forbidden "ism" of the day; or taking certain ideas off the table, prohibiting any discussion of them in the body politic. A law prohibiting speech about sex, for example, might be an attempt by government to shape public attitudes toward a fundamental human subject. This is dangerous, because in a democracy individuals, by voting and participating in other ways, must shape ideas and attitudes, not the government.

Under the First Amendment rules, laws restricting speech in this way—described in lawyer's language as regulations of speech because of its content or point of view—are presumed invalid and can be deemed constitutional *only* if the government's purpose is to prevent a grave harm, such as terrorism or lynching African Americans in the South, and if the harm cannot be avoided by any means other than regulating speech; that is, the rule that regulation of speech should not be used as a means of controlling conduct is applied with great force.

The third type of law is one that regulates speech directly but does so in a broad and indiscriminate way, not limiting its prohibitions only to some topics or points of view. One might think that such a law is worse than one that targets only one idea or topic, as it cuts a very wide swathe. But the Supreme Court has taken a different view, subjecting such laws to a scrutiny that is more exacting than that applied to regulations of conduct but less exacting than laws targeting speech based on its content (topic, point of view). The standard of review is described by lawyers as "intermediate." An example of such a law might be a noise ordinance, limiting how loudly one can speak.

The reasons for the less exacting First Amendment scrutiny are, in broad terms, twofold. First, although such laws may restrict lots of speech, they generally do not prevent a speaker from expressing his or her ideas in a different way or at a different time or place. With a noise ordinance, for example, the speaker can just turn down the volume and say whatever he or she wants to say. Thus, laws broadly restricting speech do not present the danger of censorship or of government trying to control public discussion and debate. Censorship is the principal First Amendment evil.

The second reason is, frankly, practical. Much of our conduct consists only of speech: speaking loudly, even shouting; harming people's reputation by saying false things about them; advertising a product falsely; even committing fraud, which rests on falsity and deception. In light of this, government simply *must* be able to regulate certain kinds of speech directly. If government had to prove that its interest in doing so was absolutely critical (not violent overthrow or lynching but the sale of a lemon on a used-car lot), and that there were no alternative ways of getting at the harm (such as letting the deceived consumer sue for damages after the fact), many laws that we take for granted would be unconstitutional.

Given this plain fact of life, the Supreme Court's First Amendment rules ask only whether such general (or content-neutral, in the legal terminology) laws are in fact general in application and thus do not fall disproportionately on speech about specific topics or points of view; whether they are reasonable means (not perfect, just reasonable) of achieving valid government interests (such as peace and tranquility with noise ordinances); and whether there are better and obvious ways to achieve their purposes without restricting as much speech (if so, we should suspect the government's motives). This is called intermediate scrutiny.

As might be expected, these three typologies of speech regulation make the First Amendment appear simpler than it really is. And one reason for this is the difficulty, when a specific law and a specific case arises, of figuring out exactly which type of regulation is involved. For example, how should a court view a law prohibiting destruction of a draft card when it is applied to an individual who publicly burns his card in protest of the Vietnam War? Is the law only a regulation of conduct (losing or destroying or throwing away one's draft card) that incidentally falls on speech? Or is it a regulation of speech disguised as a regulation of conduct; indeed, is it a regulation of speech expressing a specific, antiwar point of view? Should it matter if 90 percent of draft card "destruction" happened by burning them in protest? Should it matter if Congress, in enacting the law, really wanted to get at the protestors but, knowing the First Amendment law, couched this one in general terms and focused on the "conduct" of losing one's draft card?

Often, therefore, the lawyers' arguments will reflect their different views on which category of regulation a case fits into. Such arguments are essential, though they often appear sterile, not getting to the hard questions of freedom but instead dwelling on form and abstraction. But this is part of the discipline of the First Amendment, for the relevant form of regulation and the rules it carries with it serve to limit a judge's discretion. We will see much arguing about the form of the interception law in the *Bartnicki* case. At points the oral argument will seem sterile and frustrating, for dwelling too much on forms and categories has a way of diverting attention from the underlying questions of freedom, the role of the press in a democracy, and the importance of privacy.

The law at issue in the *Bartnicki* case prohibits interception of electronic communications and also prohibits distribution or publication of the contents of an illegally intercepted communication. Is this a law regulating conduct (interception) and only incidentally restricting speech (publication)? Or is it a law regulating speech (publication of electronic communications), not really one regulating conduct? If it is a regulation of speech, not conduct, is it a general one restricting publication of all intercepted conversations regardless of the topic or point of view expressed? Or is it a regulation of only certain subjects or topics, prohibiting publication only of private or secret conversations? And if the latter, should the Court apply the most speech-protective rules under the First Amendment, or is the risk of censorship or "taking subjects off the table" very low, thus justifying more relaxed scrutiny?

What about freedom of the press? Should it matter that, whatever the form of the law, speech on subjects of great public importance or interest might be prevented, even in the news—or especially in the news? Finally, what about the intercepted conversation? Is it, too, speech? Would *permitting* its publication in the newspaper or on the radio deny the conversants—in this case Gloria Bartnicki and Tony Kane—*their freedom of speech?*

* * *

Oral argument in the *Bartnicki* case began at 11:03 A.M. on Tuesday, December 5, 2000. The Chief Justice called the case.

Chief Justice Rehnquist: We'll hear argument next in Number 99-1687, Gloria Bartnicki and Anthony Kane v. Frederick Vopper. Mr. Collins.

Mr. Collins: Mr. Chief Justice and may it please the Court: In a society that values personal freedom and autonomy, there is a vital interest in securing the ability of individuals to exclude unwanted intruders from their private activities. And where the private activity consists of speech there is a particularly vital interest in preventing intrusion so that individuals may conduct their private communications freely and securely. And for that reason, Congress and the legislatures of virtually every state in this country have made it unlawful to gain access to a private communication.

Collins is attempting in this opening statement to characterize the law as a regulation of conduct that only incidentally restricts some speech. It is a regulation of the interception of a message and the sale or use of that message, just like, perhaps, a law against theft and sale of stolen property. At least that's what he wants the Justices to conclude.

Question: Well . . . presumably the state can prevent unlawful tapping of wires directly and get at the bad actor, but why should it extend to the subsequent user who didn't do anything wrong?

Mr. Collins: Because, Your Honor, as Congress and some forty states have reasoned, if there is intrusion into an individual's private communications, a tap, a bug, a scanner, whatever, and then what is obtained is broadcast to all the world . . . , the same interests that are harmed by the initial intrusion are harmed again and all the more severely because in essence, you have invited in this instance a hundred thousand people to eavesdrop. Petitioner Bartnicki stated in her deposition that when she, having no idea that anyone had intruded into her communication with Mr. Kane, heard it being broadcast on the radio, she felt that she had been violated in front of a hundred thousand people. If I, riding home today, hear a radio station broadcasting a conversation where I convey my grocery list to my wife or vice versa, I feel a violation of my person autonomy. Just as if someone—

Question: But you want to say that if I also hear that, and [then] tell my wife, that I'm committing a crime. That's what this statute says. Now maybe there'll be some creative suggestion for when it's in the public domain or something like that. But that's not what the statute says.

Question: I suppose it's very difficult, is it not, to enforce the prohibition against wire tapping against the person who actually—who actually does the tapping. In other words, that person is usually not going to come to light or publicize the thing. The way that person does the work and pushes it on to somebody else who will do the disclosure.

Mr. Collins: That's what happened in this case.

Question: An anonymous tape was sent to the radio station which is almost always the way it will happen?

Mr. Collins: Congress was told in both 1968 and '86 that it happens very frequently. I think—

Question: Well, let's change the facts just a little bit. Suppose what the conversation revealed was not some conversation about we're going to have to commit some violent acts. Let's suppose it revealed that in fact, a murder had been committed because of this very situation. And the anonymous tape then is passed on to the police and you're going to punish the person who passed on that tape when a very serious crime has been committed. Now how is the public interest served by that?

Mr. Collins: Your Honor, I believe—

Question: I actually had that very situation as a trial court judge in a murder case. I had a hard time understanding how the public interest was served by punishing the person who passed on the information.

Mr. Collins: I think there are two responses to the question, Your Honor. The first is [that] there is in the law, as the Government's reply brief points out, a doctrine of necessity which in some narrow circumstances, and it's not precisely clear how far it extends, in essence privileges what would otherwise be a violation of a statute—if the statute doesn't rule that defense out. So an action to protect life and limb may be an exception.

The second answer though, is that . . . there are important governmental interests harmed not only by the interception but by the disclosure. If those are then taken into account through a content-neutral statutory regime . . . , that [fact] in essence exhausts the First Amendment concerns. . . . I think it's essential to emphasize when I say content-neutral that this law is neutral in a way that absolutely requires a determination of content neutrality. It's neutral as to viewpoint. It's neutral as to subject matter. It doesn't allow liability to turn on disagreement with a particular message. It doesn't even target speech specifically. It targets all uses of what has been unlawfully intercepted [such as extortion], so there is no case in this Court that would characterize this law as content-based.

Question: Well, would there be a difference if the person you're talking about is the person who made the wrongful taping as opposed to the person who just passes it on?

Mr. Collins: Well, certainly, the question in this case is properly presented as to whether the statute can apply to those who are not involved in the interception.

Question: Well would it matter if it's a newspaper commenting on the information that's [already] been disclosed? Does that alter the result?

Mr. Collins: We submit that it does not for two reasons. First of all, we are applying a general statute based on important government interests, and secondly—and I do think this is critical—we then have to ask ourselves is this one of the very rare cases in this Court's jurisprudence where one would say that even though a statute is totally neutral, doesn't lend itself to Government thought control, to suppression of ideas in any way, it's not reshaping public debate, does it in some way restrict too much speech? And one area where one would worry is, does it prevent the press from doing what it needs to do? We believe this is not . . . one of those rare situations—

Question: Although this had to do with negotiations, did it not, with a public school board in a labor union context? You don't think that's sufficiently important to warrant newspaper discussion of it?

Mr. Collins: We don't deny that matters of public concern are involved. What we say is that [in] *Branzburg v. Hayes,*[3] the Court said that we know the press could get important information of public concern through wire tapping, we know the press could get important information of public concern by having a system of private informants, but we say to the press, you cannot do that. Even if you know that behind that wall is someone communicating matter of utmost public importance, you can't pierce that wall. So why then is it crucial to the press to say we can't ourselves go out and try to obtain this information of public concern through wire tapping, but if serendipitously some third person has done it, it's vital us to be able to then use the information?

Question: Well, the difference is that in one case they're acting unlawfully and in the other case they have information that they just came across because someone else acted unlawfully, and that'd be a big difference.

Mr. Collins: I think in the final analysis, no, Your Honor, because the question here is whether there are sufficient Government interests to justify [an across-the-board] application of these laws in this manner. It's not a question of is the press a bad actor or not to be punished. One has to be concerned, undoubtedly, [with whether] the press, by the rule that we advocate, [will] be chilled from performing its function. We argue "no." I don't think that the proper analysis of the issues here can ultimately turn simply on [whether or not] the press violated a law when they received the information; otherwise, of course, Congress could take a jab with the pen and say, oh, and also it's illegal to be receive any [material] that has been intercepted [thus making the press' action of receiving the tape, itself, illegal, like the crime of receiving stolen goods].

Question: Mr. Collins, may I ask you if I understand your First Amendment theory correctly? In the *Pentagon Papers* case [the executive branch tried to enjoin the *New York Times* from publishing information about the Vietnam conflict that was deemed harmful to national security. We held that the *Times* couldn't be enjoined in advance of publication. Is it your position, however, that] if Congress so provided, the *Times* or anybody else who published the materials could, *after* the publication, be held responsible in money damages?

Mr. Collins: Possibly, Your Honor, but the *Pentagon Papers* [case is] different because it was the Government itself determining what information by subject matter—

Question: A general statute.

---

3. *Branzburg* was an earlier decision in which the Court said that the First Amendment doesn't protect a reporter from the general obligation to testify about a story before a grand jury.

Mr. Collins: Well if it applied to—But it wouldn't be general because it's by definition talking only about Government information, which is arguably [based on the specific] content [of the material, unlike this case].

Question: Yes.

Mr. Collins: And there you do get into of the risk of shaping debate.

Question: Thank you, Mr. Collins.

Collins has presented a clear and coherent argument, even amid the buffeting from the Justices' questions. The law, he claims, is a regulation of conduct (intercepting communications), and although it surely falls on speech (the intercepted communications as well as their publication), it does not exclusively fall on speech and the speech it affects is not distinguished in terms of its topic or point of view. Therefore, the mildest form of First Amendment scrutiny is called for, and the law, being clearly a reasonable response to the privacy concerns Congress had, is constitutional. And even if the law is viewed as one that is focused on speech, not conduct, it applies across-the-board to all speech and therefore is not subject to the highest level of First Amendment scrutiny.

Collins then outlines the two basic rationales for enforcing the law against a person who did not do the intercepting but who, like Yocum, just found it in his mailbox. First, by prohibiting publication or distribution of intercepted phone tapes, persons otherwise inclined to intercept conversations are deprived of any incentive to do so, for no one will publish—or buy—material that is illegally obtained. The market for the intercepted material will have dried up. It's perhaps similar to outlawing possession and use of drugs to stop the production of drugs. There are big problems with this rationale, as we will soon see, but it is central to Collins's and the government's cases.

The second rationale is that prohibiting all publications of intercepted material, even by innocent parties acting for the best of reasons, is necessary to secure the right to privacy and the expectations of privacy that the statute grants users of electronic communications devices such as cell phones. Any uncomfortable applications of the prohibition on publication—such as the murder hypothetical, for example—must either fall under a common-law defense of necessity (something like a rescue argument) or, if not, be swallowed as a bitter but needed pill, a price that must be paid to guarantee privacy.

The final important point Collins made toward the end of his argument was subtle and may have been missed by most listeners in the courtroom. In response to a few Justices' concerns about punishing an innocent bystander, such as Vopper or Yocum, Collins observed that Congress *intended* to punish them if they knew the tape was illegally obtained and used it nonetheless. If the Court were to invalidate the law out of concern for innocent publishers, Congress could in a quick stroke simply enact a new provision in the law making the *knowing receipt and possession* (not publication) of illegally intercepted communications a crime, much like drug possession (or destroying a draft card) is a crime. Such a law would sweep away most First Amendment concerns, for it would clearly be a regulation of conduct alone. If Congress could do that, and if Congress's law can best be read as already having done that, the Justices should not dwell on the innocent possessor or publisher.

Collins has laid a sound foundation for the Solicitor General, who follows him to argue in support of the federal law.

Chief Justice Rehnquist: General Waxman, we will hear from you.

General Waxman: Mr. Chief Justice and may it please the Court. I do want to address the *Pentagon Papers* point and the point that Justice Kennedy made about [a person sharing] information obtained on the radio with his own wife, and Justice O'Connor's question about what difference does it make how [the publisher] got it. I first want to make the point that there is an important burden on First Amendment rights here, but we submit that the appropriate level of scrutiny is intermediate-level scrutiny because this is a totally content-neutral law of general applicability that protects fundamental values of privacy and private speech and denies third parties nothing that they otherwise would have had if the act's prohibition on interception itself was fully effective—

Question: General, isn't the problem with the easy analogy to other across-the-board regulations of speech, that here there in effect is a complete suppression of speech, whereas in the paradigmatic intermediate-scrutiny cases, somebody can speak somewhere, sometime. [The draft card burner] can tell what he thinks about the draft without burning his card. That's not so here.

General Waxman: Well, I think that is so here, and I also think that that is not an accurate characterization of all the cases. I mean, it was not true, for example, in *Cohen v. Cowles Media* [in which a newspaper was held liable for breaching a promise of confidentiality to a source], or in *Zacchini* [in which, it will be recalled from story 4, the TV station could be held liable for airing the fifteen-second film of Zacchini emerging from the cannon].

Question: But you also had a very different kind of general statute in *Cohen*—

General Waxman: That's exactly right and that's—

Question: In contract law and not speech law.

The point being raised here reveals the ambiguity of the distinctions among the three types of law discussed earlier. Is the *Cohen* case, which enforced a publisher's agreement not to publish a source's identity, merely an application of general contract law, which mainly regulates conduct and only incidentally falls on speech? Or is it a regulation of speech that falls indiscriminately on all topics and points of view and thus is subject to a higher (intermediate) level of scrutiny by the Court? Is it, in other words, an across-the-board regulation of contracts not to publish?

The *Zacchini* case illustrates the ambiguity in another way. Recall that the question in *Zacchini* was whether the airing of Hugo Zacchini's act on the TV news was a theft of his property, a performance in which he had invested his time and talent and which he sold to people attending the fair. Was the law prohibiting the taking of his property by anyone else a regulation of conduct, the equivalent of a law prohibiting trespass on private property? Or was the law instead a regulation of speech in the sense that the particular property right being enforced, control of the performance, was itself expressive, and Zacchini's right was focused on the particular subject of his act?

General Waxman: Right. And that's why—that's why we think that unlike *Cohen v. Cowles Media* where the Court applied no heightened First Amendment scrutiny, we think that heightened scrutiny is appropriate here, because there is a restraint on speech. But it is not a restraint on any topic, any viewpoint, any speaker. Anybody who [by means other than a tape recording] gets wire-tapped information or information from a bug planted in my home or my conference room, the identical information is fully available for speech or other uses. In other words, what's missing here—

Question: Well, it may be, it may not be, depending on other circumstances, but . . . it's still true that when you do the balancing, whether you call it intermediate scrutiny or you figure out some other level to put it on—what you've got to balance is that if this law is good, then the disclosure, which apparently has no other source of information, which is of concern to the public, is absolutely forbidden, and we've got to accept that as one of the prices that will be paid. Maybe as you say not in every case but it will be paid if the statute is going to be enforced across the board.

General Waxman: That is absolutely true and that is why heightened [but not the highest] scrutiny applies. It is our submission that it's significant that if the same information comes from any other source, it can be used or disseminated with impunity, which is another way, I think, of [saying] that there is no suggestion here, unlike the *Pentagon Papers* case, of a censorial motive by the Government, or an effort to take certain facts off the table—

Question: Yeah, yeah, but—to say, as your colleague did, [that] it's very rare to strike down statutes that are content-neutral, that's not accurate. What you're doing here is you're suppressing speech that is valuable to the public.

General Waxman: Justice Kennedy, I'm not suggesting that we win because intermediate-level scrutiny applies [requiring, it will be recalled, only that the law be a reasonable way to accomplish a valid, but not critical or essential, government interest]. My point here is—and this goes to the distinction with the *Pentagon Papers* case and . . . to Justice O'Connor's initial question about why we should care how the information came to be—is that the knowing use of illegally intercepted private expression implicates other constitutional values. In the *Pentagon Papers* case, this Court said that we're talking about information that was not unlawfully obtained, but instead was disclosed [leaked by a government employee] to the public as a result of a failure of a trust relationship. There are almost always less drastic means of resolving [that kind of] problem, both because you can be more careful about who you trust [with the information], and secondly, there is a much smaller universe of potential violators. Here we're talking about an interception which almost by definition is impossible of detection. People don't even know that their conversations at home or at work are being overheard, let alone who did it, and this case is a perfect—

Question: No one questions . . . that you can punish the interceptor. But what you're doing is you're taking a *class* of speech and saying this is now tainted speech and it can't be repeated by *anybody.* And there is simply no precedent for that in the cases of this Court.

The point being made by the Justice—the questioner is Justice Kennedy—is related to the very rationale for the three types of speech regulation and the differing levels of scrutiny. The First Amendment, it will be recalled, treats speech restrictions based on point of view or topic as more dangerous than restrictions that are general, or across-the-board, in character. Justice Kennedy is asking, in effect, whether that is a sound rule. Why should it be better for government to prohibit a large class of speech (even though doing so neutrally) than for the government to restrict a smaller universe of speech on a topic or expressing a despised viewpoint? The former regulation of a class of speech restricts much more speech but does not censor; the latter prohibition of speech about a topic or expressing an idea or viewpoint restricts very little speech but censors ideas in the process.

As to Justice Kennedy's assertion that no precedent exists in the Court's decisions for saying that a class of speech can be legally prohibited, there is ample reason to disagree. In *Zacchini,* the class of speech consisting of entire performances was "taken off the speech table." And the *Zacchini* rule applies not just to the human cannonball act but also to Dr. Martin Luther King Jr.'s "I Have a Dream" speech, which can't be broadcast without the family's permission. Libel law punishes anyone who knowingly or recklessly says something false and defamatory about someone else. "Reckless defamatory falsehoods" comprise a class of speech that looks pretty similar to "private electronic communications." Both classes are defined by the content of the speech and the fact of harm to personal interests.

But although Justice Kennedy may have overstated his argument a bit, his basic question about the reason behind a preference for broader, rather than narrower, speech restrictions is a good and fundamental one.

General Waxman: Well, I don't think—I do understand your point Justice Kennedy, [but] I would quarrel with your characterization of this as tainted speech that you can't do anything about. [The law] simply says that if you know that this is the result of an illegal intrusion into a zone of conversational privacy, you cannot use it until it becomes publicly known. And I'm not sure that it is fair to say that there is no precedent for taking speech like this off the table. I think we have talked about *Cohen* and *Zacchini,* but there is also the San Francisco arts case [in which the Court upheld a law restricting] use of the word "Olympic." There is trade secret law. There are grand jury secrecy rules, and rules about what employers and employees may or may not say.

Question: Mr. Solicitor General, the strongest argument is that you want to dry up the market for this sort of thing. [But] there's really no evidence that this will accomplish that goal. And I would kind of like you to comment on that because it does seem to me that an awful lot of this illegal [interception] activity will continue to go on by people who just use it for their own private illicit purposes, whether you apply this particular rule [to radio stations and newspapers or not]. And I think the scarcity of cases suggest that enforcing this rule really would not do very much to dry up the market, but maybe you'd comment on that.

The Justice's question is steering Waxman to a related but distinct argument the United States had made in support of the law, and specifically in support of its ban on publication of intercepted material by anyone, whether they did the intercepting or, as in the *Bartnicki* case, whether the material was anonymously placed in a mailbox. The argument is that without a prohibition on publication of the intercepted material, the prohibition on interception will be ineffective, because interceptors will still have an incentive to risk illegal behavior. This is essentially an economic market argument. It's like the argument that without a prohibition on sale and consumption of illegal drugs, a prohibition on manufacture and importation would be ineffective. The argument with the law in *Bartnicki* rests, however, on two disputable assumptions. The first is that most interceptions are conducted in order that the conversations can be published or sold for publication. If this is not the case, the ban on publication would be ineffective in stopping most interceptions. It would be like prohibiting use of drugs by teenagers in order to discourage drug use by everyone. Such a law would qualify under the First Amendment as unreasonable.

The second assumption is that by prohibiting dissemination of the intercepted material by the illegal interceptor, the market for the material would dry up and interceptors would be left holding the bag. But what if the market is like the drug market, which seems to operate on the rule that the higher the penalties on distribution of drugs, the higher the price a distributor can exact, and thus the higher the incentives for people to distribute more?

It is to these questions that the Justice is moving Waxman's argument. But before returning to the argument, one additional point needs to be made here, as it will creep into the argument in snippets and needs to be detected. There are actually two quite distinct justifications for the prohibition on publication of the intercepted tapes. The first is the "dry-up-the-market" theory outlined above. The second is the freestanding argument that a prohibition of all publication of the tapes is necessary to preserve the privacy expectations of those whose conversations or messages are being intercepted. If, like the *Zacchini* case, the law in *Bartnicki* is viewed as giving everyone using a cell phone a propertylike interest in the confidentiality of their conversation, then the only way to preserve that property interest is to prohibit distribution and publication of the conversation by the interceptor. This is precisely what the Court decided in the *Zacchini* case.

Would a law protecting such a privacy/property interest be neutral as to content and point of view and thus be a regulation of speech subject only to a form of reasonableness scrutiny by the Court? Or would it be a speech restriction based on content or topic—private conversations, for example, or secrets—and thus be subject to exacting scrutiny, valid only if there were absolutely no alternative ways of protecting the privacy/property interest? If so, might such a law satisfy that exacting scrutiny because without an across-the-board prohibition, people's right to have confidence in the privacy of their conversations would be fatally compromised?

Finally, does this justification require that the privacy interest be seen as a propertylike interest, as in *Zacchini*? If so, why can some interests be construed as property, and some not? Can that distinction turn on whether the expression—human cannonball act or private phone conversation—has market value and can be bought and sold? Would such a conclusion turn the First Amendment on its head, exalting speech with commercial value intended for a commercial marketplace above speech with no commercial value, such as a discussion of one's religious beliefs, one's political preferences, or even one's feelings of frustration about ongoing collective bargaining negotiations?

As the oral argument unfolds, we will see references to this alternative privacy or propertylike justification and the problems it raises. But the references will in the end be fleeting, indeed disappointing. It won't be until the Supreme Court writes its opinion in the *Bartnicki* case that the argument will emerge and have to be addressed, and even then we may find the Court's answer to it deeply unsatisfying. For now, however, the argument is turning to the market incentive theory, which some of the Justices dub the dry-up-the-market theory.

General Waxman: Well, I think that that's wrong. If you look at the cases [actually brought], a very large number of those cases involved use—at least if you take out the marital cases—involved use by third persons, and [support] the deterrence or disincentive point which is one of the three points that we make to [emphasize] the importance of the use and disclosure provisions as a means of protecting conversational privacy. The common sense point is that if you prohibit all means of exploiting stolen information, whether they are expressive means or not, you will materially lessen the incentive for many people to engage in the interception. Now, it's true there will be people who as a hobby just like to eavesdrop or intercept other people's conversations and the use—

Question: General Waxman, what about this case? This [intercepted phone conversation] was broadcast over a radio station in Wilkes-Barre, as I understand it. Now supposing the Wilkes-Barre newspaper wants to do a story about the fact that this was broadcast, how far down the line does [the law's prohibition on publication] go?

General Waxman: Well, we think that both the meaning of the word "disclose," which is in the statute, and the legislative history, demonstrate that the statute no longer applies once [the intercepted material becomes] public information or common knowledge. And we also think—we also think that—well, that's our answer with respect to how far it goes—

Question: I can't tell my next door neighbor?

General Waxman: Excuse me?

Question: If I innocently hear this tape, and I'm the second one to hear it,
but I just hear it at Yocum's house, then I can't tell my neighbor?

General Waxman: That's the—the statute precludes that use of it. It's not addressed in this case, but the statute precludes all use of it. Now if there was—

Question: I wouldn't think of doing that, of course. If somebody sent me a
tape that I knew had been illegally taken, I certainly wouldn't run around
talking to people about it. That doesn't seem to be so outrageous.

General Waxman: Well I—there has never been such a case—

Question: And Justice Kennedy lives in my neighborhood, too.

General Waxman: —a reported case in which there was either a prosecution
or a civil suit brought [against a purely private disclosure]. And of course
the plaintiffs in this case did not sue the school board members who were
told about it. But the point, it seems to me, is that what Congress was trying to protect here was the sanctity of what we all know to be critical to
our society, which is the ability to speak in an uninhibited candid fashion.
May I reserve the balance of my time?

Chief Justice: You may.

Waxman saves a few minutes following the arguments by the other side,
just in case anything needing clarification comes up during their argument.
For now he returns to counsel's table. The arguments that he and Collins have
made were on the whole general and theoretical, focused on the Supreme
Court's tests and rules developed in earlier cases, not really addressing the
facts of Bartnicki and Kane's case or, more basically, the justifications for
application of one test or another. Justice Kennedy tried to pry beneath the
smooth surface of the tests and rules, but he got no satisfaction, as Waxman
chose not to address his important question but instead to respond mechan-
ically in terms of the settled, but clearly ambiguous, doctrine.

It was now the other side's turn to present their theory of the case and
answer the Justices' questions. Yocum's lawyer had to explain why Yocum's
decision to give the tape to WILK should be exempt from the ban on distribution, and WILK's lawyer had to explain why, and when, the press should
be freed by the First Amendment from liability for publishing the tape. If the
arguments and questions had to this point been pretty abstract and theoretical, the Court's interest in the second half of the argument would become
downright specific.

The Chief Justice now called Lee Levine to the podium. Levine was representing Vopper (aka Williams), WILK, and its parent companies.

Mr. Levine: Mr. Chief Justice, and may it please the Court: Respondents are
before the Court this morning because they disseminated to the public the

contents of a telephone conversation in which the president of a public teacher's union apparently threatened to blow off the front porches of the homes of members of the local school board. Petitioners contend that such an act of pure speech is not protected by the First Amendment because that information was at some prior time unlawfully acquired by someone else.

Question: Well, I think—I think that the other side would have acknowledged that if it was indeed a clear threat to blow off somebody's porches, there might have been an exception to the statute. I don't want to decide this case on the assumption that this was a threat to blow off somebody's porch. It's at least ambiguous in the record and if all you want is a decision that you can disseminate it if it's a threat to blow off somebody's porch, I'll give you that, that's an easy case. But you want us to go beyond that and you want us to say even if it wasn't a threat to blow off somebody's porch, it can be disseminated; isn't that correct?

Mr. Levine: So long as—

Question: Okay. So let's forget about blowing up the porch.

Mr. Levine: Your Honor, I—

Question: Well, I think your argument is that blowing off—the willingness to blow off porches is a matter of some public concern in viewing the labor crisis.

Mr. Levine: That is correct, Your Honor, and that is why I gave the context to explain why this speech that was disseminated by the respondents here was truthful and involved a matter of public concern.

Question: Now, I don't understand there to be any exception in the statute for speech that threatens to blow off somebody's porch.

Mr. Levine: That is correct, Justice Stevens. On its face, the statute applies to any information concerning the content of an intercepted communication. And content is defined in the statute as any information concerning the substance, purport or meaning of that communication.

Question: And you would be content for a holding that says that a statute that does not contain such an exception is unconstitutional; is that what you're asking us for?

Mr. Levine: I'm asking Your Honors to apply the principle.

Question: You want us to decide this case on the basis that this statute does not have any exception for threatened criminal action?

Mr. Levine: No, Your Honor.

Question: I didn't think so.

Mr. Levine: The except—what it doesn't have an exception for, Your Honor, is the dissemination of truthful speech about a matter of public concern.

Question: You really don't care whether you win or not, you just want to win on the right grounds, is that what you want?

Mr. Levine: Your Honor, I'll take it any way I can get it.

Question: I'm sure.

Question: Well then stop giving out your case.

Mr. Levine: But the principle that we're advocating derives from this Court's cases: where, as here, a speaker has lawfully acquired the information he disseminates and that information is accurate and involves a matter of public concern, his speech is protected by the First Amendment, absent a demonstrated need to vindicate an interest of the highest order.

Question: Why isn't my ability to speak over the phone with some assurance of confidentiality an interest of the highest order? I mean you have speech involved on both sides of this, bear in mind. To the extent the position you urge renders the enforcement of the criminal prohibition against intercepting my telephone conversations less effective, it inhibits *my* speech. And indeed it does. I mean I don't use my home—what is it—wire free phone—

Mr. Levine: Cordless.

Question: —whenever I talk about anything involving the Court, because, you know, I don't know, I don't know who is picking it up. And you're saying it's perfectly okay for somebody not only to pick it up but to publish it in the *Washington Post* so long as, you know, so long as they didn't actually do the tap, just made a tape and mailed it to the *Post*?

Mr. Levine: Your Honor, let me make clear it is not perfectly okay to pick it up. That is prohibited by the statute.

Question: No, it is perfectly okay to give the person who picked it up exactly what that person wanted, that is, dissemination of my private conversations. I—you enable the criminal to achieve the object of his criminality.

Mr. Levine: And Your Honor, if there was any act of collaboration between the criminal and the fence, as [Yocum, Vopper, and WILK have] been called in some amicus briefs, then that person may be held liable for his own conduct.

Question: There is no collaboration but this is an essential instrument for the criminal's achieving what he wanted to achieve. And that is to disseminate to the world information which he has unlawfully obtained. It doesn't seem to me unreasonable for the Government to say "No, we're not going to let the criminal get the advantage of his criminality." We do the same thing where the highest function of Government of all is involved, the criminal law. We prevent information from being introduced, even told to the jury when it has been obtained illegally. I find it—

Mr. Levine: Justice Scalia, I'm not suggesting that it's unreasonable, but that's not the standard when you're talking about prohibition on the dissemination of truthful speech about a matter of public concern.

Question: Well, Mr. Levine, you agree that there is an exception for matters of the highest priority. How about our decisions which [have] involved, you know, protected speech on one hand but said nonetheless the government could permit a strong interest in privacy to triumph.

The kinds of cases to which Justice Scalia is referring include, for example, ones upholding bans on door-to-door peddling of products or goods or pamphlets because the laws apply generally to all speech and protect the homeowner's interest in privacy. These are most often viewed as regulations of conduct, not speech, as they are aimed at the time, place, and manner of speech. But can they be so easily distinguished from the law in *Bartnicki,* which regulates the place and manner of intruding on private communications?

Mr. Levine: Your Honor, [those cases] were time, place or manner restrictions, and the Court, because of that, properly sustained the laws. This statute, unlike the ones at issue [in those] cases, is a direct prohibition of speech itself. It is not a time, place or manner restriction. It is not a regulation of conduct that has—

Question: Well, it may nonetheless deserve intermediate scrutiny because of its content neutrality.

Mr. Levine: Your Honor, I don't believe that content neutrality is a factor when you're talking about a law that prohibits publication of matters of public concern.

Levine's argument effectively transcends the various categories or types of speech regulation. He is making the broader argument that whatever category of speech is involved, whatever test would otherwise apply, *any* law that prohibits the publication of matters of public concern by an innocent party (the newspaper, which did not illegally intercept the phone conversation) is subject to the most exacting level of First Amendment scrutiny. Notably, this is an argument that, if successful, would not only defeat the government's dry-up-the-market rationale but would also defeat the argument that an individual's interest in privacy separately justifies a flat prohibition on distribution and publication of the intercepted conversation. It is an argument, however, that was not accepted by the Court in the *Zacchini* case. Was that because the film of Zacchini flying through the air was not a matter of public concern? It certainly was a matter of public interest. What about Dr. King's "I Have a Dream" speech? Are the two concepts—public concern and public interest—distinct? How are they? And most importantly, who decides?

These questions are, in the end, the heart of the *Bartnicki* case, but the Court and the lawyers seem consciously to avoid them or gloss them over, as we will see. Is this because the questions are simply too hard to answer?

Mr. Levine: And in that regard, let me get to a point that both Justice Scalia and the Chief Justice made earlier. This notion of the laundering rationale [the dry-up-the-market theory], we submit, is not persuasive when you're talking as we are here about matters of public concern. In the Internet age, an interceptor doesn't need the press to anonymously disseminate information to a mass audience. Even if he did, there is no evidence that that provides that person with an incentive to intercept in the first place, especially where, as in this case, money does not drive the market hypothesized by the petitioner. There may well be the occasional case in which an anonymous interceptor gratuitously throws the contents of an intercepted communication over the transom, but there is no evidence that this is a systemic problem or that—

Question: Well, something like that happened here, didn't it? I mean there is an anonymous interceptor who gave it to a radio station.

Levine: But Your Honor, there is no evidence that the identity of the interceptor in this case could not have been uncovered.

Question: Well, I presume that the Government ought to have some presumption. They are saying that it's very—they enforce these laws. They are just saying it's just very difficult to find this person, the initial interceptor.

Mr. Levine: Your Honor, that is, with all due respect to the Government, purely conjecture. There is nothing in the legislative history to support that. The scores of prosecutions under the [law's] interception prohibition suggest that that's not true.

Question: Well, shouldn't the Government at least have a chance to—I mean, the Government here was cut off. There hasn't been any trial. If the question is, is it really difficult to get after interceptors, shouldn't the Government have had a chance to show that indeed it is?

Mr. Levine: Your Honor, in light of the ample evidence that is contained in the record and available to the Court, that [is not the case,] at least when you're talking about matters of public concern as you are here, where money doesn't drive the market for the interception. I think [the evidence in this case] warrants a conclusion that the Government doesn't need to be able to do that. There are so many less restrictive alternatives to prohibiting the dissemination of information, like meaningful criminal penalties against the interception itself. In this case, your Honors, the maximum criminal penalty that could be applied against the interceptor of this communication was a nominal fine with no possibility of incarceration. In another one of the cases that is pending before this Court, the interceptor of that conversation was fined $500.

Question: In—in—suppose that a stranger goes into your house, trespassing, puts his ear to the bedroom door and hears your private conversation or goes in and steals your diary and turns it over to a newspaper, [which] knowing all this, publishes it. Is it constitutional not to forbid the publication, but to collect damages from the newspaper?

Mr. Levine: Your Honor, if the information did not involve a matter of public concern—

Question: No. No. It does.

Mr. Levine: If it involves a matter of public concern—

Question: Yes.

Mr. Levine: —and there is no unlawful conduct of any kind by the person who publishes the information—

Question: All right. So you're saying that its unconstitutional to prohibit trespassers from coming into your house, steal your diaries, and listen to your most private conversations and then publish them in mass circulation dailies and you can't get damages from that as long as the newspaper itself didn't do the trespass, just knew all about it?

Mr. Levine: Your Honor, I think I misunderstood your question. The person who broke into your house and listened in—

Question: Is not a—is not a reporter.

Mr. Levine: Right.

Question: It's just someone—it's a stranger.

Mr. Levine: That person can be prosecuted.

Question: No, I'm asking if you can get damages from the newspaper and I think your answer straightforwardly is no.

Mr. Levine: That's correct, Your Honor. That's correct, Your Honor.

Question: Then I don't see how you're going to have privacy left. I mean, what kind of privacy is there if people can break into your house, steal all your information, [and the information] can be published in the newspaper that knows it and you can't get any damages from the newspaper?

The questions are now turning to the privacy, or privacy as property, argument, and away from the sloppiness of the law's dry-up-the-market justification. Levine would prefer to stay with the sloppiness argument and avoid probing questions about his broader argument, which is that government may never try to protect privacy by prohibiting publication of the private information to the world unless it exempts from that prohibition the press's (and perhaps anyone's) publication of material that is of public moment, value, interest, or significance. Levine wants to avoid that argument, perhaps, because it runs straight into copyright protection, trade secrets, Hugo Zacchini's act, and Martin Luther King's speech. Public interest doesn't grant newspapers a First Amendment right to publish in those cases. But perhaps it should.

Mr. Levine: Your Honor—

Question: It goes with trade secrets, copyrighted books and your most private information.

Mr. Levine: Your Honor, you can go after the person who intercepted.

Question: Yeah, but we don't know who that person is, you know. He takes his money and runs, all right? So the only effective redress is to stop the entire United States from knowing your most secret information or your trade secrets or your copyrighted book which was obtained with the newspaper's full knowledge through trespass, breaking and entering, any kind of stealing you want. Is that not your position?

Mr. Levine: Justice Breyer—

Question: If I disagree with that you lose—

Mr. Levine: Justice Breyer, if I understand your latest iteration of the hypothetical, you included a payment in there. If the newspaper paid for the information, that's a much closer question.

Question: No. No. I'll take it out then.

Mr. Levine: Your Honors, in the last analysis, this statute simply prohibits too much speech. In this case it prohibits Mr. Yocum from notifying members of the school board that they might be in danger. The statute also prohibits the media respondents from sharing—

Question: If the rationale of the statute is to dry up the market, it doesn't prohibit too much speech, it prohibits precisely the amount of speech that is the product of what the statute is aimed at.

Mr. Levine: But if you focus on the speech itself, Justice Stevens, and it is truthful and it involves a matter of public concern, that speech has value. That's what the [First Amendment] is all about.

Question: No, but you're arguing about the quantity. The quantity is precisely tailored to the underlying criminal conduct. It's the fruits of that, just like the fruits of an illegal search, to take Justice Scalia's example.

Mr. Levine: Not when—not when the Congress was focused on other kinds of interceptions and disclosures involving things like industrial espionage, insider trading, contested divorce. Congress did not focus on things like speech involving matters of public concern. There is nothing in the legislative history to suggest that Congress thought that that was the problem that it was trying deal with.

Question: No, the problem is illegal intercepts. And it covers the product of every illegal intercept. It exactly fits, in terms of quantity, if you're just talking about quantity, the quantity is exactly the full market for this illegal activity.

Mr. Levine: I think it's fairest to say that I'm talking about quantity and quality. Quality in the sense that the information involving truthful speech about matters of public concern is at the core of the First Amendment and that's what this statute prohibits in addition to whatever it may legitimately prohibit involving speech that doesn't involve a matter of public concern.

Question: Well, given that, then why is it worse? Why is it worse to receive a stolen diary than to steal the diary yourself? Why is it worse to receive with knowledge, the stolen diary [than to intercept a phone call and publish it]? Do you see my point?

Mr. Levine: I see your point and this may be a fine distinction in response, but I think it's an important one, Justice Breyer. The physical diary is property. Taking that, regardless of what's inside it, is not the function of the First Amendment to speak to. If you're talking about the contents of the diary, the information, and you're then penalizing someone for now knowing that information, having it in his brain and then disseminating it to other people, that is something that the First Amendment is concerned about, especially when you're talking about speech that is the truth and is a matter of public concern.

Levine is trying to distinguish physical things, which can be called property and heavily regulated notwithstanding the First Amendment, from intangible things, which cannot. But the distinction doesn't really work. Is Zacchini's act a "physical" thing? Is the broadcast of Dr. King's speech a "physical" thing? What about e-mail or Internet communication? In the *Bartnicki* case, what was published was a tape of a conversation, which is no less physical than a tape of Zacchini's act or of Dr. King's speech.

Question: I guess the case points up that chattel analogies are difficult in a modern age of digitized speech, et cetera. I mean you don't have an airline ticket anymore. It's just out there in a computer.

Mr. Levine: That's right.

Question: And what the Government is trying to do is to recognize that in this statute.

Mr. Levine: That's correct.
The Chief Justice: Thank you, Mr. Levine.

Levine has accomplished two things in his argument. He directly challenged the dry-up-the-market theory propounded by the government. More importantly, he introduced a new and simple, but compelling, argument, one that swept all of the dickering about privacy and incentives aside: when material, whatever form, is of public significance, individuals and the press have a First Amendment right to publish it, no matter what. The Supreme Court's previous decisions had never adopted such an absolute and far-reaching rule. But the Supreme Court is in the law-making business, especially when it comes to the Constitution and, in particular, the First Amendment's guarantees of individual liberty.

Taken to its logical conclusion, Levine's theory would upset a lot of settled expectations. "Public significance" exceptions to prohibitions on publication would have to be grafted onto the copyright laws, onto trademark protection, and even onto the publication of diaries. Levine had been spared tough questions on these implications. Thomas Goldstein would not be so lucky.

The Chief Justice: Mr. Goldstein, we'll hear from you.
Mr. Goldstein: Mr. Chief Justice and may it please the Court. Even if the petitioners are correct that the act's prohibition [on publication] hits the second, third, fourth person to receive it, even if that wide prohibition adds some deterrent, the prohibition is too crude a weapon—effectively a thermonuclear bomb of sorts—to be sustained in the sensitive area not of property but of free speech. It therefore should be invalidated.
Question: Well, you then presumably have other ideas as to how the Government might get at this problem, less drastic, perhaps? What are they?
Mr. Goldstein: Mr. Chief Justice, we believe that [a] narrower approach [would be to leave] in place the . . . prohibition [on publication] but [to] recognize that when the final disclosure is on a question of public significance, and is by a person completely uninvolved in the illegal interception, then the speech rights [win]. So [only] when you have the circumstance where you have speech on a matter of public significance—not just what was happening on the phone, someone came in and just overheard my conversation in my bedroom—when you're speaking on a matter of public importance, that's when the First Amendment interests are at their highest.
Question: So is it a fact—

Question: The newspaper's not going to publish it unless it has public interest? And is public interest and public significance the same thing? I mean, you know, somebody taps the phones of a prominent public official or of a prominent jurist and it turns out the guy swears like a trooper and this—you know, and the whole conversation is published in the paper. Is that a matter of public significance?

Mr. Goldstein: It is a matter of public interest. This Court—

Question: But it may well not be a matter of public significance.

Question: Well, now what's the difference if we—do our cases articulate any difference between public significance and public interest.

Mr. Goldstein: The Court has—

Question: Can you answer the question yes or no?

Mr. Goldstein: No, because it hasn't been presented, Mr. Chief Justice and I would—

Question: And you're presenting it now.

Mr. Goldstein: Yes. Mr. Chief Justice, in three lines of cases, the Court has taken—has drawn the line at public significance.

Like Levine before him, Goldstein is arguing that speech on questions of public significance, even if in the bedroom, should be freely available for a newspaper or individual to distribute to the world, no matter that the speech was legally protected against interception. The Justices immediately press him on the point, honing in hard on what he means by the term "public significance" and on whether the Court has employed such a standard elsewhere. Goldstein briefly cites a few cases, mostly in the libel field, and then tries to move on to other things, worried perhaps about the deep ambiguity of the term and the dangers of leaving its meaning to judges, who are, after all, government officials who should not be vested with the power to decide what people need to know. Indeed, the Court had years ago tried to apply a public interest standard in the libel cases, but it ultimately reversed itself out of the concern that placing the power to enforce such a standard in the hands of judges was dangerous business. Such distinctions, if enforced by legislatures or courts, would be the very kinds of content-based speech restrictions most despised by the First Amendment.

But if some idea of public value or significance is to be employed, someone must be in charge of defining and enforcing it. Goldstein might not want to explore the alternatives too deeply. Is public interest to be placed in the hands of editors? This might be likened to placing the fox in charge of the chicken coop. Might speech in the public interest mean material that the public, or a portion of it, *wants* to know or finds interesting, even titillating?

Would there be any enforceable limits if this were the standard? And how would it be tested? By Harris Poll? In some respects, the difficulties of applying and enforcing a public value, interest, need, or significance standard are the best arguments the government can make in support of the law's across-the-board prohibition on publication.

These are nettlesome questions that any lawyer would try to avoid. And that is precisely what Goldstein does.

Mr. Goldstein, continuing: But I need to return to what else we would say, what other strictures we would put on the statute in order to permit it to survive First Amendment scrutiny and still fulfill what we agree is an important governmental interest and that is that no one wants people tapping phones and breaking into homes. The real problem is that we have here a statute that is so broad that much speech that the Government has no interest or actual intent to stop from being published will in fact be published. The law applies equally—and I mean all the way down the line—in terms of punishment, identical fines to the newspaper that is the 10th party down the line to receive the information as to the intercepting.

Question: Not according to Solicitor General. He says the word disclosed means that once it has been publicly disclosed, the next person is not a discloser.

Mr. Goldstein: The radio station here played the tape in this area of northeastern Pennsylvania, Mr. Chief Justice. Now the *New York Times* comes along and listens and says oh, my goodness, look what happened here. They then publish it nationally. Under the Solicitor General's interpretation, that is a violation of the statute because it wasn't known to the people in California.

Question: Well, so your feeling is that if it's just disclosed in northeastern Pennsylvania, then someone who discloses it perhaps in northwestern Pennsylvania is disclosing it anew?

Mr. Goldstein: Exactly. And as ridiculous as that sounds—

Question: It sure does. But you don't have to read statutes unreasonably. I mean if that's an unreasonable result, don't read "disclose" to mean that. I mean you usually read statutes to produce both constitutional and reasonable results where that's possible.

Mr. Goldstein: The plain text of the statute uses a much broader term than is suggested by the Solicitor General. Let me continue with the other problems with [the law's prohibition on publishers]. The [prohibition] applies to any piece of information about the conversation, not merely the tape. [Earlier] there was a question about talking to my neighbor. In this context if you receive innocently a tape recording and merely mention the fact that you . . . know that there was a tape recording of the conversation, [the prohibition] applies equally because the definition of [material that can't be published] is so broad. It's literally any datum about the conversation.

The [law] imposes civil and criminal liability and permits the commencement of litigation even when there has been no injury at all. And the plaintiffs in this case disavowed any claim that they had actually been hurt. [And] it applies equally, no matter whether the information and indeed the conversation in question was even private. [Moreover,] and this was Justice O'Connor's first question, . . . the information that was spoken and was heard and intercepted could have been a completely public fact [already broadly known], but the fact that it was said in [an illegally intercepted] conversation would . . . [make the conversation's disclosure illegal]. The final problem—and this one is the particularly troubling one that I began with—[is that the law] applies even when the information is of vital public significance.

Now, the reason I mentioned these [problems] is that you have to look at someone who is in the position of receiving a piece of information. There is the grave concern that when you get a piece of information, notwithstanding reason to know [that it has been illegally intercepted] . . . , you [may] have real doubts about the provenance of information—

Question: Well wouldn't a reporter or a news station ordinarily want to check out a story? Are they just going to get the tape and say gee, let's put it on?

Mr. Goldstein: Mr. Chief Justice, if that's the case then I don't think that we have a problem. . . . [T]his statute operates only in the circumstance where the newspaper doesn't know the intercepting party. If the newspaper knows the intercepting party then the statute operates because the newspaper will be subpoenaed and will have to testify about who gave them the interception, and that person will be prosecuted.

Question: Well, I don't understand that.

The point Goldstein is making is pretty convoluted. The law in fact applies its prohibition on publication equally to those publishers who know the identity of the interceptor and to those who do not, contrary to Goldstein's statement. What he apparently means is that in situations in which the interceptor is known and can be prosecuted, there is no reason to apply the law. Deterrence can be had directly against the interceptor, making it unnecessary to dry up the market. There are three problems with this argument.

First, for the dry-up-the-market theory to work, all publication of the intercepted material must be prevented, for the theory operates to discourage future interceptors, not the interceptor in a case that has already happened. This was the gist of Justice Breyer's earlier observation that, so viewed, the law's absolute ban on publication fits the theory perfectly.

Second, Goldstein says that if the newspaper knows the identity of the interceptor, the interceptor will be punished because the government will force the newspaper to disclose that person's name. But it is not quite so simple. Most newspapers would mightily resist divulging the name. And federal guidelines about subpoenaing the press—and most state laws, too—deny the government the power to force disclosure of the name unless the government can prove that it has first attempted to get it by all possible alternative means. Proving that is very difficult. In any event, the government would have to slog its way through the investigation as if the paper didn't have the name, before it could then turn, much later and after considerable expense, to the newspaper. Goldstein's argument, in short, is a bit glib.

Finally, his argument goes only to the dry-up-the-market theory, not to the law's more general purpose of protecting people's expectations of privacy in electronic communications. To serve this interest—that is, to prevent one's private conversations from becoming known to the world—all publication must be barred. Whether the identity of the interceptor is known is irrelevant.

This raises one final point. Goldstein emphasizes the law's restrictions on publication of the intercepted material, even if some people already know about it—indeed, even if it has already been published by a local newspaper, for example, but not by a state-wide newspaper. At some point the continuing prohibition makes no sense, of course, and the law shouldn't be read to produce a silly result, as one of the Justices remarked. But it does not follow from this that a single publication—say, providing the material to one's neighbors—should free the local newspaper or TV station to publish the material to everyone. Privacy interests are layered: we sometimes disclose things about ourselves to some people but don't want others, or everyone else, to know. Therefore, the fact that the law may prevent a newspaper from publishing what has been disclosed to a different audience, or a state-wide paper from disclosing material that has been locally published only, does not necessarily undermine the law's interest in protecting people's privacy or their interests in confidentiality of cell phone conversations. Indeed, in *Bartnicki* none of the lawyers seriously argued that because Yocum had played the tape to some school board members, WILK was therefore free to air it on Fred Williams's radio program.

Goldstein's argument was sufficiently convoluted and obscure that it didn't present these questions clearly. Perhaps the Justices knew what he was trying to say and concluded that no further discussion was needed, given the prior questions. Instead, one Justice expressed befuddlement and another immediately turned the questions away from the dry-up-the-market theory and to the broader privacy interest the law sought to protect.

Question: I think that the Congress or States pass property laws in part to keep people away from my bedroom. And they are doing that in part for reasons better than trade secret law or copyright law, because there is something about human dignity that requires it. Well, if they can keep people away from my bedroom to hear my private conversations, even about important matters, can't they try to protect that same kind of basic dignity in respect to the new world that will come through wireless communication? Now, do you see there's a lot involved there, but that's at the bottom of what I'm trying to work out in this case?

Mr. Goldstein: Let me begin by stepping back to the variant on that question that you asked my colleague. And I do want to specify that when it comes to things like diaries, the intellectual property laws—copyright laws—still apply fully [and constitutionally prohibit their publication by anyone, innocent third party or not]. And we don't doubt that if it's a diary and it's something that is your personal information, you have written it down, that you can claim that you have [had] . . . something like intellectual property . . . stolen.

This is, frankly, a surprising concession by Goldstein. If my diary contains personal information that I expect to be private, and it is stolen, he acknowledges that the diary's later publication by a newspaper (not engaged in the theft) may be legally prohibited without any First Amendment problems. This is the necessary implication of his statement and his reference to intellectual property and copyright law and to cases such as *Cohen* (enforcing a contract with a source) or *Zacchini* (prohibiting the airing of an act on an evening news broadcast). Just what accounts for the fact that the diary is intellectual property that can be protected in this way? Is it the fact that its contents are personal and intended to be private? Is it the expectation of the diarist that the words will remain in his or her control? If it is either of these, there seems little basis for arguing that the cell-phone conversation between Bartnicki and Kane should be treated any differently. After all, the law being challenged here, which prohibits interception in order to protect people's expectations of, and security in, confidentiality, is as clear a statement of a legal right vested in the cell phone as is the copyright law or the common law of privacy in the *Zacchini* case. It might be argued that a diary is written and known only by the author, whereas a cell-phone conversation is oral and shared with another person. But the written-ness seems wholly irrelevant in an age of electronic communication, which consists really of charged electrons. And in any event an actor's performance in a play, which is clearly protected intellectual property, is neither written nor kept to the actor himself or herself. The same is true for the fifteen-second segment of Zacchini being hurled from the cannon, or for Dr. King's speech.

The only remaining distinction might be that the performance of the play and Zacchini's act had commercial value, whereas Bartnicki's cell-phone conversation did not. But this distinction would produce an odd and distasteful result: commercial information would be given greater legal protection than would noncommercial information. Happily, there is no basis in law for concluding that commercial value, only, creates propertylike interests. A diary, surely, is something that rarely has commercial value. The same is true of political discourses—most of them, anyway. But they can be made intellectual property if a legislature so chooses, or if the judge-made common law so provides.

By admitting that a diary is "property" and its publication by a newspaper, for example, can be prohibited regardless of its contents—regardless of whether the stolen, secret thoughts there revealed are of public importance (they surely would be of public interest if the diarist were a politician or a famous person)—Goldstein has stepped into a trap of his own making. So he quickly ducks and shifts to a different subject—back to the now-well-worn dry-up-the-market topic.

Mr. Goldstein, continuing: Your question to me was, can't we try hard to reduce the incentives, and I think Congress is doing that here. There is no record that suggests there is a real problem, but I think we all agree intuitively [that the law] will reduce somewhat the incentive to engage in the interception. Our problem is that it's [an absolute] ban on someone [publishing the intercepted material] and could result in massive punitive damages or jail time on someone who hasn't engaged in the primary wrongdoing. My client, [Yocum], has no idea who gave him this piece of information. He has it. It's of public significance. It's a legitimate threat on its face.

Question: He knows it was illegally obtained. He didn't know who illegally obtained it. Do you really think this phone conversation . . . what, just dropped out of the air or something? It was obviously illegally obtained. Wasn't it an obvious phone tap?

Mr. Goldstein: It was an obviously—it was obviously recorded and very likely recorded by someone who wasn't a party to it.

Question: Okay. Why do you have to know who did it?

Mr. Goldstein: Because [Yocum] is not engaged in anything that anyone believes is wrong. He has information, a legitimate threat. The court of appeals, Justice Scalia, [said] that this was not just an idle threat. [Kane] says really, truthfully, we're going to have to do some work on these people, blow off—

Question: But isn't it the case that by the time the publication which is the subject of this action occurred, the threat was over? This publication all occurred after the point at which the threat was going—

Mr. Goldstein: With respect, that is not correct, particularly as to my client. Independently after receiving it, within a day, Mr. Yocum . . . disclosed it [in violation] of the statute by giving it to the radio station and notifying the people [school board members] who were the subject [of the threat].

Question: Why didn't he just notify the people who were the subject of the threat?

Mr. Goldstein: He did.

Question: Once it goes to the radio station you're not talking about an exception for people who are performing the public service of warning victims.

Mr. Goldstein: I think that there is something to be said of warning the public. But I agree—

Question: Well, the public's porches weren't going to be blown off. The school committee's porches were going to be blown off, and they were notified. So that when it went to the radio station, we weren't worried about potential victims of porch blowings, were we?

Mr. Goldstein: When he gave it to the radio station, yes, we were.

Question: And at the same time, [Yocum] was making it known, I forget how, but he was making it known to the victims, so that the radio station was not necessary to make it known to the victims, and the people who learn through the radio station weren't potential victims. That's correct, isn't it?

Mr. Goldstein: That is correct. Our point is that when you have a piece of information . . . and it is a matter of public significance, you are not involved in anything that Congress attempted to stop. It is speech of the highest interest. If it is . . . speech on matters of public significance by someone who had nothing to do with the interception, has no idea who [the interceptor] was, that speech is protected.

Question: But [Yocum] knows that someone upon whom he is depending acted illegally.

Mr. Goldstein: Has reason to know.

Question: Has reason to know and certainly there is reason to know here.

Mr. Goldstein: That's correct.

Question: All right, and—and Congress certainly *did* intend to stop that, it seems to me, contrary to what you said. Why do you suggest that this is outside the ambit of what concerned Congress? Congress wanted to dry up a market, and I can't think of a more obvious market than the market of a radio station which has reason to know that it is publishing illegally seized interceptions.

Mr. Goldstein: Justice Souter, if I said this wasn't what Congress was trying to do, I misspoke.

Question: I thought you did say that.

Mr. Goldstein: We agreed that that [referring to the dry-up-the-market theory] was Congress' goal. Our point . . . is twofold: that neither the Congress nor the plaintiffs or the Government have attempted to develop any record that that was a serious problem. And second is that—

Question: If they knew they were required to do something beyond the intuitive judgment that people make: that of course nobody is going to do this if nobody is going to touch it, if it's going to be treated like a hot potato.

Mr. Goldstein: I think maybe you and I, Justice Ginsburg, are speaking about two slightly different things. The first is a point you identified to my colleague before, which is, isn't it really difficult to identify people and stop them when they are doing these kinds of interceptions? I think this Court can assume that to be the case. The point that I am making is that Congress when it legislated here did not operate on an understanding or any evidence that there was a problem.

The Chief Justice: Thank you, Mr. Goldstein. General Waxman, you have three minutes remaining.

General Waxman: Thank you, Mr. Chief Justice. Questions about the extent of the necessity defense which we mentioned in our reply brief or the meaning of the word disclosure are all, of course, questions of application that will be given judicial interpretation in appropriate cases where they arise. The salient point here is that the respondents have not made a case, either in their briefs or here, that going solely against the wiretapper is going to significantly protect privacy.

And contrary to their representation, the legislative history does, in fact, reflect both great solicitude for the privacy rights involved, and also, repeatedly, the recognition that wiretapping and bugging and now of course we have hacking into e-mails is almost completely impossible of interception or even detection.

The nominal fine that Mr. Levine referred to is, of course, $5,000, which is not nominal with respect to most people, and in any event exists independent of the civil remedy that Congress thought was appropriate to vindicate the privacy rights of the people whose privacy interests were [violated].

Here Waxman is directly presenting the privacy/property interest argument, which has ample support in the law itself and exists independently of the dry-up-the-market theory. He mentioned the privacy justification earlier, but lightly. Having listened to the Justices' questioning of Levine and Goldstein, however, he likely judged that a more affirmative presentation (or at least a restatement) of the privacy justification was appropriate.

He now turns to the serious problems presented by the "public significance," or public interest, argument made by Levine but largely unprobed by the Justices' questions.

General Waxman, continuing: The notion that there is a limiting principal for facts of public significance, I think, is fatal. First of all, if there were such an exception, that would not—that would deprive the statute of being content neutral. And second of all, there is almost no way to draw the line, as Justice Scalia suggests, for what is publicly significant. This court has already held twice that the name of a woman who has been raped—not the fact that there was a rape or the name of the perpetrator, but the victim—is a matter of public significance and public interest. So we don't think that there is a constitutional way to draw a line here. The [cases on which] the other side bases its [argument are] distinguishable from this case and this law. . . . [Their cases involved] laws that applied *only* to the press and not to non-expressive uses. They were content based laws reflecting a determination that society should not know certain information. They dealt with information that came from the Government that is not in the hands of private parties, and there are, we understand, reasons to suspect a censorial motive when the Government seeks to limit disclosure of information about its own activities. [Their cases] . . . all involved information that was lawfully obtained. Every single one of the persons who gave that information to the person got it lawfully.

Chief Justice Rehnquist: Thank you, General Waxman. The case is submitted.

And with the Chief Justice gaveling the argument to a close, the *Bartnicki* case was submitted. What remained was for the Justices to gather together in their conference at week's end, discuss the case among themselves, vote on its disposition, and then undertake the writing of opinions.

One might expect the *Bartnicki* case, with its many faces, complicated facts, and fundamental issues, to be decided only after long struggle and very near the end of the Court's term, in late June. And indeed it did take the Justices over five months to finally settle on an opinion. But the opinion-writing process did not drag on until late June, when many of the most contentious and difficult decisions are finally issued. Instead, the Court's opinion was issued on May 21, 2001. The Justices were divided 6-3. And this time the conservatives—Chief Justice Rehnquist, Justice Scalia, and Justice Thomas—were together in dissent.

A majority of the Justices concluded that the law was too sloppy to be upheld on the deterrence, or dry-up-the-market, theory, for most of the interceptions prohibited by the law were used for private, not public ends. Therefore, a ban on newspaper or radio publication would serve no purpose in deterring them. But the majority did interpret the law as an important and valid attempt to preserve privacy, and they saw the flat ban on publication as directly related to accomplishing that purpose. Yet the majority let Yocum, Vopper, and WILK off the hook, reasoning that the First Amendment foreclosed government, even in the face of important privacy interests, from punishing an innocent newspaper or radio station for the decision to publish intercepted material if the material is about a matter of public concern. In other words, the law remains on the books, but the First Amendment requires the carving of an exception to it for publication of matters of public concern.

The opinion was written by Justice Stevens. He wrote:

> [I]t would be quite remarkable to hold that speech by a law-abiding possessor of information can be suppressed in order to deter conduct by a non-law-abiding third party. . . . [T]here is no empirical evidence to support the assumption that the prohibition against disclosures reduces the number of illegal interceptions.
>
> The Government's second argument, however, is considerably stronger. Privacy of communication is an important interest. . . . Moreover, the fear of public disclosure of private conversations might well have a chilling effect on private speech. . . . As a result, there is a valid independent justification for prohibiting such disclosures by persons who lawfully obtained access to the contents of an illegally intercepted message, even if that prohibition does not play a significant role in preventing such interceptions from occurring in the future.
>
> The enforcement of that provision in this case, however, implicates the core

purposes of the First Amendment because it imposes sanctions on the publication of truthful information of public concern. In this case, privacy concerns give way when balanced against the interest in publishing matters of public importance. . . . [The First Amendment reflects] a "profound national commitment to the principle that debate on public issues should be uninhibited, robust and wide-open."

We think it clear that parallel reasoning requires the conclusion that a stranger's illegal conduct does not suffice to remove the First Amendment shield from speech about a matter of public concern. The months of negotiations over the proper level of compensation for teachers at the Wyoming Valley West High School were unquestionably a matter of public concern, and [Bartnicki and Kane] were clearly engaged in debate about that concern. That debate may be more mundane than the Communist's rhetoric Justice Brandeis's [classic defense of free speech was based on], but it is no less worthy of constitutional protection.

The judgment is affirmed.

It is so ordered. [Citations omitted.]

The dissenting Justices disagreed on both grounds. The dry-up-the-market rationale that Congress had used was perfectly justifiable, they said, and for that rationale to work, the whole market would have to be dried up, even if some or many of the interceptions were not market-driven. The rationale was much like the requirement that companies selling stock must provide full and accurate information to everyone why buys it, even those who don't want or don't need it; if an exception for the knowingly reckless or the knowledgeable investor is crafted into the securities laws, the dissenting Justices argued, the purpose of providing fair and accurate information to all investors would be undermined, because companies failing to provide the information would claim that an objecting investor didn't want or need the information. So also with publication of intercepted communications: an exception for cases in which the interceptor acted out of private motives and not in order to sell or distribute the conversation—or indeed an exception for publishers who believe the material involves a matter of public concerns— would simply open up two new fronts for argument and litigation, serving lawyers, perhaps, but at the same time undermining the goals of the law.

The dissenting opinion was written by Chief Justice Rehnquist.

Although the Court recognizes and even extols the virtues of [the] right to privacy, these are "mere words," W. Shakespeare, *Troilus and Cressida,* act v., sc. 3, overridden by the Court's newfound right to publish unlawfully acquired information of "public concern.". . . Perhaps the Court is correct that "[i]f the statements about the labor negotiations had been made in a public arena—during a bargaining session, for example—they would have been newsworthy." The point, however, is that Bartnicki and Kane had no intention of contributing to a public "debate" at all, and it is perverse to hold that another's unlawful interception and knowing disclosure of their conversation is speech "worthy of constitutional protection." The Constitution should not protect the involuntary broadcast of personal conversations. Even where the communications involve public figures or concern public matters, the conversations are nonetheless private and worthy of protection. Although public persons may have forgone the right to live their lives screened from public scrutiny in some areas, it does not and should not follow that they also have abandoned their right to have a private conversation without fear of it being intentionally intercepted and knowingly disclosed.

* * *

Surely "the interest in individual privacy," at its narrowest, must embrace the right to be free from surreptitious eavesdropping on, and involuntary broadcast of, our cellular telephone conversations. [Citations omitted.]

What are the implications of the Court's opinion in the *Bartnicki* case? One is fundamental yet wholly untouched in the Court's opinions. Just what does privacy mean, and what form does it take under the federal law against interception of cell-phone conversations? The Court's answer is that Congress passed the law, which contains quite specific prohibitions, and that is all that needs to be said. But should we let the Court off so easily? When a law rubs up against someone's freedom to speak or publish, it is commonplace for courts to examine the clarity and importance of the law's aims to assure that they are sufficient to outweigh the First Amendment interest in free speech and freedom of the press. If the aims of the law against interception are protection of privacy (as opposed to, for example, encouragement of the cell-phone industry's growth, a valid but less substantial interest), then we must define precisely what "privacy" means in the particular settings covered by the law and then judge whether that definition of privacy is convincing.

Why should cell-phone conversations be "private"? To prevent snooping? To prevent embarrassment by those using the phones? To give people control over what is disclosed about them? If the latter, are we sure that we want to give people control over everything they say, or might we instead limit such control to facts and statements and opinions that are deeply personal, intimate, or destructive of valuable personal and social relationships if indiscriminately known? What about things people say about crimes they are planning? Or what they say about their jobs and public responsibilities? Or what they say about the terrible stock that they are encouraging their clients to buy?

The point of these examples isn't to settle on a "best" definition of privacy. It is instead to illustrate how many different meanings privacy might have when viewed as a purpose underlying the interception law, and how little consideration the Supreme Court gave to the question. What is meant by privacy cannot be so easily escaped, for if the noninterception law's purpose were to protect all conversations, even those by criminals or rotten stockbrokers, the First Amendment claim by an individual or a news organization that publishes the tapes would surely look persuasive. Perhaps this is what the Court really meant to say when it forged its "matter of public concern" test in *Bartnicki*. But if so, this seems an elliptical and blunt-edged way of defining privacy. Depending on what public concerns consist of, some crimes don't qualify, and some deeply personal questions, such as whether to bear a child or acknowledge paternity, do. Privacy, in other words, needs to be faced head-on. We will do so in greater detail in the next story.

For now we must turn to other practical, but no less important, questions raised by the *Bartnicki* decision. What remains of a right to privacy if the law countenances publication of private matters whenever a judge, an editor, or any other person possessed of a sense of public good decides to do so? How will a journalist or a news editor decide whether intercepted material should be published, knowing that final editorial power resides in the hands of a state or federal judge—one perhaps not as enamored by the newspaper as a more distant Supreme Court might be—especially when the judge can enforce his or her final editorial judgment with a criminal conviction or an award of damages?

Will the exception carved out for publication of illegally obtained information be applied also to copyrights and trademarks and, indeed, to the purloined diary? The Court expressly disavowed any intention to answer those questions, leaving the door open for broader application of the Court's new rule. And what if Congress simply amends the law to make knowing receipt of illegally intercepted material itself a crime? This would make WILK's receipt of the tape from Yocum a criminal act quite independent of the (much) later publication of the tape. Receipt of stolen property is a crime in most jurisdictions, and it is enforceable against anyone even if the material is speech—a book, a diary, a film, and the like—without any First Amendment difficulties. Might such laws be challenged now on the authority of the *Bartnicki* decision?

The decision in the *Bartnicki* case answered few questions. Indeed, the Court professed as much, saying, "Our refusal to construe the issue more broadly is consistent with this Court's repeated refusal to answer categorically whether truthful publication may ever be punished consistent with the First Amendment." But the Court did not escape quite so narrowly. Its decision—that publication of intercepted information by a person who was not involved in the illegal interception, but who had reason to know of its illegality, is protected by the First Amendment from regulation—applies *only if the information is "about a matter of public concern."*

What, we are entitled to ask, are matters of public concern? Are they what judges deem important or valuable or legitimately interesting? Are they what people need to know, or wish to know? Are they what editors—or, for that matter, any other persons who publish an intercepted communication (such as Fred Vopper)—decide is useful or popular or even titillating? The Court simply doesn't tell us in its opinion. Indeed, in the interest of "prudence,"it explicitly chooses not to say.

The Court has thus engaged itself, with little guidance to itself or others, in the enterprise of defining the meaning of public concern and of enforcing the boundaries it places on the term. This is an enterprise the Court once before undertook, only to relent soon thereafter, saying, "We doubt the wisdom of committing this task to the conscience of judges."

Will the Court succeed now where it once failed? And if it does, should we be happy about placing final editorial review in the hands and consciences of judges, who, after all, are agents of government?

Additional Reading

Katsh, M. Ethan. *Law in a Digital World.* New York: Oxford University Press, 1995.

Schudson, Michael. *The Power of News.* Cambridge, Mass.: Harvard University Press, 1995.

STORY 7

What Is the Public's Business?
Howard v. Des Moines Register & Tribune Company
283 N.W. 2d 289 (Iowa Supreme Court 1989)

By the time the *Des Moines Register* story was published, Robbin Howard was twenty-four years old. She was married. She had a new name and a new home in a new city. In 1970, six years earlier, she was Robbin Woody, a young girl who had been committed to the Jasper County Home, a public residential facility for the care of the retarded, mentally ill, and infirm in Jasper County, Iowa. According to the *Register* story, Robbin Woody Howard "was not retarded or mentally disabled, but an 'impulsive, hair-triggered, young girl.'" For this, at the age of eighteen, she was involuntarily sterilized. Her parents and the home's doctor decided sterilization was for the best. Howard, the *Register* reported, "didn't want it at all." "She was told," according to "one source," that it was "the only way she could be dismissed from the home." Dr. Roy Sloan, the county home's psychiatrist, described her as "a very explosive, impulsive young girl . . . [who] would be a very questionable risk as far as having and rearing a baby."

All of this, and more, was published in 1976 in the *Des Moines Register,*[1] a nationally recognized newspaper serving all of Iowa. The *Register*'s story was not about Howard, as such, but about alleged illegal activities and mistreatment that had taken place in the Jasper County Home, activities that included poor care, patient deaths, scalding baths, and improper sterilizations of women. Howard was the story's rhetorical instrument, unceremoniously swept up into a larger public controversy uncovered through the investigative reporting of a very good newspaper. Her unwitting role in the controversy was not to prove the allegations but to bring them to life and to drive them home. This she did very well.

That Howard was a less than enthusiastic participant in the *Register*'s news is perfectly understandable—as was her decision to sue for invasion of privacy.

---

1. *Des Moines Register,* Feb. 15, 1976, p. 8A, reprinted in App. 61-64, *Howard v. Des Moines Register & Tribune Co.,* 283 N.W.2d 289 (Iowa 1989), *cert. denied,* 445 U.S. 904 (1980).

Robbin Howard's Story

We can't truly appreciate the difficult problems presented by privacy claims like Howard's without seeing the issues through the eyes of both parties: the person whose privacy is tragically invaded through broad public exposure of deeply personal information and whose hopes of putting the past behind him or her are permanently dashed; and the newspaper that must know how deeply a person's life will be invaded but nevertheless makes a judgment that sacrificing a person's privacy is a price worth paying in order to publish what, in its judgment, is an important story. A clear sense of these competing perspectives is revealed in the affidavits and depositions in Howard's case, which tell the story in compelling detail.

We begin with Howard's side of the story.

Deposition of Robbin Howard

Questions by Glenn Smith, attorney for the *Register:*

Q. I [want] to ask you about the more salient parts of this lawsuit and the things that have brought us here. These had to do with an article of which you complain that was published in the Sunday *Register* of February 15, 1976, and it made reference to the fact that you had been sterilized.

A. Yes.

Q. Where did this sterilization procedure take place?

A. Skiff Memorial Hospital in Newton, Iowa.

Q. What day or month or year, if you can recall, did this involve?

A. July 15th, 1971.

Q. When was sterilization of you first discussed with you?

A. It never was discussed with me. I'm the one that confronted Doctor Sloan [the Jasper County Home's psychiatrist] about it because I had heard—I don't remember who it was from, but I had heard that, you know, in order to get out of the Jasper County Home you got to do this. I confronted Doctor Sloan; he didn't confront me.

Q. You had heard that the only way you could get out of the home was to submit to this?

A. Yes.

Q. Who had you heard that from?

A. It was one of the employees. I don't remember who it was.

Q. Wouldn't have been the superintendent or anyone like that?

A. No.

Q. So you discussed this problem with Doctor Sloan?

A. Yes.

Q. How did that come up? Was he at the home?

A. He came onto the floor and I just went up and said something to him. I said,

"I heard the only way I could get out of this place was if I agree to have the operation," and he just kind of looked at me kind of funny. I says, "Well, come on, I'll sign the paper," at which time I was on medication. I didn't really know exactly what I was saying for sure.

Q. When you say "medication," what do you mean?

A. I was on thorazine.

Q. Is that a tranquilizing or similar type of drug?

A. Sort of a depressant.

Q. You told him you wanted to get out and would sign the paper if that would accomplish it, is this what I understand your conversation to be?

A. Yes, at which time I didn't really know exactly what I was saying because like I was on this medication.

Q. Well, you knew what sterilization was?

A. Yes, but when you're on this medication, the excessive milligrams that I was on, it—you were lucky if you knew your own name because it just made you kind of groggy and you just kind of walked around like you didn't know anything.

Q. Who was prescribing this medication, do you know?

A. I think it was Doctor Sloan.

Q. He produced, then, a paper for you to sign, is that it?

A. He took me down to the office and the secretary took a piece of regular typewriter paper and typed out on it that—something to the effect of that I, Robbin Woody, do agree to the sterilization operation is all it amounted to.

Q. And dated it and you signed it?

A. No, it was not dated.

Q. Wasn't dated, but at least you signed it?

A. I signed it.

Q. How soon thereafter did the sterilization procedure occur?

A. This was in April and it didn't happen till July and it was like two days later I was taken off this—I was taken off of the medication, this thorazine, at which time I was talking to one of my girl friends, Debbie Erickson, I believe it was, and she asked me if I realized what I'd done and I kind of looked at her like what do you mean and she told me my conversation with Doctor Sloan and I didn't really remember doing it. And, I confronted Doctor Sloan when he came on the floor that day and I begged him to tear up the paper and he wouldn't do it.

Q. He refused to do it?

A. Right.

Q. Did you have any discussions prior to the operation with any of the people in the surgical area about the operation?

A. You mean in the surgical area of the hospital?

Q. Yes.

A. No, not that I remember.

Q. You don't recall objecting again to—

A. All I recall is objecting to Doctor Sloan.

Q. That was some short time after you had signed the original consent, is that right?

A. If you want to call it an original consent, yes.

Q. Well, whatever it was, the paper you signed?

A. Yes. I did talk to Reva Ripper (Superintendent of the Jasper County Home).

Q. When was that conversation with Reva?

A. Well, I talked to her the night before that I talked to Doctor Sloan. And he had—I went down and signed the paper and all she could tell me was—because it was like six-thirty, seven o'clock at night and at that time you're not supposed to bother her and I went over and knocked on her door—she had an apartment—like an apartment there—and she told me that she couldn't be bothered with it and I says, "Well, who am I supposed to bother with it?" She says, "Well, just go talk to Doctor Sloan."

Q. So you saw him several days later, at least?

A. It was the next day.

Q. Is it your testimony that your adoptive parents didn't know anything about this sterilization operation between the time you signed the consent and the time it occurred?

A. They knew about it.

Q. They knew that you had signed the consent?

A. They probably knew that I signed the consent. They knew about the operation and everything, but they didn't—

Q. But that was after it had occurred?

A. They knew about it, but they didn't tell me about it. I don't know when it first was discussed with them, but I'm sure that Doctor Sloan discussed it with them prior to my even coming up and saying anything to him.

Q. How do you know this to be the case of your adoptive parents' knowledge of this signing by you of the consent?

A. I said I assume that they knew about it.

Q. But on what do you base that assumption, I guess is what I'm saying?

A. Because from what my brother Harvey said when I talked to him after I'd been out of the County Home and this and that. I talked to him and he said that they had talked to Doctor Sloan on several occasions about, like, me going home for visits and this and that and my therapy and stuff out at the County Home. Everything that Doctor Sloan said they agreed with for my benefit.

Q. Have you had any medical problems or illness or disease from the time of your confinement at the Jasper County Home to now?

A. No.

Q. Have you ever been arrested?

A. No, I have not.

Q. Have you ever been involved in any litigation—

A. Pardon me?

Q. —lawsuits other than this one?

A. No.

Q. No one has ever brought an action against you?

A. No, they have not.

Q. Have you had occasion to seek out legal assistance from others than Oscar Jones (Robbin's lawyer)?

A. No, I have not.

Q. Have you ever received injury by reason of any accidents?

A. No, I have not.

Q. Other than your adoptive brother, have you any other brothers or sisters—

A. No, I do not.

Q. Have you had any contact concerning this sterilization matter with the State Board of Health?

A. State Board—no.

Q. Did you have any contact with the Jasper County Board of Supervisors or any of its members?

A. No.

Q. Did you have any contact arising out of this sterilization or the proposed sterilization with any other public officials in Jasper County?

A. No.

Q. Did you ever slip out of your home, go out running around or dating with David Wright while you were living with the Woodys?

A. Well, they'd classify it as running away, but I didn't run away. I just took a nice long walk and went visiting. It wasn't necessarily David. I don't think I ever went and saw him. It was like some of my girl friends and stuff.

Q. But you would go out for an evening and absent yourself for a period of time?

A. It wasn't always at evening. It would be like on the weekend, maybe four-o'clock in the afternoon and I'd be back maybe by eight or nine.

Q. Did you ever stay out overnight while you were living with the Woodys against their wishes?

A. No, I did not.

Q. There's reference in this article to [your being subjected] to public contempt and ridicule. Has anybody ever actually ridiculed you on account of this?

A. On account of this, no.

Q. Have you had any remarks from these acquaintances you've mentioned or from others that know you?

A. Remarks such as?

Q. About the fact of sterilization.

A. I've had conversations with quite a few of them about it.

Q. Did any of them hold you in scorn or ridicule on account of those conversations?

A. They wasn't holding me in that, no, but, I mean, it's kind of embarrassing when everybody that you know in the whole town knows about it when you're trying to put it away, I mean, put it in the back of your mind. I mean, you know it's there, but you're putting it away so that it doesn't bother you as much and then, when it's publicly printed, it kind of hurts.

Q. But, getting back to this contempt and ridicule, you don't feel that any of your friends or acquaintances have ridiculed you?

A. They haven't, but that doesn't mean that somebody—if I went to like—

Q. Oh, I understand.

A. —like apply for a job or something, that they wouldn't.

Q. Well, is this a matter that you have discussed with others than your friends, the fact of this sterilization? You've never talked to anybody about it?

A. No, I have not.

Q. When did you first tell David Wright about this fact?

A. When he came down to Mount Pleasant the second time to get me.

Q. You told him that you were sterilized?

A. Yes.

Q. To whom else did you discuss the fact of sterilization? Did you say anything about it to your friends in Chicago?

A. I talked to Karen about it.

Q. She was—

A. Damien's sister.

Q. —Damien's sister with whom you lived?

A. Yes.

Q. Did Damien know it?

A. Yes, he knew it.

Q. You've testified to residents in Chicago and other people and employment by other people. Let's take the Carringtons. Did they know it?

A. The Carringtons didn't know it.

Q. You never mentioned it to them?

A. No.

Q. You had no reason not to mention it to them?

A. I didn't feel it was something that I needed to discuss with them.

Q. What was your purpose in going to [Mr. Jones' law] office?

A. To find out what could be done, if anything, about this article being printed in the paper.

Glenn Smith: I don't have any other questions.

Questions by Mr. Jones (Robbin's attorney):

Q. I just have a couple of matters of clarification. Robbin, how old were you when you became pregnant?

A. Seventeen.

Q. Now, you were asked, and I don't remember the exact form, after this article appeared in the paper did anyone that you knew ever come up and say to you anything about seeing this article in the paper?

A. A couple of people did.

Q. Now, you were asked if you have ever talked to anyone about the fact that you had been sterilized since the article appeared in the paper and at least I understood you to say no. Have you discussed this article with any of your friends or acquaintances?

A. When it first came out in the paper, the next day I talked to Mont and Gladys about it.

Q. Now, when people have come up to you and mentioned seeing this article in the paper, was it embarrassing to you?

A. Sometimes and sometimes not. It kind of depended on who it was or what kind of a mood I was in that day.

End of deposition

Robbin Howard's story is one of unconsented embarrassment and violation. Her secret, which she had tried to put behind her, had been laid bare, and in the process she had been denied control of the way in which she would live the rest of her life. Howard had not been retarded, nor even, it seems, impulsive. After her sterilization, she had married, changed her name, and taken a job as a nurse's aide in a rest home. She had begun taking classes in hopes of moving up in the nursing-care field that she had chosen for herself.

The *Register*'s story changed all this. It did not result in Howard losing her job. In fact, the story had few concrete consequences for her. Instead, it changed the way Howard saw herself: her self-confidence, her relationships with others, her inability to throw off the yoke of a past that to her was deeply embarrassing. In these senses Howard was a victim—a victim of the *Register*'s commitment to a story and to that story's dramatic effect.

Was Howard's tragedy the story? If so, why and to what purpose? Or was the controversy at the county home the story, with Howard serving as a particularly compelling illustration, a personification of misdeeds? Her story occupied just a few paragraphs in a very long article focused on the problems at the county home. The news story was about abuse, mistreatment, and illegal medical procedures at the county home. This was an indisputably important public issue demanding the *Register*'s attention as Iowa's statewide newspaper.

The question, though, is not the importance of the story about the county home but instead the need to bring Howard into it. How important was it for the *Register* to personify the story, rather than to just report on it? Must the press be free to use people's private lives as rhetorical instruments whenever it deems them useful, or must there be special and specific justification for a decision to do so? Must that justification go to the substance of a story, or may the press make its decision simply on the grounds that use of a person's intimate information will grab reader attention *and* give a story emotional as well as factual force?

Perhaps most importantly, why use the name? Couldn't the *Register* have told Howard's story using a different name, "Patient X, an eighteen-year-old girl . . . ," or simply using a first name, such as Mary? Would the story have really been less compelling to the reader if recounted this way?

The Register's Story

The *Register* could not simply ignore these questions in its defense against the privacy lawsuit Howard brought in the state court. It had to explain what the story was really about, and why Howard was important to its telling. But in order to do so, the *Register* had to reframe the case and the issues, making the jury see the events and the decisions through the newspaper's eyes. Margaret Engel was the reporter and author of the offending story. The *Register*'s account is revealed through the affidavit she submitted and, then, her testimony in a pretrial deposition.

Affidavit of Margaret Engel

I, Margaret Engel, on oath do depose and state that:

1. I am a reporter for *The Des Moines Register,* a morning daily newspaper published by the Des Moines Register and Tribune Company.

2. I was born July 3, 1951. From 1970 to 1973, I attended the University of Missouri, receiving a Bachelor of Journalism degree upon graduation with honors from the University. I majored in news editorial writing and English. During my undergraduate studies, I worked on the daily newspaper published by the University, *The Columbia Missourian,* in Columbia, Missouri. I received the Jay L. Torrey award from the University of Missouri's journalism faculty in 1973.

3. In June, 1973, I joined the staff of the *Lorain (Ohio) Journal* in Lorain, Ohio, the flagship newspaper of a five-newspaper group in northern Ohio, as an investigative and general assignment reporter. In 1975, the Associated Press awarded its enterprise reporting award for my series of articles on deaths and hazards at a local sandstone quarry; the Associated Press also awarded its community service award to a series of articles I co-authored on deaths due to vinyl chloride.

4. On January 12, 1976, I joined the staff of *The Des Moines Register* and was assigned to cover 14 state agencies, including the Department of Health, the Department of Social Services, the Iowa Supreme Court, and the Attorney General's Office. I continue to hold this position today. I, also, write occasional articles for the *Register*'s business section and state desk.

5. In late January, 1976, I was assigned by the *Register*'s city editor, Mr. Laurence Paul, to assist another *Register* reporter, Mr. Gerald Szumski, in a report on the

state Health Department's license revocation action against the Jasper County Home in Newton, Iowa. As a result of the assignment, I became aware of actual and rumored health and safety violations at the Jasper County Home.

6. I attended a special public meeting of the Jasper County Board of Supervisors on the afternoon of January 30, 1976, where the revocation notices, containing 120 alleged violations of Health Department rules, were read by the Jasper County Attorney, Mr. Kenneth Whitehead. Comments were given by Reva Ripper, stewardess of the Jasper County Home, Ruth Broderson, director of nursing at the Home, Dr. John Ferguson, the Home's physician, and Dr. Roy C. Sloan, the Home's psychiatrist, all of whom were in attendance. I, also, acquired copies of the state Health Department's "Notice of Revocation of Residential Care Facility License" and the "Notice of Revocation of the Intermediate Care Facility License." This meeting, along with documents and interviews by reporter Szumski, resulted in a story titled "Jasper County Nursing Home's License Pulled," which was published January 31, 1976, on page one of *The Des Moines Register.*

7. I then proceeded with an in-depth investigation of the problems at the Jasper County Home, an examination which continues to the present. In researching the difficulties at the Home, I became aware of various medical, health, safety, and administrative problems and abuses at the Home that had been reported in many news articles. . . . The article in question in this litigation, published on February 15, 1976, was the result of the initial two weeks of the in-depth investigation. Attached . . . are newspaper articles which appeared before . . . the February 15, 1976, article complained of by plaintiff, which, as a news reporter, I believe show the continuing and protracted public controversy surrounding the administration of the Jasper County Home:

"State Studies Charge of Neglect, Abuse, at Jasper County Home." By Jerald Heth, *Des Moines Tribune,* January 17, 1972.

"State Revokes License of Jasper County Home." By Jerry J. Szumski and Margaret Engel, *Des Moines Register,* January 31, 1976.

"Jasper County Supervisor Threatened." By Bonnie Wittenburg, *Des Moines Register,* February 3, 1976.

"Nursing Home Hearing Delayed." By Margaret Engel, *Des Moines Register,* February 4, 1976.

"Reva Ripper and Head Nurse Quit at Jasper County Home." By Margaret Engel, *Des Moines Register,* February 8, 1976.

"Special Problems at County Homes." To the Editor, *Des Moines Register,* February 14, 1976.

"Scalding Deaths at Jasper Home Revealed." By Margaret Engel, *Des Moines Register,* February 15, 1976.

8. During the next days, I interviewed several residents of Jasper County who had long been interested in and had dealings with the Jasper County Home. One

of these was Opal M. Snyder, of 603 W. 3rd St. South, Newton, a former columnist for the Newton Daily News and publisher of the Jasper County Free Press. She supplied me with documents including the following:

(a) Her own statement concerning the sterilization of Robbin Woody (Howard), Shelby _____, and Linda _____, three female residents at the County Home, that she had filed at the Office of Governor Robert D. Ray. Copies of Mrs. Snyder's lengthy statement are on file at the Governor's Office and are available for public inspection.

(b) A copy of a statement made by Myrle J. Corso, a former nurse's aide at the Home, who expressed her knowledge of cruel treatment and incompetence at the Home, including the sterilization of young women residents. This statement was given to the Governor, the Iowa State Health Department, the Des Moines Register and Tribune Company, Local 977 of the United Auto Workers in Newton, the area Health Planning Council, and several other public interest groups and individuals, and is available for public inspection.

(c) A copy of a statement made by Collene Blakely, a former nurse at the Jasper County Home, that Robbin Woody (Howard) had been sterilized against Robbin's wishes and that she had told Mrs. Blakely about her operation. This statement is in the files of the Office of Governor Robert D. Ray and is available for public inspection.

9. After receiving these documents, I verified the facts from public records on file in the Jasper County Auditor's and Clerk's offices. Specifically, I verified these facts in the following public records:

(a) I was aware that Jasper County Auditor's Warrant #8641 from the 1971 Jasper County Home Fund totaling $343.00 for medical services at the Newton Clinic included County funds paid out for Robbin Woody's sterilization surgery.

(b) I was aware that Jasper County Auditor's Warrant #8906 totaling $819.35 for medical services at the Newton Clinic included the surgery and hospitalization paid by the County for Linda _____ and Shelby _____.

10. Robbin Woody (Howard's) residency at the Jasper County Home was established by public documents. [A listing of documents follows.]

11. I, also, verified the instance of Robbin Woody (Howard's) sterilization with several people, including Mrs. Gladys Woody, Robbin's legal guardian; Mrs. Blakely; Reva Ripper; Dr. John Ferguson; and Dr. Roy C. Sloan. All confirmed the fact of Robbin Woody (Howard's) sterilization.

12. I made repeated unsuccessful attempts to interview Robbin Woody. Her whereabouts were unknown, even to her mother, and had been for several years. Sound journalistic investigation spanning several days and involving extensive checks of records in Jasper and Polk Counties did not disclose Robbin Woody (Howard's) whereabouts.

13. Others interviewed in connection with the story that is the basis of this suit include: [the affidavit then lists over thirty people with whom Engel spoke.]

14. In the course of my investigation, I learned that the Jasper County Home had failed to receive the necessary State approval for sterilizations performed prior to 1972. This was confirmed to me by Dr. Sloan and by Teresa Weiser, Executive Secretary of The Iowa State Board of Eugenics. Dr. Selig M. Korson, M.D., chairman of The Iowa State Board of Eugenics again confirmed, in a letter to The General Counsel, Des Moines Register and Tribune Company, that Robbin Woody's case was never reviewed as required by Chapter 145 of The Code of Iowa.

15. Based on my experience and training as a news reporter and my extensive investigation of the Jasper County Home, it became clear to me that the controversy surrounding the administration of the Jasper County Home involving the treatment, past and present, of an average of 144 people per year—delinquent juveniles, handicapped, disabled, aged, and poor adults—was a public issue ripe for investigative reporting, and resulted in the article which appeared in the *Des Moines Sunday Register* on February 15, 1976, and is the subject matter of the plaintiff's complaint.

16. As a result of the State Health Department's suspension of the Jasper County Home's two licenses in June, 1975, and the revocation action in January, 1976, the Jasper County Home became a topic of immense public concern, with emotional public hearings and heated meetings of the Jasper County Board of Supervisors. Rumors, accusations, and testimonials regarding the administration and treatment at the Jasper County Home flowed freely throughout the community and were presented at these meetings, particularly a two-hour hearing that filled the Jasper County Courthouse on February 7, 1976.

17. I felt that a news article sorting the truth from the fiction was necessary and essential to this topic of immense public concern. The news article complained of by the plaintiff dealt with sad and horrible events that occurred at the Jasper County Home during recent years under the stewardship of Reva and Clarence Ripper, who ran the Home for the last 22 years.

18. I believe that the application of the principles of responsible journalism required that no thorough investigation or news article about the Jasper County Home would be complete, thorough, or convincing without a detailing of the abuses that had been verified as fact. As described in Paragraphs 8 through 16 above, public controversy over the Jasper County Home had resulted in charges, accusations, and rumors being aired at public meetings and elsewhere. After thorough investigation, I could find no substantiation for a few of these charges. This led me to believe it was necessary, based on sound journalistic principles, to be absolutely specific, correct, and accurate in relating the instances of abuse I substantiated, rather than adding more vague charges to a rumor-plagued, emotional, and explosive public controversy.

19. I have not now, nor have I ever had, any feeling of ill-will or malice against Robbin Woody (Howard) personally. In fact, I have never met Robbin Woody Howard, and hence I do not know her personally. If anything, the news article

in question seeks to protect the rights of Robbin Woody and all young women who may in the future face the possibility of illegal sterilization by describing an actual case and the method in which a sterilization was arranged and completed on an unwilling resident of a county home. The use of Robbin Woody (Howard's) name is necessary to separate actual fact from the rash of rumors that surrounded the Jasper County Home and to differentiate her case from those of other women who were residents at the Home.

20. The news article which appeared on February 15, 1976, and which is the subject of the plaintiff's complaint, was the result of a full-time investigation lasting two weeks. Sources for the article were checked, rechecked, and corroborated; thereafter the news article was written, after two preliminary drafts, by myself and submitted to the editors where it was edited. Customary journalistic techniques and procedures were followed in the period before the article was published in order to insure an accurate and fair recital of the events disclosed in the news article.

21. [M]y only regret as the article progressed toward publication was my inability to locate her to discuss the events behind the sterilization; these efforts of communication were made in keeping with good journalistic practice and custom, but proved futile.

* * *

Deposition of Margaret Engel

Questions by Oscar Jones, Robbin Howard's attorney:

Q. Calling your attention back to either late 1975 or 1976, did you investigate the Jasper county home in Newton?

A. Yes.

Q. Why did you make this investigation?

A. Because of a massive investigation by the state health authorities into the county home.

Q. Were you ordered by anybody at *Register & Tribune* to conduct an investigation into the home?

A. My editors and I decided that this was a critical public issue and we wanted to develop a story on it.

Q. Did you write the article that appeared in the February 15, 1976, Sunday edition of the *Register*?

A. Yes.

Q. Before you published that article, did you obtain the approval of the editor or your superior, whoever that may be?

A. We don't need specific approval for each article, but they understood I was working on the story.

Q. So they understood you were working on the story. After you developed the story, you just submitted it and it was printed; you didn't have to submit it to anyone for approval, is that correct?

A. You submit to editors who approve it in their editing, yes.

Q. As a part of this investigation did you discover that several young girls had been sterilized while they were at the Jasper county home?

A. Yes.

Q. Did your investigation reveal on whose orders these girls were sterilized?

A. It wasn't specifically a matter of orders in each case. It varied from case to case.

Q. Do you remember how many girls your investigation revealed had been sterilized at the Jasper county home?

A. I learned specifically of three.

Q. Now, did your article that you had published on February 15th name all three of these girls?

A. No.

Q. Did your investigation reveal that there may have been other girls sterilized that you were not able to pin down the specifics?

A. Yes.

Q. Prior to publishing this article, did you at any time talk to Robbin Woody?

A. No.

Q. Did you ever meet Robbin Woody before you published this article?

A. No.

Q. Before publishing this article but during your investigation of the Jasper county home and after it came to your attention that some girls had been sterilized at the Jasper county home, did you discuss Robbin's sterilization with Doctor Sloan?

A. Yes. I called him.

Q. When you called him did you identify yourself?

A. Yes, several times.

Q. Had you come in contact with Doctor Sloan during your investigation?

A. Yes.

Q. During your talk with Doctor Sloan, did he furnish you with any information regarding Robbin's sterilization?

A. Yes.

Q. Did he advise you who took the initiative to have Robbin sterilized?

A. No, he didn't advise me of who took the initiative.

Q. Did he tell you that, in fact, Robbin Woody had been sterilized while she was at the Jasper county home?

A. Yes.

Q. During your discussion with Doctor Sloan, did he give you any information as to why Robbin was sterilized?

A. Yes.

Q. And what information did he provide you?

A. The information that is reprinted in the article [which is provided below].

The *Register* also learned that an 18-year-old woman sterilized in 1970 was not retarded or mentally disabled, but "an impulsive, hair-triggered young girl," in the words of Dr. Roy C. Sloan, the home's psychiatrist.

He said the decision to sterilize the resident, Robbin Woody, was made by her parents and himself. He does not recall whether Woody agreed to the operation, but a woman who was a nurse at the home at the time said "she didn't want it at all."

"For two to three weeks when I came to work she was crying," said Collene Blakely of Newton. "She was told the only way she could be dismissed from the home is if she would agree to be sterilized."

Dr. Sloan denied that, saying "We don't think in terms of punishment. That child—she was a young girl—was a very explosive, impulsive young girl largely without controls over her aggressive and, at times, irrational behavior."

He said she was sterilized because "she would be a very questionable risk as far as having and rearing a baby. The people who hold on that way are those who move on to child abuse."

Q. So the information in the article you obtained from Doctor Sloan?

A. That's correct, and other sources.

Q. Yes, but after you had obtained whatever information you had from other sources you then called Doctor Sloan, is that the situation?

A. He was one of the others I called.

Q. Were you able to obtain any information from Doctor Sloan that you had not already obtained?

A. Yes, but not basic confirmation of the fact of sterilization.

Q. How long would you say you discussed Robbin's situation with Doctor Sloan?

A. Perhaps ten minutes.

Q. Did you call Doctor Sloan specifically to gather information regarding Robbin's sterilization?

A. There were other reasons as well.

Q. After this article was published, do you recall talking to me on the telephone and making arrangements to come to my office to discuss the article that had appeared?

A. Yes.

Q. There was some conversation and I believe you asked me if this article was going to result in a lawsuit. Do you recall that, asking me if the article—

A. Not the article. I remember asking you if Robbin was planning to sue anyone and you felt that there might even be a class action on behalf of all the Iowa women who had been illegally sterilized.

Q. And do you recall making the statement that you were not concerned about *Register & Tribune* being sued because they were often sued for a million dollars or more?

A. No.

Q. At the time you started your investigation of the Jasper county home, were you particularly looking for this type of problem—that is, sterilization— or were you concerned with other problems at the Jasper county home?

A. I was concerned with all problems at the home.

Q. How long were you actively engaged in your investigation?

A. Two weeks.

Q. And I would assume you talked to numerous people at the Jasper county home during this two weeks?

A. Dozens.

Q. Do you recall talking to a nurse that advised you that Robbin was extremely upset when she discovered that they were talking about sterilizing her?

A. Yes.

Q. Did this nurse inform you as to Robbin's attitude toward sterilization?

A. Her attitude towards sterilization?

Q. Yes. Did the nurse advise you whether or not Robbin wanted to be sterilized or whether she was opposed to it?

A. Correct. She told me the details of how Robbin felt about the operation, that perhaps it was being done against her will.

Q. Did she tell you whether or not Robbin was upset because she understood she was to be sterilized?

A. There was a quote from that nurse that we used in the story that I think speaks to that.

Q. All right. But you feel that that quote was a correct quote?

A. Yes.

Q. You said that you did not talk to Robbin before publishing the article, so I'm assuming you did not obtain her consent?

A. We had hoped to talk to Robbin. We felt she had talked freely to others about it. We had every expectation she would talk to us had we been able to locate her.

Q. But before publishing the article did you, in fact, talk to Robbin?

A. No.

Q. Did you during your investigation and in preparation of publishing the article determine whether or not Robbin was a person that was mentally retarded?

A. No. That wasn't within the scope, specifically to determine whether she was judged or not judged.

Q. Did your investigation reveal this? Did you have any information regarding whether or not she was a mentally retarded person?

A. Not in the clinical sense of the term.

Q. Did you discuss this with Doctor Sloan?

A. I asked Doctor Sloan to characterize Robbin in clinical psychiatric terms.

Q. Do you recall what he told you?

A. Again, I think the article speaks to . . . his description of her. He was the home psychiatrist.

Q. Reading from the article, it says, "The *Register* also learned that an eighteen-year-old woman, sterilized in 1970, was not retarded or mentally disabled,

but an impulsive, hair-triggered young girl, in the words of Doctor Sloan."
Now is that a correct quote from what you obtained from Doctor Sloan?

A. Yes. We discussed the different categories of capabilities.

Mr. Jones: I have nothing further.

Cross-examination by Glenn Smith, attorney for the *Register:*

Q. Mr. Jones asked if you had talked with Robbin before the article was written. Can you tell us if you made any efforts to talk with her?

A. Yes. We made an exhaustive search for her whereabouts, checking many public and private sources in the course of about two straight days of simply checking for one person. Her mother had no idea of her whereabouts, had not had any idea for some time. We checked county courthouse records. Would you like me to tick them off, all the different places we checked?

Q. You did make an effort to contact her?

A. An exhaustive effort.

Q. Was it in that effort, after the article was written, that you went to Oscar Jones' office?

A. Yes. I was—We had found out that she was in Des Moines because she had contacted Oscar. We did not know that before this time, and I immediately took a cab right out to his office with the hopes of interviewing Robbin and was told at that point that the interview wasn't feasible then, but once this lawsuit was filed there would be no trouble in arranging an interview with Robbin.

Q. Mr. Jones asked you something to the effect that do you recall making a statement that you don't care about people's feelings; you only care about the article as such. Do you recall if you made such a statement?

A. What I'm trying to recall now is some of the circumstances of that confrontation. They wanted the whole thing off the record and not use it, and those weren't the ground rules that were set up initially. I think that there may have been some kind of oblique threat of what we'll do against the *Register* if we do publish it, and I may have said something to the effect, "Sure, we get these threats, but we're concerned about printing what's news," something along that line. I don't remember any specific, what was the—

Q. If you had made a statement such as you don't care about people's feelings; you only care about the article as such, would you remember that or is that the kind of—

A. Seems uncharacteristic for this story and kind of uncharacteristic for me. I wrote this story because I was concerned about circumstances of sterilization of women who didn't care to be sterilized. I obviously cared about it. I invested a lot of time and effort into—into making an exhaustive search and pinning down the facts in this case and that's why we felt it was a significant public story and that Robbin's case was a very critical fact within a mass of rumors that needed to be pinned down, and a very significant public controversy. In my professional judgment it was essential, an essential fact.

Q. Do you have any ill feeling, ill will, towards Robbin Woody?

A. Not at all. I very much wanted to locate her.

Q. Did you ever determine the names of any of the other young women?

A. Yes.

Redirect examination by Mr. Jones:

Q. I just have one additional question. You said that you did determine the names of some of the other women?

A. Yes.

Q. Did you locate or attempt to locate those women?

A. Yes, we did. We could not fully document their cases through public and private records as completely as the one case we were able to document.

Q. Was one reason that you were able to more fully document Robbin's sterilization a result of your conversation with Doctor Sloan?

A. No. He was only the final confirmation after several public and private sources preceded him. He was not the determining factor.

Q. Did you actually talk to these other girls, either one?

A. I talked to one of them.

Q. Was there a reason that you didn't talk to the other one?

A. I could not locate her.

Q. Did you make an attempt to locate all of them?

A. Yes.

Mr. Jones: I have nothing further.

* * *

Robbin Woody Howard met with no more satisfaction in court than she had in the pages of the *Register.* Her lawsuit was thrown out before trial because of the *Register's* First Amendment freedom to publish news on matters of public concern. As the Iowa Supreme Court explained:

> Here the disclosure of [Howard's] involuntary sterilization was closely related to the subject matter of the story. It documented the article's theme of maladministration and patient abuses at the Jasper County Home.
>
> In the sense of serving an appropriate news function, the disclosure contributed constructively to the impact of the article. It offered a personalized frame of reference to which the reader could relate, fostering perception and understanding. Moreover, it lent specificity and credibility to the report.
>
> In this way the disclosure served as an effective means of accomplishing the intended news function. It had positive communicative value in attracting the reader's attention to the article's subject matter and in supporting expression of the underlying theme.
>
> We do not say it was necessary for [the *Register*] to do so, but we are certain [it] had a right to treat the identities of victims of involuntary sterilization as matters of legitimate public concern. [Citations omitted.]

Two things should be said at the very outset of our assessment of the Iowa Supreme Court's decision. First, the court was curiously vague about the "matter of public concern" that it saw in the article, at one point referring to "maladministration and patient abuses at the Jasper County Home," and at another point treating the "identities of victims of involuntary sterilizations as matters of legitimate public concern." Second, the court justified the use of Howard's name because it "contributed constructively to the impact of the article," offered a "personalized frame of reference" to the reader, "lent specificity and credibility" to the article, and "attract[ed] the reader's attention to the article's subject matter." Does this standard know any limits whatever? Can't these things be said about virtually any use of a person's name and identity in news?

Yet despite these uncertainties, the Iowa Supreme Court applied the very concept of "public concern" that the Supreme Court announced in the *Bartnicki* case. Howard's case thus lets us more carefully explore the very idea of privacy and the meaning of the new "matter of public concern" rule announced in *Bartnicki.*

What, precisely, was the issue of public concern in the *Register*'s story? Was it alleged mistreatment of patients at the County Home: patients who died under suspicious circumstances, patients given scalding baths, patients who were sterilized against their will? If this was the issue, Howard's role in it was only exemplary: she was simply one of many patients who met many different fates; she was, truly, a victim, playing no part in her own fate and indeed having no say about it. Must the *Register,* then, to defend its account of Howard, explain precisely how her experience, and indeed her name, can be connected to the more general issue of public concern? Why should the *Register* be entitled in the name of the First Amendment to pick Howard out from among the many mistreated patients, and then to sweep her up into the larger public controversy? Was that decision a news decision—a judgment that Howard's case was itself significant and not simply illustrative? Or was the *Register*'s decision a purely rhetorical one, a choice of storytelling technique? Was the *Register* indifferent to Howard as a person, interested only in using her experience as an instrument of composition, a tool for telling another larger story? Should these two justifications be treated the same under the First Amendment?

Or was the matter of public concern Howard's sterilization itself, quite apart from where and at whose hands it occurred? Did the issue of public concern involve Howard's inability to understand what sterilization was? Was it her minority, the undue influence of her doctor, and the tragic and flawed consent of her mother? If Howard herself is the public issue, the *Register* must explain exactly what makes *her* case, picked out from many like it (and some worse), a matter of public concern? How is it different from any other instance of malpractice? And exactly how do the personal facts about Howard—her name at the time, her new name and place of residence (changes made to put the past behind her), her mother's name, her childhood—fit into the newspaper's argument that Howard's sterilization was itself the public issue?

What is "public" about Howard's tragic story? Is it the public's need, or desire, to know about sterilization? Or is it the gripping, novel-like and personally revealing account of a particular person? It could have been any person. Robbin Howard was just unlucky.

Or perhaps the emphasis with matters of public concern should not be on "public," but on "concern." If so, whose concern are we talking about? Is it readers' concern, even if governed by a debased standard of taste, or is it the editor's concern, looking perhaps not only to issues common and judged important to the polity or larger society but also to attracting readers and thus revenues and advertisers?

Is "news" a distinct kind of expression? Is news entitled to distinct and perhaps more generous protection under the First Amendment than an individual's right of free speech? In the *Bartnicki* case, was Jack Yocum's decision to give the tape to the local radio station a constitutionally different one than the station's later decision that the contents of the tape should be published? If so, does that mean—and perhaps require—that news publishers make decisions in particular ways, by means that separately justify a high degree of protection under the First Amendment?

* * *

"[N]ews and truth," Walter Lippmann said, "are not the same thing. . . . The function of news is to signalize an event."[2] This is the dilemma presented when the privacy tort is applied to news, or to the press, in general. As it turns out, the *Des Moines Register*'s news and editorial decision to publish Howard's story seems to have had little to do with Howard herself or even with her story, as such. It was a decision about how best—most grippingly, compellingly, engrossingly—to present an otherwise abstract and depersonalized account of the problems in the county home. The *Register*'s editorial decision was not substantive, not based on a judgment that Howard's story was important in itself, but was instead compositional. It was a choice about process, about how to communicate an issue or event to a public audience.

The significance of Howard's story was its allegorical force. It captured the imagination and focused the attention of a public audience on a current event

2. Walter Lippmann, *Public Opinion* (1922; reprint, New York: The Free Press, 1965), 358.

or issue about which the audience should be informed and with which it should, in the editor's view, be concerned. It "signalized" the issue of illegal treatment in county homes. It was, without doubt, an editorial decision in the best of journalistic tradition. But that editorial decision can be judged only in terms of process, not substance: not in terms of the story, but only how it was told.

"Objectivity," Bernard Roshco has said, "resides not in the quality of the product but in the mode of the performance."[3] The *Register*'s decision in Howard's case, in other words, can be judged not by its quality—its rightness or wrongness, the harm it produces, the importance of its subject or even its object—but by the mode of its performance. Was the decision, in other words, entitled to respect—and constitutional protection—as a news and editorial judgment? This is the question that the Iowa Supreme Court and indeed the "matter of public concern" standard in *Howard* and *Bartnicki* ultimately lead to, for it is the only sensible way in which to understand the process of news and its compositional choices.

By what criteria can we judge editorial judgment and news? Can we judge them in terms of truth, reason, independence, professionalism? And how do we feel about leaving the precise standards, as well as their application in specific cases, to judges? The First Amendment's freedom of the press, designed to protect an independent and critical press from being placed under the controlling thumb of government, surely has something to say about that. Yet if judges can't do the judging, even of process and compositional questions, aren't we left with a de facto rule that the press can *never* be held liable for privacy invasions?

Does this mean that privacy can never serve as a justification for limiting the press? That with respect to publications or disclosures by the press, at least, all privacy is lost?

Or can the privacy question be reconceived by shifting its focus away from publication of news? Can privacy be transformed into a question of the individual's control over information, of ownership of information, and of access to information? Might privacy, in short, be redefined as a question of newsgathering?

Control over information about oneself, and the resultant ability to shape one's own identity in a large and impersonal social order, may actually be a truer way to think about privacy at the turn of the millennium—more fitting, certainly, than using privacy to condemn fallen standards of decency and to compensate individuals for public humiliation and embarrassment. The time may

---

3. Bernard Roshco, *Newsmaking* (Chicago: University of Chicago Press, 1975), 55.

well have long passed for clinging to, let alone recapturing, delicate and refined standards of taste and decency, much less a now-lost collective sense of shame.

The threat to privacy today comes not from the occasional salacious publication but from the collecting, organizing, and selling of identifiable information for use not just by news organizations but more often by commercial organizations, employers, government, and persons who intercept communications or hack into databases. In view of this, perhaps privacy should now focus on the point of collection and assembly of information, empowering individuals—such as Robbin Howard or Gloria Bartnicki—to exercise control over its disclosure and its dissemination at the point of collection. This is the model now being employed to protect medical, financial, and genetic information from disclosure. Many of those new laws place restrictions on distribution of information, coupled with legally enforceable obligations of confidentiality imposed on recipients of private information.

The model is surprisingly similar to the illegal interception law in the *Bartnicki* case and thus the issue presented by *Bartnicki:* Does an exception for matters of public concern fatally undermine an idea of privacy based on control over information or a propertylike ownership of it? Can the concept of "public concern" coexist with this new regime of propertylike interests and rules of process and structure? Or will public concern become such a broad and pliable concept that it will undermine any system of rules and process and structure, indeed, undermine the idea of privacy itself?

The old-style idea of privacy, which took the form of direct restrictions on publication, gave Robbin Woody Howard no solace. The new-style idea of privacy as control over use of information seems likely to prove equally disappointing.

If so—if Robbin Woody Howard and Gloria Bartnicki and Tony Kane all must pay the price for freedom of the press—then what, exactly, are we getting in return? Is the greater appeal, force, and compositional quality that personal secrets add to a news account always worth the price? Might we conclude that in some cases, at least, we can do without knowing as much about Howard, or at least without knowing her name?

Additional Reading

Bezanson, Randall. "The Right to Privacy Revisited: Privacy, News, and Social Change, 1890–1990." *California Law Review* 80 (1992): 1133ff.

Gavison, Ruth. "Privacy and the Limits of Law." *Yale Law Journal* 89 (1986): 421ff.

Post, Robert. "The Social Foundations of Privacy: Community and Self in the Common Law Tort." *California Law Review* 77 (1989): 957ff.

Warren, Samuel D., and Louis D. Brandeis. "The Right to Privacy." *Harvard Law Review* 4 (1890): 192ff.

5. Newsgathering and Press Conduct

Must the press be free to trespass, break and enter, employ deceit, violate its own promises, and invade privacy, all in the name of getting the facts and the story? Should the means by which information is gathered be left largely to the press's own judgment? Is there some special quality that marks the press's judgment, allowing the press to claim the right to do things that would be strictly prohibited if done by individual speakers?

Those responding affirmatively claim that the information so obtained by the press may prove valuable and that if control over the press's access to information is left to government and private parties, the press's ability to provide independent fact and opinion, and thus to serve as a check on power, will be compromised.

Or should the press be subject, like all of us, to general laws that limit access to information and property? If so, is this because the press cannot be trusted to make wise and prudent decisions about which law to ignore? Or is it because, in a paradoxical way, a press that is placed above the law cannot, in the end, maintain its independence?

Those who defend the press's freedom from ordinary legal restrictions on its newsgathering activity employ a straightforward, logical argument: (1) Freedom of the press means freedom to publish. (2) Because obtaining information is essential to the press's publication, newsgathering is an exercise of press freedom. (3) Restrictions on newsgathering are therefore restrictions on the First Amendment's freedom to publish. (4) Consequently, the press should be presumptively exempt from general laws, such as trespass, that restrict newsgathering.

Those who oppose press freedom from ordinary legal restrictions employ a different argument: (1) Freedom of the press means freedom to publish. (2) Freedom to publish requires *independence* from government in *decisions* about whether and what to publish. (3) Newsgathering, as such, has little to do with independent decisions about publication. (4) Exemptions from law given *only* to the press threaten the press's independence, entangling the press with government and making the press dependent on government. (5) General laws, such as trespass, should therefore be applied to the press in order to preserve its independence.

The first argument places greatest emphasis on the information that the press publishes, maximizing the press's power to get it. The second argument places greatest emphasis on the press's independence in *deciding* what is news and whether and how to publish it. We will explore these competing views of press freedom through the stories of two recent newsgathering cases. Both cases involve quite explicit claims by the press that press newsgathering activities should not be subject to laws, such as trespass and deceit, that apply to everyone else. The Supreme Court has not yet dealt with these issues directly and explicitly. We must, then, look to the lower courts for instructive cases. There are plenty to chose from. The *Food Lion* and the *Berger* cases present the questions in the clearest light.

Story 8

Legal Privilege: Above the Law?
Food Lion v. ABC
194 F.3d 505 (4th Cir. 1999)

In fall 1992, ABC's *Prime Time Live* did a "hard-hitting" undercover report on the safety of food-handling practices employed in stores owned by Food Lion, a large grocery chain located in southeastern United States.[1] Based on allegations of unsafe and unhealthy practices lodged by a number of former and current Food Lion employees, ABC decided in early 1992 to run a story in its news magazine, *Prime Time Live*. Many current and former employees were interviewed. Food Lion was then in the midst of a labor dispute. Many, though not all, of the employees ABC interviewed were supporters of the United Food and Commercial Workers Union, which was engaged in a battle with the nonunionized Food Lion chain. The employees' allegations, if true, were serious: unsanitary food handling, repackaging and redating old meat, and selling spoiled food.

ABC decided to film the practices. The network assigned two *Prime Time Live* producers, Lynne Litt (then Lynne Dale) and Susan Barnett, to apply for positions in Food Lion stores, with the purpose of filming the food-handling practices with hidden cameras secreted in their wigs. Each applied, giving false employment backgrounds, false references, and other false information. They were hired and worked for a period of time in different Food Lion stores. Altogether the two undercover producers shot forty-five hours of tape, which *Prime Time Live* edited down to about ten minutes of footage that was used in the *Prime Time Live* broadcast.

The *Prime Time Live* report aired on November 5, 1992, more than nine months after ABC began its investigation of Food Lion's food-handling practices. The report was powerful and, for Food Lion, devastating. It showed redating of meat for which the sale date had passed, unsanitary practices, and the trimming of apparently rotten meat or produce and its repackaging for

---

1. Portions of this story are drawn from a speech entitled "Means and Ends and Food Lion," given by me as a Thrower Lecture at the Emory University School of Law in February 1998 and later published in expanded form as "Means and Ends and Food Lion: The Tension between Exemption and Independence in Newsgathering by the Press," *Emory Law Review* 47 (1998): 895ff.

sale. The piece was graphic. It was hard-hitting. It was right there on film, which meant, to virtually every viewer, that it was *real.* It spoke for itself.

But was ABC's segment really real? Marshall McLuhan warned us, long ago, to be careful about "the real." What appears real may only be the message of the medium. And Walter Lippmann implored journalists to strive to represent reality, by which he meant not events themselves but events in perspective and in a context that would lend them meaning. ABC's Food Lion segment appeared on the surface to do just that: the film of Food Lion's practices gave the events meaning—indeed all the meaning that was necessary. There they were, in full color, before our very eyes. The medium and the message conspired to declare reality, not to report it. Further questioning was made stillborn. The picture was all the perspective and context needed.

As it turns out, there was more to the Food Lion broadcast than met the eye, more than ABC and *Prime Time Live* chose to reveal. In part, the "more" consisted of the tactics that Food Lion challenged in the lawsuit it brought against ABC: the deception used by the producers to get their jobs; their unauthorized entry into nonpublic areas within the Food Lion stores; their use of hidden cameras, secreted in their wigs; the untrained efforts of Litt and Barnett in whose unschooled hands healthful and safe food practice rested for a time; the more than occasional hints of "staging" in the camera work; or the sometimes overenthusiastic efforts of the producers to get an admission or a good "shot." These additional facts were disclosed, if at all, only by inference and silent implication and thus only to the critical and very knowledgeable viewer. They were thoroughly explored in the trial.

But the "more" consisted also, and more fundamentally, of other facts that bear on ABC's newsgathering practices but lurk in the deeper background of the case. These facts concern the news decisions made by ABC: not what ABC did, but why. Why did ABC decide to pursue the story for *Prime Time Live*? Why did ABC decide to go undercover with cameras? And most importantly, why did ABC decide to delay the story in order to air it on November 5, 1992? It is these critical newsgathering and editorial choices, not just the deception, the staging, or the sloppiness in editing, that reveal the most about the newsgathering process and the nature of ABC's claim that it should be immune from the general law of trespass, fraud, and deception.

Why did the Food Lion story become a *Prime Time Live* story? In the view of many journalists, ABC could have, and should have, immediately run the story as a news piece. Indeed, with the information gathered from the disgruntled employees, including affidavits, ABC almost certainly had enough, for news purposes, to publish the story immediately. Some checking into possible incidents of sickness caused by Food Lion practices, the existence

of health department citations, or formal charges that might have been previously filed would ordinarily be undertaken before a news story was released,
but these steps were not taken even after the decision to proceed with the story
as a *Prime Time Live* segment, with the attendant delay that decision caused.

The decision to go undercover with hidden cameras to obtain filmed footage of the practices was thus not, at base, simply a news decision. It was a
broadcast news decision, and more particularly, it was a television news magazine broadcast news decision. Filmed footage was not needed to establish
the news bona fides of the story. It was not needed to produce a story that
would be believed or acted upon, thus alleviating any public health risk. It
was, instead, a necessary step to producing a television news story, a piece of
investigative journalism in which the hard-hitting facts and allegations can
be established because they are shown, and thus real. The message of the
broadcast news medium is image.

ABC's decision to air the segment on November 5, 1992, is perhaps the most
interesting one. As it turns out, November 5 fell in the fall sweeps week, the
week in which the television ratings are measured and the advertising rates
are set for the following months. Did ABC have to wait until November 5 to
get the story finished? The undercover work had been done over a two-week
period in late April and early May. Little further investigation (such as further interviews, tracking down health department records, or speaking to
health department employees) was thereafter conducted, and even if ABC
had done so, the story could have been ready by June or July. In fact, the story appears to have been "in the can" by midsummer.

Prime Time Live was not doing particularly well at the time. Its ratings were
low. A hard-hitting, undercover exposé of a very large grocery chain in the
Southeast might help the struggling newsmagazine in the ratings game—and
what better week to run such a universally appealing, titillating piece, pro-
moted by fifteen-second spots announcing an "investigation into rotten food
at a well-known supermarket chain" than a fall sweeps week? Might ABC have
made the judgment that, having discovered a health problem, it would delay reporting it in order to go undercover for video footage? Then having
gathered powerful footage, might ABC have decided, in the summer of 1992,
to wait until the November sweeps period to bolster its ratings for *Prime Time
Live* and for ABC as a whole? Might the *Prime Time Live* promotional spots
for the story have avoided using the name of the store or its location to maximize the potential national audience?

ABC's actions don't paint a very pretty picture of television journalism.
But should they make a difference to ABC's claim that it should be exempt
from laws of trespass and deceit because it was "newsgathering"? Should

courts and juries be allowed to examine the methods and motives of news organizations and editors? By what standards would they do so? If the standards would be the standards of journalism, would journalists be called to the stand to testify against journalists based on their expert judgments about the meaning of sound and reasonable editorial procedures and publication decisions? Does the First Amendment permit government to set standards by which the press's freedom is to be exercised? Judges and juries who would do so clearly represent government, the same government the press is to "check" through its publication of independent fact and opinion.

Yet do we have a choice? If the press consists of news publishers, whether large or small, who share special and common qualities and who perform special functions that distinguish them from all other varieties of persons and organizations involved in the collection and dissemination of information— such as the "spammer" on e-mail or the participants in chat rooms on the Internet—then there must be features that distinguish the press and disqualify others from claiming protection that only the press enjoys under the First Amendment.

Freedom of the press rests, at its core, on editorial judgment, on the editor's own independent decision about importance and usefulness as news, not on the will of an advertiser or the whim of an audience. This is the public side of the private and profit-oriented commercial press.

Were ABC's decisions—to delay the broadcast of the Food Lion story in order to obtain a filmed, and thus more powerful and apparently real, account of Food Lion's practices and to further delay the broadcast until sweeps week—the kinds of judgments that should be protected by the First Amendment as instances of editorial freedom? Did ABC believe that actual film, not just employees making accusations, was essential to the story's credibility? Did ABC believe that only by reaching a large national audience in the November sweeps period could the story produce the reaction needed to force changes at Food Lion? Or were ABC's judgments so affected by considerations of its audience's desires; by a felt need to maximize the forcefulness, narrowing of focus and perspective, and power of the visual medium of television; and by purely market-based and commercial considerations that they should not qualify for protection as editorial judgment?

We don't know what motivated ABC's editors and executives. The answers are in ABC's sole possession, and ABC has not said much about its decisions. But we can ask, *hypothetically,* whether decisions by ABC to go undercover to maximize the impact of the medium of television; to further delay broadcast until sweeps week as a means of helping to shore up *Prime Time Live*'s fading fortunes; and to plug it hard in advance with ads that emphasize scandal and health risk but that fail to identify the store or even its location, in order, perhaps, to appeal to a national audience should qualify as protected editorial judgment under the First Amendment.

As to the first decision—filming undercover to maximize the impact of the medium—it must be acknowledged that the medium *is* relevant to news. News, after all, must be presented in a way that people will read or watch. And this may involve some delay: delay in the writing and editing process to make the story clear, accurate, and appealingly written, as well as delay in the newsgathering process to obtain and process film footage for use on television. Was ABC's decision to go undercover to film the alleged food practices an appropriate one for a television news broadcast?

The question of whether a decision qualifies as protected editorial judgment is not, strictly speaking, an objective one, dependent strictly on the fact that a "news" organization makes it. If one person decides to don a wig with a camera hidden in it, intending just to fish around for embarrassing footage that might then be sold to the highest bidder, news broadcaster or not, we wouldn't ordinarily describe it as "editorial news judgment," much less *news* gathering. Editorial judgment concerns not just what was done but why it was done. Shouldn't the same rule be applied to ABC: its decisions are protected editorial decisions if, but only if, they are made for the right reasons?

The circumstances surrounding ABC's decision to engage in illegal newsgathering tactics suggest that the decision was, in critical measure, a product of ABC's desperation to jump-start a failing competitor of *60 Minutes* and *20/20*. It was also, it seems, a decision to maximize the image and power of video, particularly its power to transform a major, but weak, story about widespread food practices in a large grocery chain into a compelling representation of a few, perhaps even staged, instances of food handling that would "speak for themselves"; thus ABC could dispense with the need to provide broader evidence, perspective, context, and, even, balance.

What about the decision to delay the broadcast of the Food Lion story for up to five months in order to air it as a well-advertised segment during sweeps week, when ratings and thus advertising revenues are set? This decision is even more difficult to rationalize as protected editorial judgment, unless, of course, the First Amendment is interpreted as protecting decisions to maximize revenues and ratings in a competitive market. To be sure, competition is part and parcel of the press's work. It energizes a free press and also helps keep it honest and in line.

But if decisions about conduct leading to publication, including decisions about the strategic timing of publication, are to be protected by the First Amendment, shouldn't they be based in part on the public's need for information, not just on the publisher's need for profits? Can ABC's decision to delay broadcast for months in order to hit sweeps week be understood to rest in any fashion on public need? Or was ABC's decision based on what would attract an audience *at ratings time,* thereby serving the commercial will of a publisher rather than the news judgment of an editor?

The press today is experiencing a transformation from a world of monopoly to one of unrestrained competition; from a concentrated market with few choices to a decentralized market of almost unlimited choices; from an economic model of heavy fixed costs and high barriers to entry to one of low fixed costs and few barriers to entry; from a model of the press in which editors needed protection from the will of powerful publishers to one in which editors need protection from the new imperatives of audience preference, advertiser influence, and financial market demands for higher margins and profits. As the Newspaper Association of America's chief economist put it, news, like entertainment, is devoted to the enterprise of "delivering eyeballs to advertisers. . . . [L]ow income areas are not where you concentrate efforts." In a localized and decentralized market with wide choices, advertisers are increasingly the most effective surrogates for the audience in its newly defined market segments. This phenomenon is occurring in the traditional news medium of the newspaper, which is heavily dependent on advertiser revenues. It is a more longstanding and obvious phenomenon in television, a medium that is completely dependent on advertising revenues.

In this economic environment, a decision by ABC to delay the Food Lion story to maximize the power of the television medium and resuscitate ABC's poor ratings would be a perfectly rational and understandable one. But that is an entirely different matter from whether it can be described as an exercise of editorial judgment about news that should be protected by the First Amendment. On the First Amendment claim, should we indulge a heavy presumption in ABC's favor, especially when ABC is seeking immunity or exemption from generally applicable legal restrictions on its conduct—on deceit, trespass, and misrepresentation, all of which ABC purposely engaged in? Laws against such conduct apply to many other organizations and individuals who might also seek to excuse their actions by claiming that there was value or utility in their law-violating behavior. For example, corporations cannot use the device of bribery to seek new business overseas; labor unions cannot shut down public services to protect their employee-members' economic well-being; and ideological organizations cannot take the law into their own hands as a means of protest and expression. If ABC is to be immune from such laws, shouldn't it have to offer more than its logo to qualify?

Yet setting the standard of justification too high for ABC might permit the law to parse every publication decision to determine the considerations on which it rests and thus to second-guess the judgments, whether good or bad, made by editors in news organizations. Such a result, potentially destructive of ABC's independence, would be unacceptable. It would make a shambles of the private and independent press we enjoy. It would undermine the "free" press the constitution guarantees.

But does this mean that ABC must be granted automatic or absolute immunity in its newsgathering? Many would say "yes." To subject any of ABC's decisions, no matter their character or circumstances, to legal review would violate the First Amendment and press freedom. Others, however, would argue that the need to avoid legal review means that when the press engages in newsgathering conduct that violates generally applicable law, it should bear the consequences, just like everyone else. Enforcing the trespass or fraud law against ABC would involve no parsing of editorial choices whatsoever, for "getting the story by whatever means" would *never* serve as a defense or excuse for illegal conduct by the press.

Which rule, exemption or not, best serves the press's independence and editorial freedom under the First Amendment?

Additional Reading

Bevier, Lillian. "An Informed Public, and Informing Press: The Search for a Constitutional Principle." *California Law Review* 68 (1980): 482ff.

Blasi, Vincent. "The Newsman's Privilege: An Empirical Study." *Michigan Law Review* 70 (1971): 229ff.

Levi, Lili. "Dangerous Liaisons: Seduction and Betrayal in Confidential Press-Source Relations." *Rutgers Law Review* 43 (1991): 609ff.

Lewis, Anthony. "A Preferred Position for Journalism?" *Hofstra Law Review* 7 (1979): 595ff.

———. "A Public Right to Know about Public Institutions: The First Amendment as a Sword." *Supreme Court Review* 1980 (1980): 1ff.

Stewart, Potter. "Or of the Press." *Hastings Law Journal* 26 (1975): 631ff.

STORY 9

Newsgathering and Press Independence
Berger v. Hanlon
129 F.3d 505 (9th Cir. 1996)

Paul Berger was seventy-one when it happened.[1] His wife, Erma, was eighty-one. They lived on a seventy-five-thousand-acre ranch in Montana.

Paul Berger appears to be something of a character: independent and even, perhaps, a bit crusty; acclimated to the out of doors and to nature but also mindful of his livelihood and his livestock and thus not unwilling to use a strategically employed chemical or two, or even a shotgun, to control the damage done by prey, including birds of prey such as eagles and hawks. In this we might assume that Berger was typical, hardly the exception. There was certainly no reason to think that he was some kind of nut—a militia type, for example. He was a rancher in the Western mold.

Berger's alleged strategic use of poison and a shotgun to kill eagles came to the attention of the U.S. Fish and Wildlife Service and its agents in January 1993. Two of the Bergers' former employees reported to Fish and Wildlife Service agents in Montana that they had seen Berger poison and shoot eagles a few years earlier. An investigation immediately ensued. It was short and, it appears, yielded little more than the informants' tales. But it was not confidential. Montana is a country of big spaces and small places, so it is not surprising that word of the investigation got out fairly soon after it started. Everyone tends to know everyone else's business, and the doings of the federal government, whether the Internal Revenue Service or the more benign, yet powerful, Fish and Wildlife Service, were no doubt the subject of public curiosity.

Among those who found out about the investigation was Cable News Network (CNN), in the person of Jack Hamann, and Turner Broadcasting System (TBS) employees Robert Rainey and Donald Hooper. Hamann bore the title Correspondent, CNN Environmental Unit. The investigation was

---

1. Portions of this story were drawn from a speech entitled "Means and Ends and Food Lion," given by me as a Thrower Lecture at the Emory University School of Law in February 1998 and later published in expanded form as "Means and Ends and Food Lion: The Tension between Exemption and Independence in Newsgathering by the Press," *Emory Law Journal* 47 (1998): 895ff.

naturally of interest to Hamann—so much so, in fact, that it inspired him to think of the story that could be made from it. It was a story, perhaps, of environmental predation by fiercely independent, land-loving, government-despising ranchers in the West, spiced up by the story of a federal raid captured on film as it happened, calvary coming full speed to the rescue of the eagle. As the imagining grew, so, too, did the CNN and TBS staff on the scene, with lawyers now added from the CNN Legal Department and others from the CNN Environmental Unit.

It was thus a delegation of CNN and TBS employees who in early 1993 approached Fish and Wildlife Service agents in Montana. What they proposed was a straight and simple television deal: if the government would let CNN accompany the agents on a raid of the Bergers' ranch, hidden cameras running, CNN would use the footage to help the government "publicize its efforts to combat environmental crime." In return, CNN and TBS would get real-life action footage that could be used on its environmental programs—maybe the environmental equivalent of *COPS* or *Rescue 911* or *Justice Files*. It was a "you scratch my back, I'll scratch yours" arrangement. And the price was small: CNN would keep editorial control but would agree to embargo its telecast until charges were brought, the trial was underway, and the jury was empaneled.

Remarkably, as if to confirm the stakes for each party, to formalize the arrangement's deal-like quality, the parties memorialized it in a written contract. Kris McLean, an Assistant United States Attorney in Montana, and Jack Hamann of CNN, signed the contract, which provided:

> This confirms our agreement that the United States Attorney's Office for the District of Montana agrees to allow CNN to accompany USFWS [United States Fish and Wildlife Service] Agents as they attempt to execute a criminal search warrant near Jordan, Montana, some time during the week of March 22, 1993. Except as provided below, CNN shall have complete editorial control over any footage it shoots; it shall not be obliged to use the footage; and does not waive any rights or privileges it may have with respect to the footage.
>
> In return, CNN agrees to embargo the telecast of any videotape of the attempt to execute the search warrant until either: (1) a jury has been empaneled and instructed by a judge not to view television reports about the case; or (2) the defendant waives his right to a jury trial and agrees to have his case tried before a judge; or (3) a judge accepts a plea bargain; or (4) the government decides not to bring charges relating to the attempt to execute the search warrant.

The parties executed the contract on March 11, 1993. A search warrant for the Bergers' ranch, excluding the residence, was issued on March 18. The judge who issued the warrant was not told of the deal between the Fish and Wildlife Service and CNN. With the warrant issued, activity picked up speed. Presearch planning and briefings were scheduled. CNN was made aware of the material included in the warrant and other information that was supposed to be sealed until after the warrant was executed. What then transpired is described in the opinion of the United States Court of Appeals for the Ninth Circuit:

> On the morning of the search, the government team, accompanied by a media crew, gathered on a county road leading to the ranch, to discuss the execution of the warrant. The cameras videotaped that gathering. The broadcast team then proceeded with the federal agents and [Assistant U.S. Attorney] McLean in a caravan of approximately ten vehicles to a point near the Bergers' ranch. Media cameras mounted on the outside of government vehicles, or placed in their interior, documented every move made by the federal [agents]. At all times during and immediately prior to the search, [Fish and Wildlife] Special Agent Joel Scrafford was wired with a hidden CNN microphone which was continuously transmitting live audio to the CNN technical crew.
>
> Mr. Berger approached and met the caravan in a pickup truck on the road leading up to the ranch. Agent Scrafford proceeded to inform Mr. Berger of the search warrant, and asked him whether he could ride to the house in Mr. Berger's truck so that he could explain to Mrs. Berger what they were going to do. Mr. Berger allowed Agent Scrafford to ride with him in the pickup truck. Upon arriving at the Bergers' residence, the two men entered the house together. Audio recorded at the site indicates that Mr. Berger consented to Agent Scrafford's entry into the home at this time. The parties disagree on whether the agents who entered the residence with Agent Scrafford searched the residence for incriminating evidence, and whether Agent Scrafford's subsequent entries into the home were consented to. However, it is undisputed that Agent Scrafford recorded all his conversations with the Bergers inside the house.
>
> The Bergers were not informed that Agent Scrafford was wearing a microphone or that the cameras that were visible during the search belonged to the media. The media recorded more than eight hours of tape and it broadcast both the video footage and the sound recordings made in the house.

The U.S. Attorney subsequently filed criminal charges against Berger for the taking of one or more golden eagles and ferruginous hawks and one ring-billed gull and for the use of a registered pesticide, Furdan, "in a manner inconsistent with its labeling." The latter charge was a misdemeanor. He was acquitted of all charges except the misdemeanor for using the pesticide inconsistently with its labeling.

Then the Bergers sued. They sued the federal government for violation of their constitutional right to be free from unreasonable searches and seizures under the Fourth Amendment. They sued CNN and TBS for violation of the Federal Wiretap Act and for state law claims, including trespass. Most notably, the Bergers sued CNN and TBS for violating their constitutional rights. Ordinarily, constitutional rights can only be violated by the government. But this rule was overridden when the district court judge concluded that CNN and TBS were acting in concert with and on behalf of the government and thus served as an arm of the government. As the district judge put it, "[T]he 'inextricable' involvement of the media with both the planning and execution of th[e] search, the government's active involvement with the media's news gathering activities, and the mutually-derived benefits, is more than enough to make the media government actors."

The district court rejected all of the Bergers' claims. But the Bergers appealed to the United States Court of Appeals for the Ninth Circuit. The Appeals Court agreed with the Bergers, reversed the district court, and ruled that most of the Bergers' claims, including all those mentioned above, were valid if proven and should be allowed to proceed to trial.

* * *

The press's editorial freedom depends on the press's independence from those persons and institutions, most notably (but not only) government institutions and officials, about which it must make judgments in the interest of the public's need to know. Government is neither a friend nor foe to the press. It is, instead, a frequent object of the press's editorial judgments and therefore an institution upon which the press cannot afford to be reliant. Reliance on government, or dependence on government, would threaten to skew and shape judgments that might otherwise be made in the interest of public need: whether to investigate and publish, what to publish, how to publish, and when to publish.

Independence of the press connotes non-dependence, not hostility. As the Supreme Court has put it, press independence requires that the press remain at arm's length from government. The press must not be singled out by government for special treatment, whether in the form of a special benefit or burden; instead, to the extent possible, the press's interests should be the same as those shared generally by larger political constituencies of which the press is but a small part.

The *Berger* case reveals how tempting it is for a competitive news organization to sacrifice its long-term interest in independence in order to achieve short-term financial or competitive advantages. To get a good story, CNN entered into a joint venture with government agents. CNN assisted the government in achieving the government's political and public relations ends in exchange for a license to engage in cooperative activity that, if done alone, would amount to criminal trespass and invasion of privacy, if not more. What, we must ask, did CNN give up in exchange?

First, CNN gave up control over what was filmed, for its agreement was that CNN would be permitted to accompany and film only the agents conducting the search. Did CNN accompany and film all of the agents, or only some? Who decided which? Might there have been others of whom CNN was unaware?

Second, CNN gave up control over the "when" of its publication decisions, agreeing in a written contract to withhold publication until a specified point in time that was set to serve the government's prosecutorial interests.

Third, CNN compromised, and therefore effectively gave up, its ability to criticize the very government decisions of which it had become a complicit party.

—Would CNN criticize the government's decision to conduct the search, given CNN's joint involvement in its planning and execution?
—Would CNN be likely to criticize the government for allowing CNN to participate in the search? The press commentary, published after CNN's involvement in the raid became public, while distinctly muted, confirms that *CNN's participation itself* was a significant news story and the subject of public controversy.
—Would CNN be likely to use the fruits of its participation to reveal wrongdoing committed by the government agents and CNN personnel in the course of the search? Examples of wrongdoing include the facts, known to CNN, that the judge who issued the warrant was not apprised of CNN's involvement in the search, and that CNN's recording equipment was employed to effect an unconsented and unconstitutional search of the Bergers' *home*, which was not covered by the warrant. Both examples of wrongdoing benefited CNN. Disclosing them would embarrass CNN, expose CNN to potential liability, and jeopardize the prospect of future advantageous arrangements between CNN and the government.

CNN, in short, gave up a great deal. But these are not the only things that CNN gave up. At a more fundamental level, it was CNN's later claim to immunity from liability in the Bergers' lawsuit that jeopardized not only CNN's independence but that of the press in general. CNN's claim of First Amendment immunity legitimated what CNN had done. That is, a finding of constitutional immunity for CNN's newsgathering would have freed *any* news organization not only to violate general law but also to conspire with government or even with private parties to facilitate the press's law-violating techniques. Such a claim would have placed the press in a vastly increased position of *dependence* on government for leads; for information; and for the facilities of privacy invasion (including illegal participation in searches and seizures) or trespass, harassment, fraud, and deception.

It is in these respects that a rule of exemption, immunity, or privilege, even if absolute, may well reduce, rather than enhance, the independence of the press when it makes decisions about whether, what, how, and when to publish information that the public needs to know. A press that is specially exempt from law is by that exemption given a special allegiance to that law and to the legal and political system that maintains the press's special legal status. This is the concern regularly expressed by the press itself when required to participate in pooled coverage of war, coordinated by the Defense Department. How can the press be independent if it is subject to seeing only what the Defense Department decides to release or reveal?

A benefit specially conferred is one that can be specially withdrawn. And a press possessed of a special stake in the existing legal order is not in a position to criticize fiercely and independently that legal order. It is more likely to curry its favor, to cooperate with it, to join it, and to benefit further from it.

There are limits on the press under the Constitution, limits on what qualifies as the press, limits on the actions the press may freely take, limits on the kinds of judgments it may make. An Internet chat room is not a press publisher, though it is a publisher of fact and opinion on current affairs. The telephone company is not a newspaper or its equivalent, though it is engaged in the business of transmitting current information on the widest possible scale. What's different about the chat room and the phone company?

A most instructive recent case involved a lawsuit against Compuserve, a Web browser, alleging that Compuserve was liable for a defamatory statement that was published on one of the chat rooms provided for customers by the company. Compuserve had published the false and damaging statement as fact to others and therefore should be liable just as a newspaper would be liable for a story it writes or pulls off the Associated Press wire. The interesting thing about the case was Compuserve's defense. Compuserve disclaimed having made *any* editorial judgment, any selection choices about what to publish and what not to publish. Compuserve was a forum for speech, but it wasn't a press publisher because it exercised no editorial judgment at all. It was simply like the telephone company, the spam distributor, or most cable operators.

Is the press different than Compuserve and the phone company? Does the difference lie, among other places, in the fact that the press makes judgments about publication within the framework of its constitutional role of providing useful and interesting information and opinion to the public? If so, is it possible to avoid drawing and then enforcing the lines of demarcation that separate press claims from claims of other publishers and speakers?

For some, the distinction is critical and must be drawn, though drawn carefully when it is the government—its courts and juries—that are acting. The press performs special functions, and it is those very functions and responsibilities that underlie claims such as ABC's and CNN's in the *Food Lion* and *Berger* cases. If the press's role is disseminating information about government to the public, it must enjoy special discretion in choosing how to obtain the information.

Many others, both scholars and journalists, argue that no judgments about the meaning of the press and no distinctions between the chat room and the daily newspaper need be made. This is because the press's freedom under the First Amendment is no different from the freedom afforded individuals and companies under the free speech guarantee. The press is simply another speaker with the same First Amendment rights to speak—and the same limitations on those rights.

But can this be the proper view? Doesn't the press perform constitutional functions, disseminating information and opinion widely, checking the exercise of government and private power through fact and truth, affording a source of information independent of government and, indeed, any other form of ideological or political allegiance? The free speech guarantee protects individuals in their liberty of belief and thought and expression, and more lately corporations in their liberty and freedom to speak and advertise. These aims have little to do with checking government and informing decision making in a democracy. Different purposes may require different measures of protection under the First Amendment.

More fundamentally, if those who argue that press and speech freedoms are the same are correct, then our inquiry has come full circle to the privilege claims presented by ABC and CNN in *Food Lion* and *Berger*. If the press's rights are the same as those afforded individuals when they speak, then the result for ABC and CNN is clear: the press is subject to the same rules as apply to individuals. The press enjoys no special privilege from laws that prohibit trespassing or deceiving or defrauding.

It is not the press's self-interest that the First Amendment protects. It is instead the press's independence that is protected, for it is independence that enables the press to make difficult, sometimes costly, judgments, including the judgment that law violation is occasionally necessary *and worth the consequences* in order to serve the public's need for information on the subjects of "politics and political economy." It is this higher obligation that was voiced in the appeal of the People's Charter Union in January 1849 at a critical moment in the struggle against the stamp tax in England and at a formative moment in the emergence of a free press:

> We are told that Englishmen are too ignorant to be entrusted with that franchise which is now nearly universal in Western Europe; we demand, then, that ignorance should no longer be compulsory. It is not always easy to know who are our real friends; but we think we are safe in denouncing as our enemies all those who desire to perpetuate our ignorance. By the penny stamp not only are we debarred from the expression of our thoughts and feelings, but it is made impossible for men of education or of capital to employ themselves in instructing us, as the price of their publication would be enhanced by the stamp to an amount which we cannot pay. A cheap stamped newspaper cannot be a good one. And if we are asked why we cannot be satisfied with the elegant and polite literature which may be had cheaply, we reply that we can no longer exist upon the earth without information on the subjects of politics and political economy. . . . And we say to those who are within the pale of the Constitution, "if you cannot give us this knowledge, at least do not prevent us from seeking it ourselves; to tax the light of knowledge was ever a crime—see that you commit not the crime of perpetuating that tax." Those who should do so would brand themselves indelibly as the willful oppressors of the poor, and would be justly responsible for all the inevitable results of our ignorance.[2]

It may seem strange to conclude that independence of the press is guaranteed by making the press, without exception, subject to laws that apply generally to the press and nonpress alike, but in many respects that is the moral of the English struggle to free the press. A press that is given special exemption must defend its exemption, politically if not legally, without the benefit of a claim to equal treatment with everyone else; the press, in other words, must justify itself continually as deserving such a special position. And a press that is able to receive special benefits must, in accepting them, submit a portion of its independence to their dispenser, which in most cases will be the government, a government agency, or an officer or employee of the government. Isn't this the very reason why most news organizations prohibit journalists from taking gifts from sources or news subjects?

In the *Berger* case, CNN and TBS sought special benefits from the government. Compromised independence is precisely what did, and almost always will, result. CNN was made a party to the planning of the search, its tactics,

---

2. Collet Dobson Collet, *History of the Taxes on Knowledge: Their Origin and Repeal* (Ann Arbor, Mich.: Gryphon Books, 1971), 45.

and its strategy. CNN's cameras were there to serve two masters: the news and video-based publication objectives of CNN and the government's interest in publicity. And if the government's planned raid had turned sour, CNN would have been a party to the mistakes and therefore an unlikely discloser of them. CNN was unlikely to complain or criticize the hand that fed it. And CNN was even less likely to assess independently the situation of the Bergers, the grounds for the government's decisions, the conduct of the search, or the possible political ends served by a major raid. With cameras running and five vehicles of agents spreading out on a small ranch owned and operated by a crusty seventy-one-year-old rancher who believes in private property and his ability to exercise control on it, CNN transformed itself into a participant in the government's actions—a partner in the government's acts, not an independent observer and reporter of them.

Like ABC, which did little independent investigation of prior complaints about Food Lion or comparisons with other chains or investigations into the conduct of health authorities, CNN would do no independent work in the *Berger* case. CNN let the government define the story and shape its news content. Why?

In today's news business, profits are a function of audience, and audience is defined not in terms of raw numbers but in demographic characteristics—buying power, wealth, attitudes and habits, and the like. The profitable firm is now the firm that focuses content on the best segment of an audience, the segment for which the advertiser will pay the most. And just as newspapers around the country are happily shedding circulation as a conscious strategy to create a well-defined audience for advertisers, and making more money doing so, broadcasters also are looking for their markets, focusing their content, including news content, on those markets, and worrying less about loss of nonpreferred audiences.

In this way the audience's preferences have been brought home to the editors of broadcast news programming, and those preferences are being brought home in terms more specific than ever before imagined. Geraldo Rivera is kept by NBC, not lost to Fox, by giving him the dignity of a news anchor. This is done, in part, by broadening the organizational reach of the NBC news division to encompass more entertainment programming, anointing it as news. Economics don't explain everything in life or in journalism, but they tell a lot about why ABC, CNN, and other news organizations have taken certain actions.

Is the rise of new, and often demographically and competitively driven, techniques bad or good for news and journalism and press freedom? The new techniques would be bad if they took control of the news judgments and the news process itself, as a tail wagging the dog. If, on the other hand, the news judgments remain well-grounded—based on public importance and *need* to know—but are simply adapted to new economics and new audiences, there would be little ground for concern, for the techniques would be employed in good faith and in pursuit of important ends.

But neither extreme—means dominating ends (technique dominating content or news decisions) or ends dominating means—seems to be the case. The picture is more complicated than that. So we have to think about ways in which we can distinguish the legitimate use of new techniques—in service of effective communication of independent news judgment—from the illegitimate. Not surprisingly, the criteria for making that distinction lie in the very distinction itself: whether the question of technique precedes or follows the substantive news judgment; whether technique serves news content, resting on a good-faith judgment that news content will be improved and its communication to an audience enhanced, rather than the opposite; and whether the news judgment itself is premised on a good-faith belief in what is important and on what the audience needs to know, not just what the audience might want to see. Is technique employed to achieve a higher purpose than commerce and market and advertiser and passion? Could *Prime Time Live*'s actions in the *Food Lion* case or CNN's in the *Berger* case meet this standard?

The question, in the end, is the same for ABC's hidden camera as it is for an act of civil disobedience: was it undertaken with knowledge of the legal consequences, in service of a public interest, as a selfless act made in the interest of news, which is the dissemination of information on public and private matters about which people need to be informed? Or was it an instance of important news being consciously delayed in order to maximize the visuals, increase an audience, and raise the ratings and the advertising revenues?

Was CNN's participation with the government the only, and thus a necessary, means of obtaining a very important news story, or was it a Faustian selling of CNN's journalistic soul to get material that would titillate but not inform, sating the audience's thirst for commercial purposes only? Can selflessness coexist with dependence? Can the press be independent of law yet occupy a place of special privilege under law, possessed of a special legal status? Can the press devote itself to independent reporting of fact and opinion, critical not only of people or policies or law, yet at the same time have an institutional stake in the existing legal order? Can a press with special privileges not enjoyed by the public it serves perform as a skeptical chronicler and critic of the existing legal, political, and economic order?

The press must be institutionally agnostic in its editorial choices. Many would argue that ABC crossed this line in the *Food Lion* case, serving its corporate and advertiser interests at the expense of its audience's interests in news—and at the expense of those consumers at Food Lion stores whose food, ABC believed, was unsafe but who were not informed of this fact until November 5, although the story *as news* was essentially complete nearly six months earlier. Many would also argue that CNN crossed the line in the *Berger* case by entering into a formal arrangement with the government, making itself a party to, and thus an unlikely critic of, the government's action. CNN's was an act of entertainment, not of journalism.

Would privileging ABC's and CNN's shortsightedness by excusing them from liability serve to legitimate conduct that undermines journalism and jeopardizes the very independence that the press has achieved only after hundreds of years of struggle? Would a rule that takes as its starting point—its presumptive result, if you will—that the press should be subject to generally applicable law better respect the press's constitutional interest in independence from government? Would such a rule also give respect to the moral force of the press's self-conscious decision to violate law in pursuit of ends it considers more important?

The law's normal response when an individual violates society's rules for a moral or just end is to give the act a decent name—civil disobedience—and then to hold the law violator to account, on the theory that if the "end" is very important, it must be important enough to achieve at the price the law exacts. Jesse Jackson recently went to jail overnight, a price he was willing to pay for taking the law into his own hands in service of his own ends. Whether we agree with him or not, we should respect him for that. We would discount the importance of Jackson's act by ignoring it or excusing it.

Why should ABC and CNN be treated differently?

Additional Reading

Bevier, Lillian. "An Informed Public, and Informing Press: The Search for a Constitutional Principle." *California Law Review* 68 (1980): 482ff.

Cranberg, Gilbert, Randall Bezanson, and John Soloski. *Taking Stock: Journalism and the Publicly Traded Newspaper Company.* Ames: Iowa State University Press, 2001.

6. How Free Can the Press Be?

In a wonderful, yet little-known, volume titled *History of the Taxes on Knowledge,* which recounts the struggle against the Stamp Act in eighteenth- and nineteenth-century England, Collet Dobson Collet, the author and chronicler, begins with the following fictional account: "When the King of the Tonga Isles, in the Pacific Ocean, was initiated by Mr. Marriner, the missionary, into the mysteries of the art of writing, he was alarmed at the idea of his subjects learning to read: 'I should,' he said, 'be surrounded with plots.'"[1]

A free press is a "bulwark of liberty," an essential restraint on tyranny—perhaps even more essential in a democracy. The press's stock in trade is knowledge; its duty is public dissemination. Knowledge is common property. In a free and democratic society dependent ultimately on the consent of the governed, the broad diffusion of knowledge is the most basic premise upon which we have cast our fate.

Press freedom, in short, exists to serve a purpose that is constitutive of democracy and freedom. Trading in knowledge, the common property of self-government and liberty, necessarily requires that the press be independent of government and private centers of influence and authority. Judgments about fact, truth, and importance must be made free of coercion or inducement by government. Guaranteeing that independence means, as the Pentagon Papers case illustrates, that the press must have a right to publish that which is embarrassing or harmful or unpopular.

Yet the press is both constitutive of democracy and obedient to it; the press is not just an observer but also a participant in the American experiment in

---

1. Collet Dobson Collet, *History of the Taxes on Knowledge: Their Origin and Repeal* (Ann Arbor, Mich.: Gryphon Books, 1971), 1.

self-government. Thus, the press's freedom, like all other important freedoms (speech, private property, due process, equality), is not absolute. The press is not above the law. There are limits, difficult as they may be to identify and administer. And the first limit, reflected in the Pentagon Papers case, is that the press's freedom may not be exercised in a way that threatens the foundations of democracy or equally important premises on which our democracy rests, such as human life, personal liberty, or the government's capacity to govern. Enforcing this limit is where the contested questions of immediacy, directness of causation, and seriousness of harm come into play.

Other limits are equally important, but equally difficult to calibrate. The press is not just a disseminator of information. It is an exerciser of judgment about the information to be disseminated: its truth, its importance, its public value or utility. This is what is commonly called "editorial judgment." Information is the form press publication takes; judgment is the substance. Only if the press offers its own independent publication judgment can readers or listeners or viewers accept or reject it for what it is rather than who it serves. Does independence transcend freedom from government censorship or control? Does it necessarily imply, and perhaps even require, a private and competitive system of knowledge dissemination, free of government, free of private authority or interests, and free also of a monopoly of the information providers—the press actors—themselves? This, of course, is the dilemma presented in the *Tornillo* case. In many ways the Supreme Court's answer— "editing is what editors are for"—has a shallow and unsatisfying ring.

And then there are the equally basic, but more particularized, questions about the scope of the press's freedom—the ends to which it is directed. Does the press owe a duty to truth? Is truth, or perhaps more accurately *truth seeking*, a necessary premise upon which readers must rely, lest the press's democratically constitutive function break down in a world of data anarchy? And how can truth be measured for this purpose—by truth itself, judged in courts of the government, or by the reporter's and editor's genuine, though imperfect, aspiration for truth?

Is the press no different in function or freedom or constitutional stature from any speaker or writer or publisher? Or is its stock in trade knowledge, which means fact and opinion on matters of general importance in a self-governing society? If so, can the line—say, between news and entertainment, fact and imagination—be measured by what is published, or rather by how and why something is published? A used Chevrolet, even its price, may be useful and important public information in some contexts (perhaps in relation to odometer fraud), but in the hands of a used-car dealer is the price of the used Chevy quite the same? Hugo Zacchini claimed that his human cannonball act was entertainment, pure and simple: factual to be sure, but not really more than a satisfying sensation of danger and awe even in the hands of a television station's nightly news broadcast.

The Pittsburgh Commission on Human Relations claimed that employment want-ads served no purpose other than commerce in jobs. Dressing up the want-ad columns in sex-designated terms could not convert them into statements of social policy. But how can we know when, for example, the Marlboro Man ad is just an advertisement for cigarettes, and when it serves instead as a cultural icon? Is intention relevant here, too? If so, how far dare we probe the mind of an editor who claims to be exercising independent editorial judgment?

Or is the distinction instead, as the Court suggested in the *Pittsburgh Press* case, that the activity fostered by the want-ad columns—sex discrimination— was itself illegal? But how can such a distinction be squared with the Pentagon Papers case, in which the tendency of the disclosure was admittedly the occurrence of serious harm, even death of soldiers? But absent direct causation and immediacy, tendency simply won't suffice.

And of course how can an "illegality" rationale be squared with the *Bartnicki* decision, which said in effect that aiding and abetting a crime and thereby directly causing the harm of public disclosure of protected private information, is not sufficient to justify limiting publication? *Bartnicki* seems to hold that the First Amendment prohibits, almost absolutely, a decision to regulate speech in order to prevent or punish illegal conduct. Yet this is precisely what happened in the *Pittsburgh Press* case. With the issue of privacy, is the difference that the disclosed conversation was of public relevance or importance—or that those who made the editorial decision so believed— but the decisions to publish sex-designated want-ad column headings or Zacchini's act involved no matters of public relevance or importance? If so, the distinction is, at best, vague.

And for those who sympathize with Robbin Woody Howard, whose sterilization was indisputably part of a public controversy, "publicness" alone seems insufficient as a criterion, as does purpose or editorial integrity. The serious harm caused to Howard was immediately, directly, and clearly produced by, and only by, the publication itself. Did Howard lose because her "harms"—loss of dignity and personal identity and social and professional relationships and self-worth—were less important than disturbing ongoing peace negotiations with North Vietnam, discouraging sex discrimination by Pittsburgh employers, or compromising the commercial value of Zacchini's act? Why should privacy count less than an author's copyright or a performer's ability to profit from an act?

Finally, what should be done with press claims of freedom to engage in illegal *conduct*, not just to publish information? To be sure, the press must obtain information before it can publish it. But how far can that be taken? I must have a computer to write this sentence. May I therefore claim a First Amendment right to steal a computer from someone else as long as I use it to produce protected speech? And there is another problem: the press's motives are not always unsullied. The press can be self-serving, profit max-imizing, and base. Few would likely defend the press's right to trespass or commit fraud in order to publish sex-designated want-ad column headings. The Supreme Court refused to let the press trespass (in effect) to steal Zac-chini's act. Can courts of law sort out the differences in motive or value among conversations on a labor strike, want-ad column headings, use of il-legal substances to kill wildlife, unhealthy food-handling practices, or dirty tricks in a political campaign? Most fundamentally, if the press is given an exemption from trespass law, for example, but only for stories *judged by a court, not by an editor,* to be important, has the press not lost its independence in the bargain, and thus an important ingredient of its freedom?

These are the questions, the problems, and indeed the paradoxes of press freedom. Without the press we would not be free. But as the terrorist exam-ple suggests, might too much of it kill us? It is hard to say that the Supreme Court has done a thorough job of defining, much less consistently protect-ing, press freedom. But the Court is just beginning its work. For a long time the press was a small, professionally monolithic, and largely self-governing group. You knew it when you saw it. But those days are now long gone. In-formation is now an adjective for our new American economy. Information is commerce and power and enterprise and product. We are literally drown-ing in it. It is now becoming evident to those who value and rely upon the press that the press's sorting, selecting, and judging functions are more im-portant than ever before. Without the press, readers, viewers, and citizens seeking to be informed would have no capacity to select, to believe, or to assess the information they want and need.

For public information, then, and for the public in America, the press is today more important than it has ever been. The press simply needs to come to grips with what its own identity is—to have the courage, in short, to dis-tinguish itself from the pornographer or the chat-room conversant or the advertiser or the anonymous Web site or the calculated lair.

The press's freedom will depend on how well the press succeeds in doing so.

Index

RANDALL P. BEZANSON is the David H. Vernon Professor of Law at the University of Iowa. His books include *Libel Law and the Press: Myth and Reality* (1987), *Taxes on Knowledge in America: Exactions on the Press from Colonial Times to the Present* (1994), *Speech Stories: How Free Can Speech Be?* (1998), *Taking Stock: Journalism and the Publicly Traded Newspaper Company* (2001) and *How Free Can Religion Be?* (2006).

The History of Communication